D1740469

The
Syrian Princesses

The Syrian Princesses

The Women Who Ruled Rome, AD 193-235

Godfrey Turton

CASSELL · LONDON

CASSELL & COMPANY LTD

an imprint of
Cassell & Collier Macmillan Publishers Ltd
35 Red Lion Square, London WC1R 4SG
and at Sydney, Auckland, Toronto, Johannesburg

and an affiliate of The Macmillan Company Inc, New York

First published 1974

ISBN 0 304 29394 6

To Elvira

Printed in Great Britain by Butler & Tanner Ltd, Frome and London

F574

Contents

Author's Note

The purpose of this book is to interest the general reader in an important but not very well-known period of Roman history. The facts given are to the best of my belief accurate; but I have not supplied references or footnotes, which, however indispensable in a work of scholarship, would be out of place here in a popular introduction to the subject. Readers wishing to study the period in fuller detail will find a list of sources and authorities in the Bibliographical Appendix.

There is an apparent inconsistency in my spelling of Roman names ending in -*anus*. As it is a longstanding custom in English to omit the Latin suffix in names sufficiently well known, I have written Papinian, Ulpian, etc., instead of Papinianus, Ulpianus; but in those too unfamiliar to have earned abbreviation, e.g. Maternianus, Antiochianus, I have left the last syllable intact.

Roman Emperors

from the Foundation of the Empire

AUGUSTUS	31 BC–AD 14
TIBERIUS	14–37
CALIGULA	37–41
CLAUDIUS	41–54
NERO	54–68
GALBA	68–69 ⎤
OTHO	69 ⎟ The year of the four
VITELLIUS	69 ⎟ Emperors, AD 69
VESPASIAN	69–79 ⎦
TITUS	79–81
DOMITIAN	81–96
NERVA	96–98
TRAJAN	98–117
HADRIAN	117–138
ANTONINUS PIUS	138–161
MARCUS AURELIUS	161–180
COMMODUS	180–192
PERTINAX	193 (1 January to 28 March)
(DIDIUS JULIANUS)	193
SEPTIMIUS SEVERUS	193–211
CARACALLA and GETA	211–212
CARACALLA alone	212–217
(MACRINUS)	217–218
HELIOGABALUS	218–222
ALEXANDER SEVERUS	222–235

Those of doubtful status are shown in brackets.

Moray Firth
Carpow
Cramond
Firth of Tay
Firth of Forth
Luguvallium
(Carlisle)
Hadrian's Wall
Eboracum (York)
Deva (Chester)
BRITAIN
Londinium

North Sea

Baltic Sea

Atlantic
Ocean

GERMANY
Moguntiacum (Mainz)

Rhine

R. Danube

GAUL

RHAETIA
NORICUM
Vindobona
(Vienna)
Carnuntum
Aquin
(Buda
PANNONIA

Lugdunum
(Lyon)

R. Rhone

Alps

Singidunum
(Belgrade)
Viminaci

HISPANIA

CORSICA
Rome
ITALY
Adriatic Sea

SARDINIA

Tyrrhenian Sea

Mediterranean

MAURETANIA
Cirta
NUMIDIA Carthage
Hadrumetum

SICILY

Leptis Magna

A
F
R
I
C
A
Cy

0   100   200   300   400   500   1000   Miles

THE ROMAN EMPIRE

circa A·D·200

N

Caspian Sea

ACIA

R. Danube

S I A

THRACE

Byzantium
Bosporus
Chalcedon

BITHYNIA

NIA· Perinthus·

Nicomedia

·Nicaea

Cyzicus

LEMNOS Sigeum
Illium

·Pergamum

A S I A

M I N O R

Taurus Mts.

Cilician Gates

ARMENIA

MEDIA

PARTHIAN EMPIRE

Edessa·

Nisibis

·Arbela

Athens

PAROS

Aegean Sea

RHODES

CILICIA

Issus·

Carrhae

Hatra·

R. Tigris

MESOPOTAMIA

PERSIA

CRETE

CYPRUS

Antioch·
·Apamea

·Emesa
Laodicea·

PHOENICIA

R. Euphrates

S Y R I A

Seleucia·

Ctesiphon
·Babylon

Persian Gulf

S e a

Tyre·

Caesarea·

·Jerusalem

ICA

Alexandria·

Pelusium·

Memphis·

E
G
Y
P
T

R. Nile

A R A B I A

Red Sea

Thebes·

·Philae

Black Sea

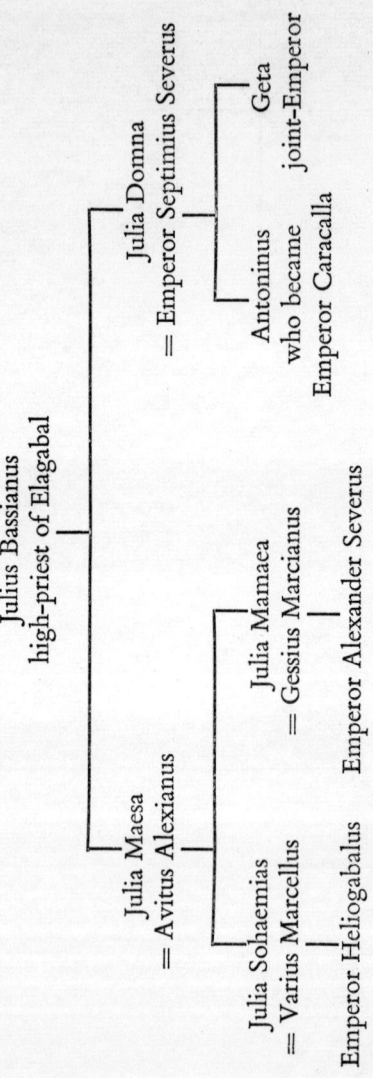

Genealogical Table

1

A Rising Star from Syria

Roman history tends to fade out for the general reader towards the end of the first century. When the characters familiar from Shakespeare's plays, *Julius Caesar* and *Antony and Cleopatra*, have left the stage, and the more notorious of the early Emperors like Nero have followed them, few names are left that have earned immortality, and the story comes to be regarded as material only for the specialist. The result is to draw a curtain over a period that can claim with justice to be the golden age of Rome. During the Age of the Antonines, as it is usually called, covering the years from 96 to 180, most of the second century, the Empire attained its greatest size and prosperity. There is no other example in history of a State whose frontiers were so nearly conterminous with those of the known world. The only neighbour fit to be regarded as a rival was the Kingdom of Parthia, whose territory extended over Persia and parts of Central Asia. In other directions— beyond the Rhine and Danube in the north-east, or the fringes of the Sahara desert in the south—the frontiers of Rome were the limits of civilization. In the Age of the Antonines it was possible to travel from the Tyne to the Nile, or from Mesopotamia to the Atlantic, without leaving territory under Roman jurisdiction and the security of the Roman peace.

The political cohesion enjoyed by this vast area owed much to a succession of capable and public-spirited rulers in Rome, a dynasty that depended for continuity not on blood relationship but adoption. The custom was for each Emperor to choose his own heir, whom he then adopted as his son. The man chosen was already of mature years, one whose career revealed qualities worthy of high office. While his adoptive father lived, he bore the courtesy title of Caesar, Emperor designate. The system worked smoothly until Marcus Aurelius, the Emperor renowned as a Stoic philosopher, allowed parental affection to sway his judgement. Departing from precedent, he chose his son Commodus to succeed him. Commodus lacked the necessary strength of character. The dizzy eminence turned his head, and he acquired the arrogance and succumbed to the suspicious anxiety of a tyrant, till his behaviour provoked the very result that he feared, and he was murdered late at night on the last day of the year 192.

The event was a grave shock to Roman stability, but the fabric of the Empire was strong enough to survive. After a short period of anarchy a new dynasty came to power, under which it seemed to people living at the time that the Age of the Antonines was restored. The new Emperors by a legal fiction retained even the name, and the State, recovering from the temporary jolt, resumed, or seemed to resume, its steady progress. There was disappointment in store, as history has shown. Roman civilization stood on the brink of an abyss, into which it was destined to fall in spite of the efforts made to save it. The story of the years from 193 to 235, with which this book is concerned, is that of Imperial Rome enjoying the final glow of its heyday before its sudden collapse into chaos. Much later, at the end of the century, the State would rise again from ruin under strong Emperors such as Diocletian and Constantine the Great, but in a changed form that had little in common with the Empire founded by Augustus.

The period is of interest not only as a turning-point in Roman history, the downfall from Imperial greatness, but also because of the part played in the direction of affairs by feminine genius. The dynasty established by Septimius Severus after the murder of Commodus gave Rome five Emperors covering three generations; but its achievement, the respite that it earned for the Roman world, owed most to the work of four remarkable women of the Imperial family: the two sisters, Julia Domna and Julia Maesa, and the latter's daughters, Sohaemias and Mamaea. The Syrian Princesses, as Gibbon calls them, were active not only in politics but with even greater vigour in the field of religion. Living a hundred years before Christianity earned official recognition, they cherished a dream of reconciling religious differences throughout the Empire in an all-embracing monotheism founded on ideas current in the temple of the god Elagabal at Emesa in Syria, where the two elder were born. The plan was inspired by a breadth of vision rare in any age, more especially that in which they lived. The aim was to abolish strife between rival creeds and to promote harmony between them, to which each would contribute its own glimpse of eternal truth. If the work had been successful, the conditions fostering the rise of Christianity would have been changed so fundamentally that it is open to doubt whether the Christian hierarchy would ever have attained the power which corrupted it in later ages.

Although the Syrian Princesses were defeated by events, they better deserve to be remembered than many more loudly publicized heroines of antiquity, a Cleopatra or a Messalina. Their portraits can still be seen on coins struck in their lifetime. The aim of this book is to restore them as far as possible to life.

Emesa, the birthplace of Julia Domna and Julia Maesa, was a town of importance standing on the upper waters of the river Orontes in Syria, near the site of the modern Homs. The river rising in the mountains of the Antilebanon emerges into a plain so fertile that some versions of the Jewish legend claimed it as the original Garden of Eden. On the outskirts of Emesa the swift stream was interrupted by a lake, of which traces still remain. On a hillock overlooking it the temple of Elagabal rose, dominating the landscape, a holy place of Semitic religion whose gilded colonnade and pediment bore witness to the lasting influence of Greece in the land conquered by Alexander the Great. The temple enjoyed great prestige. Pilgrims flocked there not only from the Roman province but also from Parthian territory beyond the Euphrates and Tigris, bringing offerings of value, a treasure accumulating through the years. The high priest, Julius Bassianus, was a rich man. He was the father of Julia Domna and Julia Maesa, and as he does not seem to have had a son they were his heirs.

The office of high priest had been hereditary in the family from time immemorial. Formerly it embraced civil as well as religious authority. Emesa was an independent kingdom, of which the high priest was King; but soon after 66 BC it became tributary to Rome, subjugated by Pompey during his campaign in the East. The distant ancestor who held office at that date bore the name of Samsiceramus, and whether because of its outlandish sound in Roman ears, or because Samsiceramus himself was known as a flamboyant character, Cicero uses the name in his letters as a nickname for Pompey, who loved to boast of his Eastern triumph.

Samsiceramus died before the murder of Julius Caesar plunged the Roman world into civil war. His son, who succeeded him, became involved in the troubles and was put to death by Antony; but after Antony's defeat at Actium and the restoration of peace under Augustus, the next heir, grandson of Samsiceramus, received his reward and was reinstated in his ancestral domain. It was probably on this account that he adopted the family name of Julius, which was that of Augustus himself. The practice of adding a Roman name to their own was common among native magnates of the Roman Empire, usually in recognition of a grant of Roman citizenship.

Thereafter for the best part of a century the high priests reigned undisturbed at Emesa under Roman suzerainty, holding a position not unlike that of a Prince Bishop in medieval Germany. They intermarried with neighbouring families of similar rank, with, amongst others, daughters of the house of Herod. A time came, however, when the provincial administration was reformed and civil authority transferred from native rulers to the Roman governor of Syria. Only his religious functions were left to the high priest at Emesa, but these were enough to assure him dignity and wealth. Both daughters of Julius Bassianus could expect a handsome dowry when they married.

Julia Domna was the younger of the two, but as the man whom she married, Lucius Septimius Severus, was destined in the course of events to become Roman Emperor, she had precedence over her sister when she grew up, and it will be convenient in the following pages to use the family name, Julia, for her alone. The meaning of her personal name, Domna, is open to doubt. It is almost certainly not Latin in origin and has no connection, despite apparent similarity, with the Latin *domina*, 'mistress'. A seal has been found at Cyzicus on the southern shore of the Sea of Marmara on which it appears as title of a goddess of the underworld, and although Cyzicus is a long way from Emesa this is an appropriate meaning for a name given to a daughter of the high priest of Elagabal. It was the custom for a Syrian god to have a female consort.

Julia was nearly seventeen when Septimius Severus took her as his second wife, but he had had an earlier opportunity of making her acquaintance when he was stationed in Syria in 179 in command of a legion, the fourth Scythica. She was barely ten years old at the time, but it is likely that she was an attractive child, to judge from the lively charm of expression shown on coins that portrayed her and the reputation that she enjoyed for beauty in maturity, and that the impression made on him lingered in his memory so that seven years later, when his first wife, Paccia Marciana, was dead, he proposed himself to the high priest at Emesa as suitor for the hand of his younger daughter. The elder sister, Maesa, either failed to attract him or was already married.

Later, when he became Emperor, a story was told that he chose Julia because her horoscope predicted that she would marry a king. Marvels of the sort suited the fashion of the age, and the prediction as usual followed the event. There is no need to look farther for a motive to urge his ambition than his father-in-law's wealth. The marriage, however, was not wholly to his advantage; it could even in certain respects be regarded as a misalliance. In marrying the daughter of the high priest of Elagabal he defied the prejudice still attaching in conservative circles to a Roman officer with an Eastern wife, and in later years the admixture of Syrian blood afforded opportunity for gibes to enemies of the dynasty. He was without doubt an ambitious man, but there was also, as can be seen from the events of his career, an introspective side to his character, susceptible to emotional impulse. The atmosphere of supernatural mystery evoked by the rites in the temple at Emesa was of a sort to appeal to his temperament, especially when it became incarnate in a girl as intelligent, charming and high-spirited as Julia.

At the date of this second marriage he was forty-two years old, propraetor—chief magistrate—of Gallia Lugdunensis, a district extending over much of central France with headquarters at Lugdunum, the modern Lyon. This was an important rung on the ladder of official promotion, and it is a tribute to his ability or to the weight of influence exerted on his behalf that he had risen so high from comparatively humble birth. His family came from Leptis Magna, a busy port on the African coast situated not far from the modern Tripoli, where he was born on 11 April 145. His father was of equestrian rank, that is to say of the well-to-do middle class insufficiently aristocratic to qualify for the senate, and probably of indigenous stock descended from the Carthaginians who reigned in ancient times over all this part of North Africa. Punic rather than Latin was the language spoken in the household, and when the young Septimius went to school both Latin and Greek were among the subjects whose elements he studied. He never wholly outgrew this belated introduction to the language. Even when he became Emperor his Punic accent provoked sneers, a tendency to drop the *h* at the beginning of a word, to give a single *l* a sound like that of *ll* in modern Italian, and to lengthen a short vowel in the first syllable of a word, as if one were to say 'peeper' for 'pepper'. If his pronunciation offended fastidious ears, it was at least more intelligible than his sister's. The story is told that after his rise to power she came to Rome to visit him; but she spoke Latin so atrociously that she put him to shame and, loading her with presents to soothe her feelings, he packed her off home on the next boat to Leptis.

From his earliest years he was mindful of his dignity. Although sturdily built he was below normal height, but he impressed himself on his schoolmates by the force of his character. A favourite game was to play the part of a judge while the other boys stood respectfully round him submitting disputes to his decision. Later, in his twenties, when he had been to Rome to complete his studies and was beginning a career in the service of the State, he returned to Africa as aide-de-camp on the governor's staff. He was walking in the street at Leptis, preceded by lictors carrying the *fasces*, the emblems of authority, when an old friend recognized him and ran forward to greet and embrace him. Septimius pushed him away and ordered the lictors to arrest him and take him off to be flogged. Afterwards he issued a proclamation broadcast by the town crier: 'Members of the public are warned that it is a punishable offence to embrace a Roman officer.'

In spite of his jealous insistence on the respect due to his rank his manners were neither arrogant nor pompous. On military duty he made a point of sharing the discomforts of the campaign, marching in person with his soldiers, readily accessible to those who wished to speak to him. When he presided in the law courts he listened with patience to the pleas of the litigants and with courtesy to the opinions of his assessors. He was as strict in his demands on himself as on others, mindful of the rights of each in their proper place, fiercely resenting any transgression of established order.

While he was at Rome to complete his studies he cultivated the acquaintance of his cousins living there, who, unlike his father, had been promoted from equestrian to senatorial rank. Their influence was successful in obtaining for him, by a special decree of the Emperor Marcus Aurelius, the right to wear the broad-striped toga of a senator, without which no one was eligible for the higher grades of an official career. A series of appointments followed of rising importance, including that in his native province of Africa, and in 179, the last year before Marcus Aurelius died, he was given his first military command, that of a legion stationed in Syria, where, as has already been said, he met the child Julia who was destined to become his second wife.

Little is known of his first wife, Paccia Marciana, beyond the fact that she bore him two daughters. Later, when he was Emperor, he put up a memorial to her at Cirta, the modern Constantine in Algeria, next to another in honour of his father, who moved from Leptis to Cirta just before his death. It is probable that she herself was a native of the town, and that Septimius met her either on a visit to his father or when, as is recorded, he was recalled from duty in Spain by news of his father's death to wind up his affairs. He made no mention of her in the memoirs that he composed later in his life. His silence can perhaps be regarded as evidence that his feeling for her lacked warmth.

At the time of his military service in Syria the governor of the province was Helvius Pertinax, a man in his middle fifties whose successful career was the more remarkable as he was born a freedman's son (his father was a timber merchant) and earned a living as a schoolmaster in his youth until he obtained a commission in the army. He and Septimius became close friends, and they were at one in their dissatisfaction when the Emperor Marcus Aurelius, conducting a campaign on the Danube, died of a digestive complaint at Vienna on 17 March 180, leaving as heir his son Commodus, a boy of eighteen. There were many in the Empire who deplored the breach of the tradition, respected for more than a century, which ensured on an Emperor's death a mature and experienced successor.

As soon as he began his reign Commodus made it his purpose to shake off the influence of his father's old advisers and replace them with cronies of his own. The exposure of a plot to assassinate him in 182 brought the struggle to a climax and, with the help of his ambitious favourite, Perennis, who held the crucial position at Rome of Prefect of the Praetorian Guard, he exacted fierce revenge, carrying out a purge of the leading figures of the former régime and those who supported them. Both Pertinax and Septimius were among the sufferers and were luckier than most in escaping with their lives. The former was exiled to his estates in northern Italy on the borders of Cisalpine Gaul, the latter to Athens. Syria received a new governor, the legion a new commander.

Kicking his heels in Athens, cut off from public affairs, Septimius consoled himself with the study of religion and visits to the monuments of antiquity. He had a connoisseur's eye for the treasures of sculpture and architecture still adorning the Acropolis, so that he incurred blame when he became Emperor by the extravagance of his zeal for building temples. Religious ideas too and the rites in which they found expression were an interest that persisted through his life, and which he shared with Julia. In Athens there was abundant opportunity to gratify it. The city retained its reputation for learning and its claim to be the intellectual capital of the Empire, filled with citizens as ready as on the occasion of Saint Paul's visit some century and a half earlier to spend their time 'in nothing else but either to tell or to hear some new thing'. Neither occult speculation, however, nor architectural sightseeing could make up to Septimius for the check to his career. The Athenians, no respecters of persons, renowned through the ages for their ribaldry, did nothing to soothe his feelings. They were more inclined to mock than to sympathize with the fallen pride of a Roman officer in disgrace, and the very insistence with which he stood on his dignity provoked them to bolder impudence. He resented their behaviour angrily at the time, but there is no evidence that he bore them a lasting grudge. Honorific inscriptions survive from a later date testifying to the loyalty felt for himself and his family by the citizens of Athens and the supreme Council of the Areopagus. By then he was Emperor, lord of the Roman world, and could afford to forget the slights put on a legionary ex-commander.

His troubles came to an end in 185 when Perennis, his powerful enemy at the Imperial court, was overthrown, and the new Prefect whom Commodus appointed to the Praetorian Guard rehabilitated most of those formerly in disfavour. Septimius went as propraetor to Lugdunum, where he remained undisturbed by the continuing struggle at Rome, the intrigues besetting the reign and the suspicious Emperor's savage reprisals. Securely established in an honourable position in the service of the State, with good prospects of advancement, he was an eligible suitor to seek the hand in marriage of the daughter of the high priest at Emesa.

Whether or not Julia remembered him from the days of her childhood when he was serving in Syria, it is likely that she accepted his proposal without regret. A Syrian girl was brought up to expect a marriage arranged by her father. It could be a source of relief and satisfaction to one of Julia's lively intelligence, enterprise and insatiable curiosity that the choice fell on a rising officer in the service of the Roman Empire, a man much older than herself but still in the prime of life, rather than on an inexperienced boy, the heir of a local princeling. She had less reason than girls educated in a different tradition to feel alarm at the prospect of giving herself to a stranger. It was a time-honoured custom of her religion, denounced more than a thousand years earlier by the Hebrew authors of the Old Testament but still preserved in Syrian ritual, that every girl on attaining nubile age should present herself naked in the temple and kneel prostrate at the altar, waiting for a stranger to deflower her. The duty was imposed on all from the highest to the lowest. To fail to submit was to incur the guilt of impiety. The stranger represented the god, to whom her virginity was owed.

It has been suggested that the custom had its origin in the principle of exogamy, the need of the community to ensure a healthy mixture in its blood and avoid degeneration from inbreeding. There was the further advantage that it protected immature girls from rape, a crime equivalent to sacrilege when it forestalled the god in the exercise of his privilege.

Although the evidence of the Old Testament dates from a period in the distant past, it remains applicable to that in which Julia lived when it insists on the prevalence of erotic rites in Syrian religion. The gods and goddesses of the Syrians were spirits of hill, wood and stream, worshipped in groves and high places. On their bounty depended the fertility of the earth, of crops and cattle and of the human race. Their benevolence was encouraged by rites of sympathetic magic, like those practised according to the account in the Book of Kings by Maacah, backsliding grandmother of the righteous King Asa of Judah. In her youth she had been the favourite wife of Rehoboam, son of Solomon, and it seems that she clung even in her old age to the pagan beliefs for which Solomon earned the disapproval of the priesthood of Jehovah. She set up a priapic idol under the trees beside a stream, and the young men and girls of the neighbourhood came to worship there with games and dances, till the news reached King Asa's ears. He arrived with a band of zealots to interrupt the proceedings, hacked the idol to pieces, burnt it and stamped the ashes into the ground. He punished his grandmother by depriving her of her rank and fortune. The story reveals the nature of one of the principal sources of disagreement between the religion of the Jews and that of their pagan neighbours. The rites suppressed in Judah persisted through the ages in Syria. Idols such as Maacah's still presided, when Julia was born, over woods and meadows haunted by the nymphs of the Orontes.

There is another aspect of Syrian religion of which the Old Testament speaks with abhorrence, the practice of human sacrifice, the rites celebrated by worshippers of Moloch and at other indigenous shrines causing 'their sons and daughters to pass through the fire'. Few traces of the custom remained in Syria when Julia lived, none at all in the temple of Elagabal where her father officiated as high priest. The barbarity was not only condemned by public opinion, it was expressly forbidden by Roman law, which made this exception to the general tolerance that it extended to native religions, just as the no less tolerant British Raj in India prohibited *suttee*, the self-immolation of a widow on her husband's pyre. Human victims might still be sacrificed surreptitiously in back streets by shady practitioners of sorcery, but no such violation of the law was conceivable in a famous temple whose rites were conducted in public under the eyes of the Roman authorities.

Julia's own views are revealed in a book, the *Life of Apollonius*, written at her request and under her inspiration by her friend, Flavius Philostratus, a leading member of the literary and scientific circle over which she presided when her husband became Emperor. More will be said of the book and its author in a later chapter; it is enough for the present to remark that, purporting to write the life of an itinerant sage, Apollonius, who had lived in the previous century, Philostratus expounds the ideas on religion and philosophy held by himself and Julia. There is disapproval for the slaughter even of animals as sacrificial victims, and the conduct of the ancient Greek philosopher Empedocles is praised, who, when custom prescribed the sacrifice of a bull, brought for the purpose a model made of pastry. As for human sacrifice, it is denounced as blasphemy to expect favours from a rite for which any god worthy of the name should strike the murderous priest dead.

Another important change in Syrian religion was that which it owed to the influence of Chaldean astrology, a study which, persisting from the far-off days of the greatness of Babylon, spread through the centuries into most of the neighbouring countries of the East. The ideas that made the widest appeal were those linking the movement of the stars to human destiny, and it is evident from the surviving literature of the period that Julia and her friends were firm believers in horoscopes and similar means of prediction. Observation of the stars led on, however, to more fruitful fields of speculation. It revealed a world of order and light remote from the troubles of earth and encouraged belief in a divine power, omnipotent and ubiquitous, reigning there. It was no great step to the doctrine that this sublime world was the destined home of human spirits after death, of those at any rate who deserved admission. Early teaching, as in other Semitic religions, offered little comfort about the after-life. The dead were assigned to a gloomy abode, of which the Hebrew Sheol is a typical example, described in the Book of Job as a land 'of the shadow of death without any order, and where the light is as darkness'. The ideas borrowed from the Chaldeans transformed the prospect, banished the nightmare. The sun, ruler of the stars in heaven, became the symbol of godhead on earth, able to lead the human spirit to interstellar felicity.

Syrian religion was polytheistic in the sense that each community had its own divine protector presiding in its temple; but there was little tendency to create a pantheon of gods and goddesses related to one another in terms of a traditional mythology. In early times it was sufficient function for the tribal god to protect his people, and no heed was paid to the gods of others except to hope that in war one's own would prove the stronger. As communal life began to cohere into larger units, this attitude became an anachronism. Local rivalries lost their importance. When war broke out, the enemy was a distant nation as foreign in religion as in language and customs. The idea took root that local gods were all aspects of a single spirit, the same godhead whose emblem in the sky was the sun.

This view was reinforced in Syria by the custom of giving all gods alike the title of Baal. The word, made familiar by its use in the Old Testament, is a generic term meaning 'Lord', and it was even applied, according to the prophet Hosea, by the Jews themselves to Jehovah. A wide divergence, however, developed on the subject between Jews and pagans: among the latter the identity of title fostered assimilation of the natures of different gods, so that the distinction faded between one city's Baal and another's. In so far as rivalry persisted between them it resembled that which survives to this day between neighbouring shrines of Christian saints, where local patriotism insists without theological controversy on the superior virtues of its sacred relics. The Jews, on the other hand, denied that Jehovah was the equal of other Baals, one aspect among many of the godhead. They claimed that he was the one and only god, whose jealousy would bear no rivals, and the very word Baal acquired an opprobrious meaning, associated in their minds with idolatry. Syrian tolerance was the foundation on which Julia and her successors built to give the Roman Empire a religion acceptable to all and including all that was best in existing cults. In contrast, Christianity inherited and relied for much of its force on Jewish exclusiveness.

By the time that Julia was born the process of religious assimilation had been carried so far in Syria that the doctrines and ritual of the worship of Elagabal, the Baal of Emesa, differed little from established custom in other temples of the country. Various interpretations of the god's name have been offered. The first syllable contains a root meaning 'god', common to most Semitic languages, seen in Elohim in Hebrew, Allah in Arabic. A possible derivation of the second part is from the Syriac *gabal*, 'a hill'. The title, 'god of the hill', would be appropriate in a flat country to a deity whose temple crowned even a low eminence. There is, however, a homonym, *gabal*, meaning 'creates'. If this is the source of the name, Elagabal was God the Creator. It is a function that conflicts with the claims asserted on behalf of Jehovah alone in the Book of Genesis, but the title would have sounded less challengingly in pagan ears, denoting no more than that Elagabal shared the divine power of creativity.

Something is known of the elaborate ritual with which the god was worshipped from accounts given of it at a later date when for a few years he had a temple dedicated to him at Rome. The principal details are of a sort common to nearly all Syrian cults, the splendour of the appointments and sacred utensils, the jewelled vestments worn by the priests, the ecstatic wail of flutes and thunder of drums, the jubilant singing and dancing leading at appropriate seasons of the year to erotic rites of fertility. Scenes like this were to be found in any of the famous temples of the neighbourhood. If there was anything unusual at Emesa it was the form in which the god was manifested there, a boulder of black rock, probably meteoric in origin, conical in shape with a striated pattern of grooves and ridges, whether natural markings or characters of occult meaning. Attribution of sanctity to a stone in its natural shape was not without parallel in antiquity. Aphrodite, for instance, was worshipped as a cone of white limestone in her temple at Paphos in Cyprus. More often, however, at this date the emblem of deity bore human or other recognizable likeness, which it owed to the art of a sculptor. To that extent Elagabal was eccentric.

In view of the part played by Julia in the intellectual life of her husband's reign it is relevant to ask how much she was indoctrinated with the teaching of the priests of Elagabal when she left Emesa to be married to Septimius and live as propraetor's wife in Roman society at Lugdunum. She was not yet seventeen, scarcely of an age to have developed the strength of mind evident in her later career. The gorgeous ritual and passionate excitement of the services in the familiar temple were among the earliest memories of her childhood, and it is probable that she missed them with homesick longing as she attended the routine of conventional piety at the altar of Jupiter Optimus Maximus and the rest of the official pantheon of Rome. That is not to say that she retained a blind faith in the tenets in which she was brought up: the magical efficacy of the black stone worshipped at Emesa. Such credulity is out of keeping with the active intelligence to which her career bears witness, the curiosity with which she explored every available variety of religious experience. The book written by her friend Philostratus in harmony with her own ideas insists that respect is due to all religions alike. It is certain that she would have resented any sneer at the rites of Elagabal or the hallowed meteorite; but in defending them she could accommodate loyalty to speculative reason by following the example set by many leading thinkers of the day, who attributed to sacred tradition a symbolic meaning. This was the method used by eminent philosophers to extract spiritual edification from the Iliad, and with equal ingenuity by the Christian Fathers, Origen especially, to elucidate refractory texts in the Bible. Tenuous as the connection might be between the literal and the imputed sense, the symbolic interpretation offered freedom to the quest for truth without offending the sacrosanctity of Holy Writ.

At Lugdunum she had to adapt herself to change in other fields as well as that of religion. The Western provinces of the Empire lagged behind the Eastern in intellect and culture. During the two hundred years which had elapsed since the conquest of Gaul by Julius Caesar much had been done to build towns equipped with handsome buildings, to connect them by a system of roads and establish law and order for the encouragement of trade and agriculture; but the Roman way of life was too newly implanted to foster a spirit of the sort that flourished in the East, rooted in tradition inherited from the great civilizations of the past—Greek, Babylonian, Egyptian. A Syrian girl transferred to Gaul was in a similar position to an officer's bride in the British Empire who, brought up in a cathedral city or university town in England, accompanied her husband to his post in one of the brasher colonies. The contrast was especially poignant between Lugdunum and Emesa, where the shrine of Elagabal enjoyed fame as a centre of learning. Julia was accustomed to the constant excitement of a flow of pilgrims to the temple, the most eminent and cultivated of whom her father entertained in his house, and when the topics reflecting their interests, philosophy, literature and science, were discussed at the table it is probable that she herself took part in the conversation. Syrian girls behaved with a freedom that earned condemnation in countries where stricter convention prevailed.

She had other matters, however, to occupy her attention when her first child was born at Lugdunum on 4 April 188, a son known to history as the Emperor Caracalla. She employed a wet-nurse to feed him, and it is of interest that the woman was a Christian. Throughout her life she had contact with many adherents of the sect, protecting them and treating them with sympathy; but the refusal of Christianity to tolerate any other religion was uncongenial to her, and she cherished her independence of mind.

At the end of the year her husband's appointment in Gaul came to an end, and she accompanied him to Rome with her baby son. The swiftest and most comfortable method of travel was by sea; but Septimius, who had to be in Rome on New Year's Day when official appointments were re-allocated, was travelling at a season when navigation was dangerous, and no one without urgent reason would be bold enough to take ship, least of all if he had his wife and child with him. The Rhône offered safe passage for the first part of the way; but thereafter it would be necessary to disembark and complete the journey into Italy by road. The excellent roads built in the Roman Empire afforded better communication than there was ever to be again in Europe till the end of the eighteenth century. A high officer of State like Septimius could rely on prompt relays of horses at frequent post-houses to speed him on his way, a military escort to protect him from interference and the hospitality of a wealthy citizen to provide lodging for the night, to save him the discomfort of crowded and filthy inns. Nevertheless, in spite of these advantages, the journey was a severe ordeal for a woman so soon after the birth of her first child and with another already in her womb. Although the vehicle was long and spacious and was fitted with benches (it could be adapted in an emergency for sleeping), its four wheels were rimmed with iron and the springless carriage jolted painfully. Even in the most favourable conditions, with a team of eight horses, the best speed to be expected was an average of five miles an hour.

The party reached Rome in time for the New Year ballot held to allot official posts in the provinces. Septimius received that of governor of Sicily.

Julia gave birth in Sicily in 189 to her second son, Geta. After that there were no more children. Even at this stage it seems that she cherished ambitious dreams for her husband's career. Contemporary historians writing after the event relate many marvellous portents foreshadowing his coming greatness. However much they owed to hindsight, they are an indication of his readiness to believe in supernatural guidance, a propensity encouraged by his Syrian wife. Arts of fortune-telling flourished in Syria, as the story already quoted of her horoscope illustrates, and she herself was too open-minded to despise them. It is possible to see her imagination at work rather than his own in some of the omens recorded, especially the dream said to have come to him while he was still at Lugdunum, in which someone lifted him on to an eminence overlooking a limitless panorama of land and sea; he reached out as if to play on a musical instrument and the effect was melodious harmony. The imagery is worthy of Julia, the future Augusta, who was to earn renown for her patronage of the Muses.

It was dangerous to show too much interest in divination in the reign of Commodus. Reports of visits paid by Septimius to practitioners of the occult in Sicily reached the ears of the authorities in Rome, arousing the Emperor's restless suspicions. Septimius was recalled and put on trial, charged with magical practices directed to purposes of treason. More fortunate than many in a like predicament under Commodus, he was acquitted and his accusers were crucified. He owed his safety in all probability to the influence of Pertinax, his friend in the old days in Syria, who by now was restored to Imperial favour and held the office of Prefect of the City, a position second in importance only to that of Prefect of the Praetorian Guard. The Prefect of the City was responsible for the maintenance of order in the streets and commanded for the purpose an armed police force. These were the only troops allowed in the capital apart from the Praetorian Guard, the Emperor's bodyguard, quartered in barracks on the outskirts.

Warned by his escape, Septimius was careful to avoid further offence and lived quietly at Rome under the protection of Pertinax, while he waited for renewed employment in the service of the State. It was a time indeed when prudence was needed. After the fall of Perennis, to whose enmity both Pertinax and Septimius owed their former disgrace, Commodus transferred his favour to a freedman called Cleander, originally a Phrygian slave. The new favourite was soon as unpopular as his predecessor, earning the hatred of high and low alike by his arrogance and rapacity, till at last a shortage of corn on the market, for which the blame was laid on his mismanagement, provoked the crowds at a show in the Circus Maximus to so violent a riot that Commodus in panic abandoned him and had him beheaded. This took place early in 190, while Septimius was still in Sicily, and during the months that followed the political situation at Rome was in ferment with plots and counterplots. Commodus was eager to avenge the loss of his favourite, his opponents to take advantage of his discomfiture.

In this tumultuous atmosphere the political outlook was so uncertain that Julia was not entirely guilty of fantasy in dreaming of the topmost pinnacle for her hitherto undistinguished husband. He and Pertinax took care not to expose themselves in the struggle; but it is clear from events where their sympathy lay, that they were among those who longed with bitter regret for the orderly government of Marcus Aurelius and his predecessors. For more than a century Rome had forgotten what it was like to be governed by a weak Emperor, who mistook arbitrary ferocity for strength and relied in the direction of affairs on the advice of upstarts as incompetent and irresponsible as himself. To misgovernment Commodus added a fault which gave particular offence to the traditionally-minded: he was a man of superb physique and loved to show off his prowess by fighting in person with gladiators and wild beasts in the show-ground. Even if the gladiators were under orders to let the Emperor win, no such deference could be expected from a lion or rhinoceros; but Roman senators watching the feats were less impressed by the Emperor's skill and courage than by the indignity of his behaviour. They were readier to forgive his errors of administration than the impropriety of a public performance in which he played a part usually reserved for slaves and condemned criminals.

As discontent mounted and suspects suffered ruthless punishment, powerful conspirators in high places went quietly ahead with their plans. The Praetorian Prefect recently appointed, Aemilius Laetus, was a fellow-countryman of Septimius from North Africa. His adherence to the conspiracy meant that it could count on the commanders of both the armed forces in Rome—Laetus with the Praetorian Guard, Pertinax with the urban cohorts, the police force under the control of the Prefect of the City. In addition steps were taken to ensure that men of suitable views were chosen to govern the most important provinces, among them Upper Pannonia bordering the Danube in territory that today forms part of Lower Austria and Hungary between Vienna and Budapest. This was an uneasy frontier, the scene of a recent dangerous invasion of unsubjugated tribes barely repelled by Marcus Aurelius. It was also—a fact peculiarly relevant in the circumstances—a point where the frontier of the Roman Empire lay nearest to Italy, so that the three legions stationed there had a shorter journey to the capital than any other army in the provinces. The post of governor went by custom to an officer of proved ability and achievement, preferably with previous experience on the Danube or Rhine. It testifies to the power exerted by his friends behind the scenes that Upper Pannonia was offered to Septimius, who had had little experience of military service beyond a legionary command in Syria.

The plan, according to a story circulated later, was that when the time was ripe Pertinax should replace Commodus as Emperor and, in obedience to Antonine precedent, adopt Septimius as his son and heir, Emperor designate. With this expectation in mind Septimius set out with his wife and two little boys in the late summer of 191 to take up his new appointment. In view of his increased importance he could enjoy to an even greater extent than before the benefit of all official services available to promote speed and comfort; but it was a journey unlikely nevertheless to be completed in less than a month, a distance of some 680 miles round the head of the Adriatic to circumvent the Alps and across present-day Slovenia and Burgenland to the headquarters of his province at Carnuntum on the Danube.

2

Murder on New Year's Eve

Carnuntum occupied a site near the modern village of Petronell, between Hainburg and Deutsch–Altenburg. The Roman town looked eastward across the Danube to pathless woods beyond the bounds of civilization. If life in Gaul lacked amenities to which Syrian Julia was accustomed, it was a haven of comfort in comparison with her new home. Pannonia was added to the Roman Empire by Augustus more than half a century after Julius Caesar's conquest of Gaul. Roman institutions were less firmly established there, not only because of the shorter time that had elapsed, but also because of the situation of the province on a part of the frontier seldom free from anxiety. Whereas Lugdunum was a thriving centre of commerce surrounded in every direction by the peaceful fruits of Roman government, Carnuntum was a military outpost standing on guard on the verge of hostile wilds and an important staging-post for the import of amber from the north.

Excavations carried out in recent times on military sites of Roman antiquity have revealed how greatly the standard of living, manners and sanitary conditions in such places fell short of those prevailing in civil society elsewhere in the Empire. Such discomforts, repugnant to Julia's fastidious taste, were more easily endured, however, than the tedious isolation, the dearth of congenial companionship. In the subsequent course of her life she was in the habit of accompanying her husband on his journeys and campaigns, regardless of physical hardship; but, taught perhaps by her experience at Carnuntum, she was careful on such occasions to be attended by friends of her own, who shared her interests and were capable of intelligent conversation.

Her husband had more to occupy him while he awaited the expected news from Rome of the overthrow of Commodus, the elevation of Pertinax and his own promotion to the dignity of Imperial heir. The province that he governed lay, as has been said, at a sensitive point on the frontiers of the Empire, the scene during the reign of Marcus Aurelius of an irruption of German tribes so formidable that the invaders penetrated the Alps and advanced deep into Italy. More than a decade of fighting was needed to expel them finally from Roman soil. Although the work was accomplished by the time that Septimius became governor of Upper Pannonia, the fear of a renewed outbreak called for constant vigilance. He was reminded of the danger whenever he looked across the river from the ridge on which Carnuntum was built. The farther shore was a no-man's-land, an uninhabited wilderness of scrub and woodland from which the German tribes were excluded by the terms of the peace treaty. It was a strip extending ten miles deep in either direction along the river with a palisade to mark its limits and a chain of watch-towers.

This was his first experience of the outermost fringe of the Roman world, unlike anything known to him in his earlier service in Syria and Gaul. It is possible that as he surveyed the belt of solitude bounding the frontier the idea took shape in his mind destined to bear fruit in later years, a plan to extend Roman influence imperceptibly into unsubjugated territory, so that no sharp line of distinction remained. Hitherto the Roman soldier, forbidden to marry at any time during his military service, had been an intruder without roots in the country where he served, having no social contact with its natives except the daughters by way of rape and prostitution. An entirely new relationship was established during the reign of Septimius when he removed their prohibition on marriage. Soldiers, free to choose brides, sought them from villages on either side of the frontier. They raised families related by blood to the native inhabitants and shared their attachment to the soil. A community grew up in which political boundaries yielded importance to ties of kinship.

The Roman Empire suffered many incursions in later years, but the frontiers, breached and patched up again, survived for another two centuries. They owed their durability to the work of Septimius, who substituted for a barrier of desolate no-man's-land the living sympathies of a mixed population, a fringe of territory cherished as home by soldier and tribesman alike.

All this lay far in the future while he waited at Carnuntum for news of the outcome of events in Rome. He had more than a year to wait, but even so it seems that the climax came sooner than was expected. Circumstances suddenly arose which forced the conspirators to act before their plans were ripe. To understand the reasons it is necessary to leave Septimius and Julia at Carnuntum and describe what was happening in Rome on the last day of the year 192.

New Year's Day, the Kalends of January, was a public holiday; it was also the date on which the consuls for the year began their term of office. These officers, who in the time of the Republic held supreme authority in the State, had been deprived of effective power since the foundation of the Empire by Augustus; but they retained honour as a symbol of Roman continuity, a venerable archaism linking the present with the past. Traditional sentiment lent importance to the gesture which the Emperor Commodus had in mind for the celebration of the New Year 193. His intention was to announce at an appropriate moment in the proceedings that the appointment of the two consuls designated was annulled and to take their place himself in solitary dignity. It was to be a signal of his final release from the influence of his father's old advisers. Henceforward he would reign as absolute potentate.

It was in keeping with his character that he could not resist the temptation to add a whimsical touch to shock convention. He would appear for his inauguration wearing, instead of the official regalia, the dress of a gladiator, with a procession of gladiators to escort him. The effect would be rather as if a reigning monarch or other head of State today attended a solemn ceremony in football jersey and shorts, escorted by a team in similar outfit.

He was so tickled by his own humour that he could not refrain from boasting of it in confidence to his mistress, a girl called Marcia; but there were details of the programme, a sanguinary sequel, that he was careful to keep to himself. Even so, she was disturbed by what she heard, knowing him too well to believe that the proceedings would be limited to a parade of sportswear. She did her best to dissuade him, but her protests were unavailing. Their only effect was to irritate him without deflecting him from his purpose. It was the same when he confided in Laetus, the Praetorian Prefect, and Eclectus, his Egyptian chamberlain, from both of whom he needed co-operation to see that the gladiators were mustered and suitable arrangements made for a dressing-room in their quarters, from which he would emerge fitted out for the pageant. They listened to his plans with apprehension and a guilty conscience, wondering what lay behind them. Both Eclectus and Laetus were involved in the conspiracy already set on foot to depose him. So too was Marcia.

She was a young woman of determined character who had maintained her influence over the Emperor for several years, enjoying most of the privileges of a wife except that of connubial status. He was so enamoured of her face and figure that he made her pose for her portrait as an Amazon, naked but for helmet and sword, and he used an intaglio engraved from it in his signet ring as his personal seal. In her heart, however, she hated him for his brutality and drunkenness. She had resigned herself to him unwillingly when he put her former lover to death on a charge of treason, and she escaped from his embraces as often as she could to seek comfort in those of Eclectus, with whom she was in love. As a child she was brought up by Christian foster-parents, and whether or not she herself accepted the creed she regarded its adherents with favour, intervening with powerful effect to defend them from persecution and rescue those already condemned to the silver-mines in Sardinia. A contemporary Christian writer, Saint Hippolytus, describes her as a 'God-loving woman', virtuous at least in her zeal to relieve the oppressed.

Her influence was less successful in deterring Commodus from his present resolve. When she made a last attempt on New Year's Eve he dismissed her with angry abuse and retired to his room for his siesta, taking writing tablets with him. Later he went across to the bath-house, leaving the tablets on his bed. These consisted of thin sheets of wood or other material (the Emperor's were probably of ivory) coated with dark wax, on which messages were written with a pointed stick, the *stilus*. A cord threaded through a hole pierced in the tablets held them together. While the Emperor's bedroom was empty, a little boy attached to the staff wandered in, saw the tablets on the bed and took them to play with. He ran with them into the passage, where he collided with Marcia and fell; as she stooped to pick him up and kiss him she caught sight of what he held in his hands. Recognizing the toy as the Emperor's tablets she grabbed them for fear that they would come to harm, but before putting them away she had the curiosity to read what was written. She found a list of victims destined for execution the next morning. Her own name was the first.

She ran to find Eclectus, her lover.

'Look,' she exclaimed, 'how we're to celebrate New Year's Day.'

She showed him the list. His name was on it as well as hers, also those of Laetus and most of the other conspirators. The preparations for revolt were still incomplete, but they could afford to wait no longer. It was evident that an informer had betrayed them, and that unless Commodus died within the next few hours they themselves would die on the morrow.

Eclectus sealed the tablets and sent them in secret to Laetus in the

Praetorian barracks. The soldiers stationed there were for the most part devoted to Commodus, who took care to confirm their allegiance by abundant largess. It was important therefore to notify Laetus without delay, so that he would be ready to control any outburst that the crisis might provoke. He had means too to warn the others who were in danger.

Laetus arrived in person in reply to the message, using the pretext that he wished to consult Eclectus about arrangements for the procession of gladiators on the following day. The Emperor's household had moved recently to a mansion on the Caelian hill, a district inhabited by the well-to-do, as he complained that he was unable to sleep in the noisy palace. This was fortunate in the present emergency. There was more chance here than in the palace, his official residence, to take action appropriate to the circumstances without attracting attention. All three of them, Laetus, Eclectus and Marcia, were agreed on the need to act at once. At any moment Commodus would return from his bath. When Marcia, more Amazon than Christian, suggested that she should poison him, the other two accepted her offer with relief, and Laetus returned to the barracks to await news of the outcome of the operation.

Commodus lingered in the bath-house drinking with a group of boon companions, and Marcia had time to make preparations before they departed. Knowing that it was his custom to invite her to pledge him from the same cup, she left the wine undoctored and put the poison in the meat. This was an art in which she had no skill, but when she brought him the food he ate it, too drunk or too hungry to notice anything peculiar in the taste. He fell asleep, and she gave orders for everyone to go away and leave him undisturbed.

In an hour or so he woke up groaning and shrieking with pains in his belly. The poison was working at last; but whether because of an error in the dose, or because the quantity of wine he had drunk earlier provoked his stomach to erupt, he suddenly began to retch and vomit. He kept on so long that she feared, as she watched him, that he would purge his system completely and restore it to health. She left in dismay to seek help.

She found an attendant called Narcissus, a powerful athlete. Exerting all her charm on him, she persuaded him to accompany her back into the room. Commodus was scrambling shakily to his feet in a pool of vomit, aware that he had been poisoned and swearing vengeance. Before he could recover his strength Narcissus seized and strangled him.

By now it was long after dark. With help from Narcissus she wrapped the corpse in a pile of old blankets, which she gave to two slaves to carry out of the house, telling them that it was a bundle of rubbish. The guards at the gate let them pass without demur, seeing nothing suspicious in the burden whose shape was in any case barely distinguishable in the darkness. The bearers put it on a cart, pulled it beyond the bounds of the city and dumped it there. There were few people about in the streets in the chill of the winter night. Most were at home entertaining friends and making preparations for the New Year festival.

Eclectus set out for the barracks to tell Laetus of their success and to discuss what to do next. He found a group of conspirators already assembled there, but Pertinax, too cautious to commit himself, was not among them. His absence was a setback to their plans and they went together to his house to summon him. The outer door was locked, everything shut up; but their knocking aroused the porter, who opened to them reluctantly, unwilling to admit them till he recognized Laetus, the Praetorian Prefect, whose authority he dared not disobey. He told them that his master was in bed, and he would go to him and announce their arrival.

Pertinax, without any doubt, knew the purpose of the visit. It is inconceivable that Laetus had failed to warn him, in common with the other conspirators, of Marcia's discovery of the fatal tablets. It was not in character, however, for Pertinax to take precipitate action. He was a man of sixty-six who had raised himself by prudence and industry from humble origins to a high position in the State, and he set too great a value on his achievement to risk a mistake. He could allow himself, tempted by the glittering prospect of the purple, to take part in a conspiracy of which every step was carefully prepared to ensure a successful outcome; but he shrank back in alarm when matters came suddenly to a head before the time was ripe. He preferred to go to bed and wait quietly to see what the morrow had in store. It is possible that his own name was not on the list.

He received his visitors with suspicion and apprehension, fearing that, deliberately or not, they would lead him into a trap, and even when Laetus assured him that Commodus was dead he remained unconvinced. He insisted on sending a trusted officer to inspect the body where it lay on waste ground in the suburbs. When the result of the inspection confirmed the news, and it was clear that the prize was his for the taking, he at last overcame his hesitation and agreed to accompany the others back to the barracks to present himself to the soldiers as their new Emperor. In view of their devotion to Commodus it was necessary to proceed with care. Nothing must be said of the murder: the story would be that Commodus died of apoplexy. The same officer was sent again to the body to retrieve it and take it to be kept in a safe place, where something could be done to remove the marks of violence inconsistent with a natural death. There was need too to protect it from the fury of the many enemies who bore Commodus a grudge, especially those in the senate who would gladly order it to be dragged through the streets with a hook like that of a common criminal. Any such affront to the dead Emperor would give mortal offence to the Praetorian Guard.

A couple of hours and more remained before dawn, but Rome awoke early on the morning of the New Year when it was the custom for clients of powerful patrons to assemble ready at the door to greet them and solicit favours. The streets were already beginning to fill as Pertinax and his party rode to the barracks, and word spread, deliberately propagated among the passers-by, that the Emperor was dead. It suited the purpose of the conspirators that the news should be known. They were not sorry when a crowd collected to follow them, eager to satisfy curiosity and to report the event to patrons who, like most men of substance in Rome, would be delighted to hear that they were rid of the hated Commodus. Although Laetus hoped that the respect due to him as Prefect would be enough to keep the soldiers in order, vociferous support from the public could be a useful reinforcement. No effort was made when the party reached the barracks to prevent interlopers from entering too. In consequence there were present almost as many unauthorized spectators as soldiers, and the soldiers themselves, bewildered and drowsy, called on parade at so unexpectedly early an hour, were under the additional disadvantage that, as it was a day of festival, they were forbidden to carry arms.

They listened in gloomy silence as Laetus announced the death of the Emperor Commodus from apoplexy and invited them to acclaim Pertinax successor to the Imperial purple. A few half-hearted voices were raised in assent. Professing to regard these as an expression of unanimous approval, he made haste to declare that Pertinax was Emperor by military acclamation. Any protests were drowned in the vociferous cheers of the gate-crashing crowd.

Pertinax himself stepped forward to thank the soldiers for the honour conferred on him, a stately figure with a long beard, inclined to corpulence but dignified in bearing. Although easy and affable in

B

conversation he was a poor orator, and his speech made an unfavour-able impression, especially the closing words: 'There are many difficul-ties in the present situation, fellow-soldiers, but with your co-operation *some* can be straightened out.'

They took him to refer to the burdensome cost of the privileges granted them by Commodus, high pay swollen at frequent intervals by a lavish distribution of bonus, and they listened with angry mis-givings. They were in no mood to co-operate in economies enforced at their expense. For the time being, however, they kept their feelings to themselves.

The new Emperor and his friends returned from the barracks into the city to seek confirmation of his title from the senate. There was still a little time before dawn, and the senate-house stood locked and deserted. The janitor was not to be found, having slipped off to a tavern to drink to the New Year. While they looked for him, Per-tinax took shelter from the cold in the neighbouring Temple of Con-cord; he was joined there by an elderly senator, Claudius Pompeianus, son-in-law of Marcus Aurelius, who, like many of that Emperor's intimates and advisers, had fallen into disfavour under Commodus and retired from public life. Pertinax and Pompeianus were old friends; Pertinax owed his first start in the army to Pompeianus's powerful influence, and the two had been in close association throughout their careers. Their meeting this morning seems, however, to have been by chance. Pompeianus explained that he had been awakened and come out of doors to gather news on hearing of the death of Commodus, about which he professed deep regret. It is probable from what is known of him that his words were sincere, and that he himself had no part in the conspiracy. He had been devoted to Marcus Aurelius, and in spite of his disappointment in Commodus and estrangement from him he was incapable of wishing harm to come to the great man's son, his own brother-in-law.

The effect of their conversation was to put Pertinax to shame and deprive his ambition of lustre. There was nothing to encourage him in the manner of his recent acclamation by the soldiers, and as he brooded in the foggy chill of the winter dawn over the dangers and difficulties in which he was involving himself his spirit failed. He told Pompeianus that he was waiting for the senate to accept him as Emperor, and invited him to take his place. Pompeianus had the good sense to refuse.

By this time the senate-house was open, and the senators were already gathering. All were jubilant over the tyrant's overthrow. An account of the proceedings is given by an eye-witness, the historian

Dio,* who as a senator himself was present in person. He describes the enthusiasm when Pertinax entered, the eager throng jostling to approach. When Pertinax spoke, however, his mood remained diffident.

'I've been named Emperor by the soldiers,' he announced, 'but I don't want the office and am ready to resign it here and now on the grounds of my age, my health and the distressing state of affairs.'

The first two of these grounds, as Dio points out, had little validity. He was in his middle sixties, hale and hearty, except for a slight limp; but the third ground lies nearer the true source of his reluctance. It was evident that details were leaking out already of the manner in which Commodus had met his death. The only incident to mar the harmony of the proceedings occurred when Sosius Falco, one of the consuls designated to take office that day (whose appointment Commodus had intended to annul in gladiatorial majesty), intervened to ask whether power entrusted to Pertinax would not be exercised in fact behind the scenes by Laetus and Marcia. Both were unpopular in the senate, the one as mistress of Commodus, the other as commander of his bodyguard. Both were guilty in the eyes of many of those present of the still graver fault of a lack of aristocratic credentials. This was a charge to which Pertinax also was vulnerable. As Emperor, he could expect enmity on two flanks. The Praetorian Guards would not easily forgive the murder of Commodus, or the senators forget for long their jealousy of an outsider.

For the moment, however, there was little room in the senate-house for any emotions other than relief and exultation. All who sat there had lived for years in fear of Commodus, of his savage temper and incalculable vagaries. The sudden removal of the threat provoked an outburst of uncontrollable joy. Falco's objection was overruled and Pertinax invested with the customary titles and attributes of Imperial dignity. As the news spread through the city there were scenes of wild rejoicing, the mobs milling through the streets, hacking to pieces every statue of Commodus that they found and defacing inscriptions which bore his name. They called fiercely for his body to be surrendered to them so that they could vent their hatred on it with appropriate mockery and outrage, and there was indignation when the demand was refused. Pertinax, anxious to spare the feelings of the Praetorian Guards, ordered that his predecessor should receive decent burial.

The Praetorian Guards were not alone in viewing the course of

* See Bibliographical Appendix, page 201, for fuller details about him.

events with alarm and despondency. To the comfortable middle class, farmers, tradesmen and artisans, the news of the murder of Commodus came as a disagreeable shock when the details leaked out. They knew him only as head of the State and had no experience of his personal idiosyncrasies, or the reign of terror imposed on the court. It was enough for them that his government afforded the political stability that they needed to earn a living and bring up a family, and they had no sympathy with the demonstrators, the rootless, the adolescent, the criminal fringe, who grasped the opportunity of his downfall to run riot in the streets. For the best part of a century Rome had enjoyed and grown accustomed to the secure prosperity of the Age of the Antonines, with its orderly transition of power from Emperor to Emperor designate. The nearest parallel to the present crisis lay beyond living memory, the murder of the Emperor Domitian in 96. Men hoped devoutly that the outcome would be as harmless as it was on that occasion. In place of the hated Domitian a mild and well-meaning senator was chosen, the elderly Nerva, who reigned without offence and was succeeded in due course by a young man of promise whom he adopted, the Emperor Trajan.

There was an earlier precedent, however, than the murder of Domitian, one less comfortable in retrospect, to show what might happen when the Empire was left headless. In 69, the notorious year of the four Emperors, the vacancy created by Nero's suicide encouraged generals commanding armies in the provinces to advance on Rome, where each in turn tried to seize the purple for himself. Chaos and civil war were the result, till at last Vespasian, the fourth, emerged victorious and established by force a dynasty of his own. It was urgently necessary for Pertinax to convince public opinion that events would repeat the example of 96 and not of 69, and he sent word at once into the provinces to inform the governors of his accession and demand their allegiance. Many refused to believe what they heard, so long was it since any such upheaval had disturbed the capital of the Empire, and the messengers were put in prison as bearers of false news. It was not, Dio explains, because the governors concerned were unwilling for the report to be true, but that they were afraid of the anger of Commodus if they prematurely assumed him to be dead, whereas they counted on indulgence from Pertinax if it proved in fact that the messengers were wrongly imprisoned.

The new régime was still far from secure. On the third day of the reign there was a riot in the Praetorian barracks when the soldiers were called to take the oath. Nursing a grievance against their Prefect for the way in which he gerrymandered the acclamation and foisted Pertinax on them, they turned suddenly to a spectator at the ceremony, Triarius Maternus, a senator of distinction, offered to acclaim him Emperor and take the oath to him instead. Triarius was cousin to Falco's colleague, who shared with him the consulship of the year; but whether or not he came by prearrangement at Falco's instigation, he took fright and ran away when the soldiers saluted him. They caught hold of him to detain him, and in the struggle that followed his clothes were pulled off. When at last his too-zealous supporters let him go, he fled naked through the streets to the palace to be first with his explanation to Pertinax and disclaim any treasonable intent. Pertinax accepted his excuses and exonerated him; but Triarius left Rome shortly afterwards to live in the country, unable to bear the ridicule and lewd comments which the memory of his undignified figure provoked.

Laetus was in a difficult position, sharing with Eclectus and Marcia responsibility for the murder of Commodus, which the men under his command deplored. He saw that the only way to retain their loyalty and reconcile them to events was to persuade them that they would receive as generous treatment from the new Emperor as from the old. It was a distasteful idea to Pertinax, who was frugal by nature, having been taught by stringent circumstances in his youth to prefer saving to spending. He was bent on curtailing the extravagance of the largess enjoyed by the soldiers, as he hinted not too tactfully in his speech in the barracks in the early hours of New Year's Day. In justification of his policy he could point to the dwindling resources left in the treasury by Commodus. A plan was found at last that offered a temporary solution to the dispute: to raise money he put up for sale all the luxuries amassed by Commodus for sport and pleasure, costly armour and weapons for gladiatorial displays, magnificent racing chariots, fine clothes, jewellery, many objects of art of lubricious design, and a bevy of pretty slaves. The sale served a double purpose, both replenishing the Imperial treasury and attracting fresh obloquy to Commodus whose vices were exposed to envious disapproval.

Laetus co-operated by rounding up former favourites of Commodus living in well-heeled retirement on their ill-gotten gains. He not only confiscated their wealth, but also put them to public shame by revealing the services by which they earned it and the insulting nicknames attached to them. It was a favourite habit of Commodus's with his minions to gloat over their degradation and taunt them with their compliance.

Enough money was raised from these sources to appease the soldiers
and buy a respite from their demands. Pertinax was careful at the same
time to retain and foster the goodwill shown him in the senate. In
proof of the leniency and justice to be expected under his government,
in contrast with the arbitrary tyranny of the previous reign, he ordered
the cases of many prominent people put to death by Commodus to
be re-examined, the false accusers to be punished and the bodies of the
victims exhumed and reburied with appropriate honour in their
ancestral tombs. As few changes as possible were made among those
in charge of high offices of State. The only important post that he
refilled was his own of Prefect of the City, to which he appointed his
father-in-law, Flavius Sulpicianus. Eclectus was kept on as chamberlain
and married Marcia. Both were devotedly loyal to the new régime,
in whose accession to power they had played so active a part. For those
who cherished Antonine precedent, recalling the stability that was its
fruit, there was encouragement when Pertinax refused for his son the
title of Caesar, Emperor designate, offered by the senate. The reason
that he gave was that the boy was too young, not yet fit for the
honour; but his behaviour is in keeping with the view that he had
already promised to adopt Septimius Severus as his heir and was only
waiting for a suitable opportunity to announce his intention. Meanwhile he sent his own son and daughter away from court to live with
Sulpicianus, their maternal grandfather. Both were still children, born
of his marriage to a wife much younger than himself.

The conciliatory policy was not without effect. Many leading
figures from the past, eminent under Marcus Aurelius, reappeared in
public life, among them Pompeianus, the companion in the Temple of
Concord to whom Pertinax offered to resign the purple in the cold
dawn of New Year's Day. Dio records his surprise at seeing Pompeianus again in the senate-house and notes that his eyesight, whose
failure had been his excuse for absence while Commodus reigned,
made sudden recovery. Pertinax treated the ageing statesman with
marked respect, inviting him during the deliberations of the senate to
sit beside him on the presiding bench, but not, Dio adds, in a way that
reflected on the others: 'With all of us he was on terms of utmost
equality, easy to approach, ready to listen to an opinion that anyone
expressed, and replying as man to man with his own.'

Dio may be guilty of partiality, but he speaks from personal observation, and it is clear that Pertinax, a self-made man, preserved the
unpretentious manners and simple tastes of his upbringing. His thrifty
habits earned sneers from his enemies. Even Dio, who attended banquets

in the palace, comments on the plainness of the cooking; but if the entertainment failed to satisfy the gourmet at least it provided food for the intellect. Pertinax enjoyed literary conversation. When he dined in private with his wife a favourite guest was an old friend of his youth, who had been his colleague when he was a schoolmaster.

Another side to his character is revealed by the successful course of his military career. His affability could be misleading, and many accused him of duplicity when suave words bore fruit in stern action. In the army he was known as a strict disciplinarian. Whether in spite of or because of the reputation, he enjoyed respect and popularity among the soldiers under his command, especially those on the Danube where he served in the wars of Marcus Aurelius. In 186 when he was governor of Britain a rioting legion urged him to set himself up as Emperor in rivalry to Commodus. The proposal was offensive both to his native caution and to his hatred of military indiscipline. He denounced the men as mutineers, punishing them the more ruthlessly because their misbehaviour put his own life in danger. He made haste to write to Commodus to exonerate himself.

The face presented to the world was that of a hard-working servant of the State, amiable, trustworthy and law-abiding; but it covered an ambition ready to respond when his friends in Rome invited him to join them in a conspiracy to seize the reins of government. This was no wildcat scheme such as that proposed by the mutinous soldiers in Britain. The conspirators were men holding high office and exerting powerful influence. He knew moreover from information available to him as Prefect of the City that Commodus provoked mounting resentment and was ripe for overthrow, and he may fairly be credited with the belief that a change of government was in the public interest. Even so, he drew back in alarm when premature disclosure called for precipitate action to avert disaster, and although he yielded to persuasion when he had proof that Commodus was dead his hesitation persisted. No success ever banished it entirely. It was as if in his heart he was unable to believe that he was truly Emperor. Yet he was well qualified in many respects for his position, and high hopes were entertained of him by his friends. He had ideas which might have been fruitful if he had been given time to carry them out, such as his plan to make over to working farmers any land lying unfarmed and derelict, whether under private ownership or on the Imperial estates, and to accord the occupant immunity from taxation for ten years and permanent security of tenure. It was his intention to publish a programme of reforms during the celebration of the Parilia, a pastoral festival traditionally regarded as the anniversary of the foundation of Rome. The date fell on 21 April, but by then he was dead.

Trouble came as soon as the money raised from the sale of curios in the palace was exhausted. The problem returned: to satisfy the demands of the Praetorian Guard he had to drain the treasury of resources needed for the administration of the State. His attempt to solve it at the expense of the soldiers by lowering their rate of pay provoked angry discontent and accusations of parsimony. They were jealous of their privileges, an *élite* founded by Augustus when the Empire was first established to serve as his bodyguard, the only armed force in the city apart from the urban cohorts, the police. An Emperor strong enough to control them found them useful to enforce his policy and suppress revolt; but when the Imperial government was weak, and discipline neglected, they were ready to turn from servant into master and assume the functions of kingmaker. For a long time they had been given no chance. They were impatient to grasp it now.

The part played in events by Laetus is obscure. It is known that disagreement arose between him and Pertinax, and it is likely that the cause was the cut in pay for the soldiers, which he deplored because the mutinous spirit that it fostered in the barracks threatened his own authority as Prefect. When Pertinax rejected his advice he began, according to Dio, to look for a more amenable candidate to replace him, and his choice fell surprisingly on the consul Falco, who had denounced Pertinax at the meeting of the senate in the early hours of New Year's Day as the puppet of Laetus and Marcia. It seems that Falco belonged to the party in the senate unable to forgive Pertinax for his lowly birth, that Laetus approached him as the most prominent of the malcontents, and that he himself accepted the incongruous ally for the sake of the immediate advantage. There was a weakness, however, in the alliance between the most conservative senators and the Praetorian Guard. The former commanded no majority in the senate-house. When the revolt broke out Pertinax was at the port of Ostia, discussing problems relating to the supply of imported corn on which Rome depended. He hurried back at once, summoned the senate and appealed for support. Soldiers from the barracks were among the spectators, also freedmen and others to whose fortunes, accumulated under Commodus, the accession of Pertinax put an end. These muttered threateningly against Pertinax when he spoke, but the effect was the opposite of that intended. The senate retorted with a vote pronouncing Falco a public enemy, a verdict carrying the penalty of death. There was disappointment when Pertinax expressed reluctance to shed a senator's blood and insisted on granting a reprieve. Falco suffered nothing worse than banishment to his estate in the country.

Less mercy was shown to the soldiers who supported him. Laetus, whose own part in the affair had been either kept secret or forgiven, picked out the leading troublemakers for ruthless punishment. It is probable that he was glad of the opportunity to be rid of them, hoping that their removal would bring the others to a submissive frame of mind so that he could carry on his duties unmolested in renewed harmony with Pertinax.

His hopes were not fulfilled. The punishment inflicted on a few wholly failed to intimidate the rest of the soldiers, provoking them instead to fury. They were determined to avenge the victims and were convinced that violent resistance alone would save them from sharing the same fate themselves. Laetus could do nothing with them. They had no respect any longer for his authority. When news reached the palace on 28 March of scenes of disorder on a scale bordering on open rebellion Pertinax sent the Prefect of the City, his father-in-law Sulpicianus, to the barracks to reason with the demonstrators. The negotiations had at first some success. Many were favourably impressed by the arguments that Sulpicianus put to them to persuade them to moderate their demands. Only a militant minority of about two hundred stood out against him; but when these saw that they were losing support among their comrades, and that moderate counsels were prevailing, they decided to act on their own and confront the Emperor in person. Marching in closed ranks with drawn swords, they entered the city (the barracks lay outside at some distance from the walls) and advanced through the streets to the palace on the Palatine hill. It was still quite early in the morning.

Pertinax had arranged to attend a recital of poetry that day at the Athenaeum, but when he heard of the outbreak of rioting he put the engagement off and stayed at home. He was waiting anxiously for news from Sulpicianus when his wife ran to tell him that there were soldiers coming up the hill, and as he looked from the window their shouts of defiance and brandished weapons showed him clearly enough that they meant harm. His first impulse was to summon Laetus, who was with him in the palace. Low as the credit of the Praetorian Prefect had fallen, it was his duty in such an emergency to go out and restore discipline. The sight of their commanding officer, however, and the sound of his voice served only to inflame the men's ill-humour. They greeted him with threats and jeers, and he pulled his cloak over his face and fled.

The soldiers entered the palace unopposed, favoured by treachery among the officers on guard at the gate, many of whom owed their places to Commodus and resented the stricter rules introduced by Pertinax to discourage fraud and corruption. It was unlucky for Pertinax that when he cancelled his visit to the Athenaeum he dismissed the armed escort waiting to attend him. Nevertheless he had forces available in the palace to defend him, a night-patrol from the urban cohorts still on duty at that hour of the morning and numbers of loyal retainers. His friends urged him to seek refuge in an inner room till these could be mustered; but he refused to hide, regarding it as beneath his dignity, and insisted on going out in person to face the rioters and remonstrate with them. His behaviour resembled that recorded of him when he suppressed the mutiny in Britain, exposing himself so fearlessly to danger that he was gravely wounded. In political decisions he was cautious to excess, but he had no lack of personal courage. Perhaps too he relied on his own suavity of speech to persuade and conciliate.

He came out into the courtyard accompanied by a few attendants including the Egyptian chamberlain Eclectus, husband of Marcia. His appearance took the soldiers by surprise. They were abashed by the dignity of his bearing, and when he addressed them, reminding them of the allegiance that they owed to their Emperor, most of them listened in crestfallen silence and sheathed their swords. Not so their ringleader, a Tungrian recruit from the upper Meuse. This man, fearing retribution if his comrades failed him and called the riot off, strode forward waving his sword in the air.

'Here's what the soldiers owe you,' he shouted, and lunging at Pertinax he struck him a savage blow. The others, fired by his example, drew their weapons again and fell on the Emperor, stabbing him to death. His attendants fled, all except Eclectus, who fought fiercely to defend him till he himself also was killed. He was a man, it was said, ruled by his emotions, whether they took the form of passion for Marcia, hatred of Commodus or loyalty to Pertinax.

After a reign of eighty-seven days Pertinax was dead. The soldiers cut off his head, stuck it on a spear and returned with it in triumph to their barracks. The news provoked consternation in the city, especially in the senate where, as was seen at the time of Falco's revolt, Pertinax had many supporters. Even those senators who held it against him that he was not one of themselves, and would gladly have replaced him, became alarmed now that the deed was done by the Praetorian Guard, in whose insubordination they saw a threat to their own authority.

Among the general public there was unqualified regret, less from love of Pertinax himself than from fear of the future for a Rome again left without an Emperor.

The soldiers however were jubilant. They regarded themselves as conquerors able to order events to their will. There was no armed force fit to contend with them in the city or the neighbouring region of Italy, and in any case the barracks that they inhabited were a walled fortress all but impregnable. They shut themselves up there to decide what next to do. Sulpicianus was still among them, no longer an Emperor's emissary but a prisoner unable to escape. Restraining his feelings when they showed him the bleeding head impaled on a spear, he tried to negotiate his succession to the purple in his son-in-law's place. Whether his motive was ambition or genuine concern to save the State from anarchy and protect the dead Emperor's wife and children, his own daughter and grandchildren, he made sufficient impression on the soldiers to persuade them to take him seriously as a candidate; but the negotiations ran into difficulties as they haggled over the price to be paid by the new Emperor for military support and acclamation. At last the soldiers lost patience, and a few with the loudest voices came out and stood on the ramparts announcing to all and sundry that the Empire was for sale and inviting competitive bids.

A crowd gathered beneath to listen to them, and words of the proposed auction passed quickly from mouth to mouth; but for a time there were no bidders. Most senators who heard what was happening were appalled by the insult to Imperial dignity, a scandal without parallel in Roman history. There was present in Rome, however, a man of great wealth called Didius Julianus who was renowned for his greed for money and haste to spend it. He was of sufficiently exalted rank to aspire to the purple and had held a number of responsible posts, rising without remark through the usual stages of an official career, except for a period of disgrace under Commodus, a misadventure common to many others. This Didius was at dinner when news of the auction reached him. Several of his guests, anxious to flatter him, told him that there was no one better fitted for the appointment than himself. His wife and daughter eagerly agreed, urging him to go at once and bid for the prize. He needed little persuasion. Interrupting his meal, he hurried out into the street and made for the barracks.

The soldiers were still on the wall waiting to do business. Didius stood beneath and shouted his bid up to them, indicating the amount with his fingers when his voice was lost in the noise. The auctioneer took the bid and repeated it to Sulpicianus behind him within, who promptly raised it. The price offered mounted rapidly as each outbid the other. Didius tried to sway the issue in his favour by warning that if Sulpicianus won he would take revenge for the death of his son-in-law, Pertinax; but Sulpicianus himself, standing inside the fortress with the soldiers around him, was able to reasure them, and they refused to be diverted from trade. The bidding went on, but Sulpicianus was approaching his limit. He was not as wealthy as Didius, and he knew from his own observation of the difficulties with which Pertinax had to contend that he could rely on no substantial contribution from public funds. When Didius made a culminating bid more than doubling the preceding rise, the contest was over. The auctioneer's hammer fell, and the prize was knocked down to Didius for a sum equivalent to a bonus of five years' pay for every man serving in the Praetorian Guard.

The spectators looked on with sullen hostility. The murder of two Emperors within three months confirmed their gloomiest forebodings of insecurity and anarchy, and the farce of the auction was an added outrage to their feelings, an insult to the majesty of Rome. When the soldiers hailed Didius with the Imperial title, the popular outcry became so threatening that he was in danger of being lynched until a ladder was lowered from the ramparts and he climbed up it to safety. The soldiers dared not open the gate to admit him for fear that it would be rushed. Having escaped ignominiously into the barracks, he found protection but little honour. He was a puppet Emperor created by the soldiers, and they were in no mood to let him forget his dependence. They demanded that all the perquisites and privileges which they had enjoyed under Commodus should be restored, and that in token of the changed direction of affairs the name and titles of Commodus which Pertinax had removed should be reinstated on their standards. In place of Laetus, whom they deposed, they put forward two nominees of their own to be Praetorian Prefects. Sulpicianus was deprived of his post of Prefect of the City, but allowed to depart unharmed. Didius agreed to everything demanded of him. He was in no position to deny his protectors their will. They provided an escort to conduct him back into the city, heavily armed to guard him from the angry populace. Stones were thrown at the procession as it passed through the streets. Jeers greeted the victorious bidder in his fancy-price purple.

As he entered the palace he recovered his spirits, able at last to enjoy the prestige of Imperial dignity. In the dining-room a meal prepared for Pertinax was still laid out on the table. Didius stared with a grunt of contempt at the homely fare and sent servants to a fashionable restaurant to bring back whatever was most expensive on the menu. Having eaten, he joined a party of friends to play dice. The headless body of Pertinax was stored out of sight in a shed.

3
Civil War

Messengers galloping on horseback kept the capital in touch with the most distant parts of the Empire. The Imperial post was well organized with frequent relays, by which news travelled to inform the governor of Upper Pannonia in less than ten days of the course of public affairs. Septimius would have known by the second week in January of the successful outcome of the revolution that overthrew Commodus on the last night of the year 192, and he could announce to the legions under his command that Pertinax was their Emperor and call on them to swear allegiance to the new government. Unlike the Praetorian Guard at Rome, the soldiers stationed on the Danube had no reason to regret the change. Commodus was a mere name to them; but Pertinax they knew personally and liked and respected, remembering him from the days when he held command there in the wars of Marcus Aurelius. Septimius could count on their loyalty and on the benevolence of the governors in neighbouring provinces, including his own brother, Septimius Geta, in Lower Moesia downstream near the Danube's mouth. He profited too from the care with which Laetus and his friends, organizing the conspiracy against Commodus, filled key positions in the Empire with men who shared their views.

For the best part of three months the news remained cheerful, reporting the success achieved by the new Emperor in allaying discontent in the Praetorian Guard and winning the support of a majority of the senate. Septimius had special cause for satisfaction when he heard that Pertinax refused to accept for his son the title of Caesar, Emperor designate. It was evident that this was held in abeyance in accordance with agreement for Septimius himself, and the announcement would probably be made in April at the festival of the Parilia together with the other reforms that Pertinax had in mind. Septimius could reasonably expect that he would then be recalled to Rome to a position of power at the Emperor's side, and that this was the last winter that he and Julia would spend at Carnuntum.

Nevertheless it seems that even at this stage he was uneasy in his mind. He had a dream which, like those at Lugdunum, haunted his imagination in vivid detail. He saw Pertinax riding on a splendidly accoutred horse along the Sacred Way, the busy street leading into the Forum in Rome. At the entrance to the Forum the horse threw Pertinax off, then sank on its haunches for Septimius standing at its side to mount and ride on in safety. Belief in the prophetic meaning of dreams was generally accepted among men of his time, and it was not uncommon for the credulous to reinforce the dreams with stories made up after the event. In this case, however, there is evidence that the dream, whether precognitive or not, was an authentic experience retained in his memory. When he became Emperor he put up an equestrian statue at the spot in the street in Rome of which he had dreamt as he lay in bed at Carnuntum.

The first week in April brought news that confirmed his worst fears: the murder of Pertinax and sale of the Empire to Didius added the frustration of his prospects to personal sorrow for the loss of an old and trusted friend. His dismay was shared by the officers and men of the legions under his command, and when he appealed for their help to avenge Pertinax they responded with enthusiasm. There were veterans among them who had served under Pertinax and esteemed him for his justice and benevolence. Even those to whom he was only the distant Emperor in Rome were attracted by an adventure that promised excitement and profit, and all of them as legionary soldiers on active service felt contempt for the pampered *élite* of the Praetorian Guard.

The scandal of the auction shocked them to the heart. To their simple minds the Imperial office had inviolable sanctity. It needed little prompting for them to acclaim Septimius himself as Emperor, and he accepted with the barest show of reluctance. The purple was his by right. If Pertinax had lived he would have appointed him Emperor designate.

Messages went out to the governors of neighbouring provinces demanding their allegiance to the new Emperor Septimius Severus. Many of them owed their position to Laetus, picked to support the conspiracy against Commodus, and now when they heard that Pertinax was dead they accepted Septimius as his successor without question. They sent favourable replies, promising co-operation in overthrowing the usurper at Rome. An expeditionary force began to assemble at Carnuntum, drawn from the military establishment along the entire frontier from the Black Sea to the North Sea.

While the legions were gathering, many from a distance, Septimius heard that he had a rival who disputed his claim to the purple: Pescennius Niger, governor of Syria. It seemed that the example set in 69, the year of the four Emperors, was after all to be re-enacted. Niger, like Septimius, was of middle-class origin. He was the older of the two, already in his middle fifties, with a career very similar in many respects to that of Pertinax, rising from humble beginnings to a succession of offices of mounting importance in the army. He held a military command in Gaul in 186 when Septimius was propraetor at Lugdunum, and the two were associated in suppressing a dangerous gang of deserters running riot in the province. Septimius spoke with approval of the competence shown by Niger in the task. There is no reason, however, to suppose that they maintained contact afterwards, or that Niger was privy to the conspiracy in which Septimius and his friends were involved later in Rome. He owed his appointment in Syria, not to Laetus, but to one of the favourites in the palace to whom Commodus gave ear. The events of New Year's Day 193 took him by surprise.

Dio describes him as dull-witted, of faulty judgement. This is not inconsistent with the character of a soldier who could earn promotion by his competence in the ordinary run of duties, rounding up bandits in Gaul, for instance, but whose mind lacked the subtlety needed for affairs of state. It could be that the second-rate quality of his talents made him a more useful, more tractable tool for powerful interests. His name first provoked attention when it was heard on the lips of demonstrators in Rome calling for him to come and punish Didius and the Praetorian Guard. They were unlikely to pick out the obscure governor of Syria unless the idea was put into their heads by timely suggestion. The Eastern provinces, on which Niger relied for support, were the richest in the Empire. The magnates who controlled the wealth wanted an Emperor of their own choosing, no matter if the price to be paid were civil war.

When the news reached Septimius his immediate care was to ensure that the war was a duel between him and Niger, not a three-sided contest. The only remaining governor able to threaten him, of whose sympathies he was in doubt, was Clodius Albinus in Britain, formidable not only on account of the legions under his command but also of the influence that his noble birth earned him in the senate. Septimius wrote at once, offering him the title of Emperor designate if he refrained from intervening in the coming struggle. For the time being the promise had the desired effect. Albinus was content to remain an onlooker.

Meanwhile, with as much of his army as was already mustered, Septimius set off to march to Rome. Many legions coming from a distance were still on their way, but he was unwilling to wait for them. Inactivity was uncongenial to his impulsive nature, and he had had enough of it in recent months watching from the outer edge of the Empire the course of crucial events at the centre. The need to forestall Niger provided a motive for haste. He urged the men on, forcing the pace with such vigour that at night they slept without unbuckling their breastplates. He himself shared all their hardships, sleeping as rough as they did. In less than a month the army was at the head of the Adriatic, entering Italy.

The effort could have been saved. Niger was still at Antioch, his headquarters in Syria, making preparations at leisure, encouraged by reports of the unpopularity of Didius and demonstrations in his own favour at Rome to believe that the purple was his for the taking. He saw no need to hurry. Even if he knew that he had a rival in Septimius, he was unaware that the Pannonian legions were already advancing.

Didius awaited the invasion in a state bordering on panic. He had enemies enough surrounding him at home, senators jealous of their constitutional rights who resented his usurpation of the purple, and a turbulent population whose contempt for the hero of the auction sale was inflamed by paid agitators, mainly agents of Niger. He was losing favour even with the Praetorian Guard. Apart from a small instalment on account, the purchase price offered for the Empire was still unpaid. To restore his credit and earn acclaim in the barracks he ordered the arrest and punishment of the murderers of Commodus, to whose bounty the soldiers looked back with nostalgia. Laetus was dragged from retirement and put to death; so also Marcia, no longer the naked Amazon adorning an Emperor's seal, powerful protectress of Christians, but still in the eyes of Didius a dangerous conspirator, passionately mourning her husband killed in defence of Pertinax. To these victims Didius added a number of children sacrificed with magic rites to conjure help from the underworld.

Nevertheless Septimius advanced unhindered through Italy. Except for the raid of trans-Danubian tribesmen in the reign of Marcus Aurelius, there had been no war on Italian territory for more than a century. The cities unaccustomed to an armed invader sent envoys to meet and come to terms with him as he approached. Didius in Rome got the

senate to declare him a public enemy and even appointed a successor
to replace him as governor of Upper Pannonia; but these were empty
gestures as power to enforce them was totally lacking. A detachment
of the Praetorian Guard sent to Ravenna to take control of the Adriatic
fleet and cut the invader's communications in the rear failed ignominiously; the sailors went over to Septimius, and the Praetorians returned in haste to Rome. The latter, demoralized by their comfortable
life in barracks, were ill fitted for active service in the field.

Didius enjoyed no better success when he sent agents from his force
of secret police to assassinate his rival. Seeing how well their victim
was guarded the assassins lost their nerve, confessed their design and
earned pardon by working for Septimius instead. As the enemy relentlessly drew nearer, frantic preparations were made at Rome to repel
the attack. Dio who was present describes the mockery that Didius
provoked by an attempt to enlist the elephants from the circus, putting
turrets on their backs with armed gladiators inside. The elephants,
unaccustomed to the load, stampeded, tipping the garrison to the
ground. Another plan, no less abortive, was to send out a procession
of Vestal Virgins, votaresses of the sacred fire, the most venerated of
Roman institutions, to restrain the invaders by an appeal to religious
sentiment. The priests discouraged it, apprehensive of the response that
the little bevy of chastity would elicit from Pannonian legionaries.

In despair Didius offered to resign the purple to the respected elder
statesman, Pompeianus, on condition that his own life was spared. It
was the second offer of the sort to be made to Pompeianus; he refused
it as firmly as on the occasion in the Temple of Concord with Pertinax
on New Year's Day. With Septimius already at the gate a last hope
remained for Didius. He summoned the senate and asked for a vote
dividing the Empire into half, one for himself, the other for the man
pronounced at his request so recently a public enemy. There was no
need for the senate to debate the question. Septimius let it be known
that he demanded the whole Empire and would share it with no one.
His forces entered the city unopposed. The Praetorian Guard, intimidated and outnumbered, deserted to his cause, and the senators,
yielding to superior force, most of them with relief and satisfaction,
condemned Didius to death.

An officer went at once to the palace to carry out the sentence.
Didius lay cowering on a bed, and his last words are recorded: 'What
harm have I done? Whom have I killed?'

He played no part in the murder of Pertinax, but there were many
of less exalted rank whose blood he shed to sustain him in his brief

glory. His wife and daughter who urged him to bid for power received his body for burial.

The senate made haste to salute Septimius as Emperor and to atone by present deference for the affronts, including the stigma of public enemy, put on him in the recent past in obedience to Didius. He himself was ready enough to overlook them. He had a hot temper, and when need arose he could be ruthless; but he was not vindictive by nature, preferring conciliation to vengeance. Consistent in loyalty and gratitude to his friends, he took care to reward those whose work contributed to his victory. These included many senators, former supporters of Pertinax, who regarded him as the rightful heir. He chose two of them to become his sons-in-law, husbands of the daughters born of his first marriage. The girls, now in their late teens, were living in Italy, where, less fortunate than their half-brothers, Julia's two small sons, safe with their mother at Carnuntum, they had been in grave danger from the events following the death of Pertinax. It was a favourite tactic in civil strife, one adopted by Septimius himself in his struggle with Niger, to hold a rival's children as hostages. Didius however was kept too busy and reigned for too short a time to find and seize the prey, and the girls could now emerge from hiding for a fashionable wedding in Rome. Little more is recorded of them or their husbands, but if they lived for the normal span of years they were witnesses from beginning to end of the history of the dynasty founded by their father.

Even those in the senate who were known to be opponents of Septimius, and were unable to plead that they acted under duress, suffered no worse punishment than a heavy fine. It was assessed with scrupulous exactitude. A senator accused of correspondence with Niger and speeches urging his claim explained in defence that he only wanted to get rid of Didius, that it made no matter to him whether Niger or Septimius accomplished the task, and it was by chance that he picked the former. Septimius found him fifty per cent guilty, and half the fine was remitted.

No mercy however was shown to the murderers of Pertinax. The men who took part in the riot at the palace were identified and put to death. Towards the rest of the Praetorian Guard Septimius acted with more caution. He was determined to be master in Rome, to put an end to the insolence of soldiers who claimed licence to set up an Emperor at their pleasure; but he wished at the same time to avoid open conflict with a well-armed force occupying strongly fortified barracks. He summoned them to a parade ground between the barracks and the city, announcing that it was for a ceremony to celebrate his victory. They themselves had been waiting in suspense to know what was in store for them, and when the order came they obeyed with relief, taking it to mean that they were restored to favour to play their traditional part in a public celebration. They appeared, as was the custom on such occasions, in ceremonial dress without weapons except the purely ornamental. Unarmed and crowned with laurel, they stood drawn up in front of the platform from which Septimius addressed them.

There was nothing conciliatory in his words. His voice rose angrily as he denounced their treachery to their Emperor, his friend Pertinax, their effrontery in putting the Empire up for sale and the brutal violence of the reign of terror that they had imposed on peaceful citizens. They listened with eyes intently fixed on him, not observing what was happening behind their backs, where his own soldiers from the Pannonian legions were ready to close in on them and surround them. As Septimius came to the end of his speech the legionaries sprang forward, brandishing swords and spears. There was no battle, no one was hurt. The Praetorians, unarmed at the mercy of armed enemies, submitted without resistance while their tunics were stripped of belts and badges of rank. Helpless and humiliated, they waited for the Emperor to pronounce sentence. He told them that their lives would be spared if they left Rome and never again came within a hundred miles of its walls. Then he dismissed them, and they fled from the field.

A few tried to return to the barracks, but they were forestalled. While the fortress was empty a detachment of legionaries had been sent to occupy it and bar access to the weapons stored there.

The disgrace of a body of men hated for their turbulence and arrogance earned Septimius popularity in the city. The crowds that had shouted for Niger transferred their allegiance without hesitation to a deliverer present in overwhelming force, able to banish the troublemakers, depose their puppet and restore peace. The relief was shared by many in the senate who despised Didius and were appalled by the prevailing anarchy. Even those who were of Niger's party, having interests in the Eastern provinces, were content for the time being to lie low, thankful for the clemency extended to them. It helped to reconcile the senators to Septimius that he was on good terms with Albinus in Britain, his designated heir. Albinus with his aristocratic credentials enjoyed esteem as a pillar of the senatorial order.

Septimius remained in Rome for thirty days from June to July 193.

He presided with appropriate pomp and mourning over the funeral of Pertinax, whose ministers, removed by Didius, he reinstated in office. Other positions of importance in the government were filled with followers of his own who had proved their loyalty in the recent troubles. Having dismissed the Praetorian Guard to the last man, he re-established it on a new basis. Enlistment in the corps of *élite* had been reserved hitherto for the sons of well-to-do families in Italy, who enjoyed a rate of pay and other conditions of service that were the envy of the rest of the army. The new Praetorians whom he installed in the barracks were not Italians at all but soldiers chosen from the legions accompanying him, Pannonians and other natives of the frontier. He hoped that, untainted with urban manners, they would fulfil their duties with simple-minded devotion. For a time indeed their conduct earned approval; but as they grew accustomed to civilization and lost their awe of it, they succumbed to temptation and were often as guilty as their predecessors of insubordination and arrogant abuse of their privileges. On such occasions their outlandish speech and appearance aggravated popular resentment.

Having done what he could to provide for stable government in his absence, Septimius led his army back round the head of the Adriatic to complete his conquest of the Empire. In spite of his success in Rome and the recognition of his title by the senate he still had to contend with Niger, the rival claimant, who, stirred from complacency, was ready at last to take action. Egypt, the vital granary on which the supply of corn for the Roman population depended, already lay under Niger's control, and he himself with the forces available in Syria and neighbouring provinces was advancing north to the Bosporus to invade Europe. He made his headquarters at Byzantium, the town chosen a century later by Constantine the Great to be the eastern capital of his Empire under the name of New Rome, known still later as Constantinople. It was a stronghold without rival in the East, renowned for its massive fortifications and built on a site that gave it command of the narrow seas. Septimius descended with his army through the Balkans to confront him there.

Little is known of Julia's doings at this time. In later years it was her habit to accompany her husband on expeditions, even when the purpose was a military campaign; but on his march to Rome in the spring of 193 the urgency was too great and the issue too uncertain. Her presence would have been an encumbrance, especially with her two little sons, aged five and four. After the defeat of Didius and his own acceptance of the title of Emperor from the senate Septimius conferred on her that of Augusta, borne by the Emperor's wife, and coins were struck representing her appropriately as Venus. She was with him in Rome to receive the honour, and when he left for the East she followed him, probably travelling in greater comfort by sea. Her native Syria, being the enemy's heartland, was no safe refuge; but she had a wide choice of cities farther north ready to offer her their hospitality in the wake of her husband's formidable army. Prominent citizens in Illyria and Thrace would be eager to earn gratitude from Septimius by offering a country house to the Augusta to accommodate her household, which included at this time not only her own family but also Niger's wife and children held as hostages, enforced guests. Niger, fearing for their safety if Syria were invaded, had sent them abroad; but their hiding-place was betrayed to Septimius, and they were hunted down and caught. Their captor was Fulvius Plautianus, an old friend since his boyhood in Leptis, of whom more will be heard later in the reign.

While the hostages were under Julia's care they were treated with consideration, as if they had been her own kin; but they were none the less in an unenviable position. Septimius hoped to use them as a lever to persuade Niger to abandon his claim, promising that if he did so he would be allowed to live unmolested in retirement. Niger, an obstinate man slow to move but tenacious once he took action, rejected the terms. The most to which he would agree was that they should share the Empire between them, but this was a proposal that Septimius refused to consider. Niger's wife knew her husband too well to believe that her danger would play any decisive part in the negotiations. He prided himself on the sternness of his principles and was heard to describe his wife as an easily replaceable apparatus for bearing him offspring.

For the present, however, the hostages were left in peace in Julia's house, while Septimius pressed on to enforce his terms by victory in battle. He laid siege to Byzantium; but the fortifications were too strong to be taken by storm, and he was unwilling to delay there. Detaching a part of his forces to keep the town invested, he himself with the rest crossed the narrow sea into Asia, where Niger and his army awaited him. In the battles that followed Septimius was victorious. Although his own experience of military command was small he could recognize talent in others and chose capable generals to serve him. They drove the enemy southwards through Asia Minor, subjugating on the way and demanding allegiance from the Greek cities along the coast. The jealousy among these was such that it was sufficient reason if one of them adhered to Septimius for its neighbour to declare for Niger. Nevertheless the work was accomplished at last, and before the end of the year Niger and his army were in flight across the Taurus mountains into Syria. Septimius retired to spend the winter at Perinthus on the northern shore of the Sea of Marmara, where Julia joined him, and on 4 April 194 they celebrated their elder son's sixth birthday.

At this time Niger's cause suffered a grave blow from the defection of the Prefect of Egypt, which saved Septimius from fear of an embargo on corn for Rome. There were revolts too in a number of Syrian cities, especially those where Julia's family had influence. As soon as the passes were open in the mountains, Septimius sent his army through the Taurus to invade the fertile plain of Syria beyond. Niger mustered his own men to block the way, and a final battle was fought at Issus at the head of the Gulf of Alexandretta, a site already known to history for the decisive defeat inflicted on the Persians more than five hundred years earlier by Alexander the Great. The result for Niger was crushing defeat, and as his army scattered he took a fast horse and galloped back with a small party to Antioch; but he found no support in the town, only lamentation and panic, and he rode on in despair hoping to reach the Euphrates and sanctuary beyond the frontier with the King of Parthia. He was overtaken by his pursuers, and they cut off his head and brought it back to Septimius, who sent it to Byzantium, still besieged and still resisting, to prove to the citizens that their leader was dead and the cause lost for which they fought.

Not even their putative Emperor's severed head could persuade the Byzantines to surrender; but elsewhere Niger's death was regarded as the end of the civil war, to the great relief of the Roman world. For the past year and more there had been crisis after crisis threatening collapse of the established order, the *Pax Romana*, the settled condition of life familiar since far beyond living memory to a population extending from the Atlantic Ocean to the Persian Gulf. The outcome of the battle of Issus seemed to dispel the nightmare. Once more an Emperor reigned undisputed, strong enough to maintain authority so that people could live undisturbed. Few grieved for Niger, as few would have grieved for Septimius if he had lost. The Roman world cared little who the Emperor was, only for stable and capable government.

Septimius himself did his best to encourage the sanguine mood. He refrained from vindictive reprisals. Niger's wife and children, no longer useful as hostages, left Julia's care to live in retirement, where, it was supposed, they would play no further part in public affairs. The only senator put to death was Asellius Aemilianus, governor of

Asia, who was in command of a part of Niger's army. Taken prisoner while the struggle was still in progress, he was considered too dangerous a man to leave alive. In punishing others who opposed him Septimius was content with a heavy fine. It was said of him that he preferred money to blood.

Expediency was the predominating motive also in his administrative changes. He dismissed Niger's supporters and replaced them with his own in important offices of state. In Syria, where Niger's influence was deeply entrenched, the old administration was entirely abolished and the province cut into two with a governor allotted to each part. There was lamentation and panic again at Antioch, as when Niger fled from the battlefield of Issus. This had been his provincial capital, acclaiming him Emperor and pledged to his support. The citizens expected the same treatment from Septimius as Niger had inflicted on communities ill-disposed to him while he held power, Laodicea for instance and Tyre, which he condemned to be looted and burnt. Antioch, queen of cities in the Eastern Empire, famous for its luxury and wealth, offered greater temptation to the plunderer. It was a relief to its fears but a blow to its pride that, instead of material damage, it suffered only loss of prestige, being degraded to the status of a village under the jurisdiction of its despised neighbour, Laodicea, which became the capital of the reconstituted province.

The aim of the conciliatory policy pursued by Septimius after the defeat of Niger was to restore concord to the Empire, to unite senate, people and army behind him; but he attached greatest importance to the third of these. He never forgot the debt that he owed to his soldiers, through whose support he rose to power, and his dying advice to his sons was to care for them and put their interests first. At the same time he made it clear, as was shown by his treatment of the Praetorian Guard on his arrival in Rome, that he was no puppet Emperor like Didius willing to submit to dictation. He was concerned to improve the pay and conditions of service of the men under his command, but he demanded in return their loyal obedience. There were occasions at first when this response was not forthcoming, when he was threatened with mutiny; but he learnt by experience how to impose his will, and his blend of solicitude and severity had its reward at last in a disciplined army ready to serve him with devotion. It was an instrument that needed handling with strength and skill, and when it fell into the hands of weaker successors it became a menace to the peace of the Roman world. The fault was not of his making; it was inherent in the Empire founded by Augustus, who himself won his title by victory in civil war. Septimius, like Augustus, had a strong enough character to use and not be used by his army, to provide under military protection a stable administration fostering public welfare.

When he was guilty of injustice the impulse sprang from a hot temper. There were still traces in him of the young officer in his first appointment at Leptis who, affronted by the familiarity with which a friend embraced him in the street, condemned him to be flogged by the lictors. Even now, when he was bent on conciliation, he could be provoked to rage by a philosopher—father of the poet Oppian, a member of Julia's circle of learned and literary friends—who refused, with ostentatious disdain for worldly pomp, to attend victory celebrations at Issus. Septimius had him arrested and sent into exile on a small island, from which not even Oppian's literary reputation and influence with Julia could procure his recall. No subsequent incident of a similar sort is recorded, and it is likely from the evidence that Septimius, aware of his own failing, grew more careful not to lose his temper over trifles. He exercised no such restraint, however, where the issue was of real importance. Circumstances were shortly to arise in which he gave vent to anger that invited comparison with Commodus at his fiercest.

Meanwhile, for the rest of the year 195, the prospect remained untroubled except for the obstinacy with which Byzantium still held out on behalf of the dead Niger. Septimius was unwilling to return to Rome till this last pocket of resistance was wiped out. Leaving sufficient forces to maintain the siege, he took the opportunity while he waited in Syria to lead the main body of his army across the Euphrates. He had the excuse that many of the Arab tribes living there had supported Niger's cause, and that fugitives from the beaten army found refuge among them; but he was tempted also by hope of annexing the whole of Mesopotamia and fixing the frontier of the Roman Empire on the Tigris. The effect would be not only to earn him useful prestige at the outset of his reign: it would also relieve Roman administration of troublesome contiguity with a Tom Tiddler's ground of semi-independent princedoms and tribal leaders nominally subject to the King of Parthia.

This was the only part of the world where the Roman Empire bordered on the territory of a power of rank approaching its own. In the course of the centuries Rome had conquered and supplanted rival after rival, first the Carthaginians, then the Seleucids and Ptolemys, successors of Alexander the Great. The Parthians alone survived indestructible, winning as many battles as they lost against Roman armies.

Their Empire, extending from Mesopotamia to the borders of India, had its origin more than four hundred years earlier in the turmoil resulting from Alexander's conquest of the East. They themselves, nomads of central Asian extraction inhabiting the hilly country to the south-east of the Caspian Sea, had been subject to the Great Kings of Persia from Cyrus to Darius. When Persia was overthrown by Alexander, and he himself dying left his conquests to be split up among his generals, the Parthians were unwilling to submit to the Greek overlord. Under the leadership of a talented bandit called Arsaces they carried on a long struggle, winning at last independence for their homeland. In the years that followed, as the heirs of Alexander grew weaker and their Empire fell into decay, the Parthians extended their territory till they gained control of most of western Asia. The Parthian Empire came into being, ruled by the Arsacid dynasty named after the national hero, the bandit Arsaces.

The Empire was an ill-assorted conglomeration of subject nations, most of them on a higher level of culture than their Parthian rulers, whom they despised as barbarians. Nevertheless in spite of frequent dissension it held together for centuries, thanks to the genius shown by the Parthians for riding on a loose rein. The Parthian King of Kings, as he styled himself, demanded allegiance; but he was no oppressor either in taxation or the claims of military service. For the most part he left his subjects to themselves, abstaining from interference in their religion or social customs. The laxity of the administration encouraged turbulence, but rebellion seldom gathered strength as sufficient motive for disaffection was lacking. Recently however a new danger had appeared, a rebirth of national sentiment in the Persian provinces, where after centuries of subjugation the Persians aroused themselves to throw off the yoke of Parthian barbarians and revive the ancient glory of the days of Cyrus, Xerxes and Darius. Religious zeal added fervour to the movement. The rebels were champions of the traditional religion of Persia founded on the teaching of the prophet Zoroaster, and they resented the freedom accorded to rivals by Parthian tolerance.

The Parthian King, Vologaeses IV, was too occupied with this threat in the heart of his dominions to spare attention for foreign affairs. He took no advantage of the opportunity given him when Niger withdrew the legions from the frontier to lead them against Septimius in the north. Even now when Septimius, victorious in the civil war, brought them back to invade Mesopotamia, no Parthian army came to oppose him. The local princes were left to defend themselves, and the Romans overpowered them with little difficulty. The climate was a more formidable enemy than the Arab tribesmen. Much of the journey lay through the desert, where the army suffered great hardship from dust-storms and thirst. Even when water was found the men were afraid to drink it, repelled by its appearance and smell, till Septimius himself took a cup, knelt down and filled and drained it, and others followed his example. In his boyhood at Leptis he lived at no great distance from the Libyan desert, and he was accustomed to this sort of well.

In spite of the dangers and discomforts Julia accompanied him on the campaign. There were no roads here along which it was possible to travel in a carriage. Septimius marched on foot with his men. The only conveyance available to Julia was a litter carried on the shoulders of six or sometimes eight bearers. The litter was in common use for short journeys in the streets of a town, and in such circumstances it was the most comfortable means of transport, a substantial ark with roof and curtains, gaily decorated, in which the passenger reclined at ease. No such luxury could be afforded to Julia on campaign in the wilds of Mesopotamia; but even a litter supplied from military stores would have a canopy to protect her from the sun, and her zest for exploration made up for the lack of other comforts. Her presence and advice were useful in dealing with the local Arabs, many of whom came on pilgrimage to Emesa to the shrine of Elagabal. At Nisibis at a ceremony held to celebrate the annexation of conquered territory she received from the soldiers the title of *Mater Castrorum*, Patroness of the Camp.

In the autumn of 195 the news reached Septimius of the fall of Byzantium. The siege had lasted more than two years, such was the spirit with which the besieged held out. When supplies ran short, the women cut off their hair to braid into ropes for the ships and engines of war, and the temples were stripped of bronze statues to use as missiles. The walls were among the strongest in the Roman world, legendary walls that 'sang'. There were seven towers from the Thracian gate to the entrance of the Bosporus, and if anyone approached the first of these and shouted, an echo answered from the next, then from the next beyond and so on in succession, till all seven had spoken. Neither their strength nor their fame, however, could save them. Septimius was determined that the fortress should not threaten his communications again: he ordered the walls to be razed to the ground. The town was left defenceless with its theatres, baths and other public buildings in ruins, till in the next century a Roman Emperor chose it to be his capital, the New Rome destined to outlive the Old.

The surrender of Byzantium removed a principal reason for linger-
ing in the East. There was no urgency about the campaign in Mesopotamia. Some progress had been made, some territory annexed. If the
task was broken off, it could be resumed later. The Parthian King,
beset with troubles at home, was unlikely to intervene to undo the
work in the meantime. Septimius himself was not free from anxiety
about his own home front. Disturbing rumours reached him of negotiations between disaffected senators in Rome and Albinus in Britain.
He knew that he had opponents in the senate who disapproved of him
as an African upstart with a Syrian wife, and who would have preferred
the aristocratic Albinus as Emperor regnant rather than Emperor
designate. Letters found afterwards when the correspondence of
Albinus was seized proved that there was ground even at this stage for
suspicion of a *coup d'état*.

To reinforce his position and enhance its prestige Septimius issued
a proclamation describing himself as son by adoption of Marcus
Aurelius. It had been the custom for the past hundred years, as has
already been said, for the reigning Emperor to adopt his intended
successor; but there was no precedent for a posthumous adoption
claiming the relationship fifteen years after the Emperor's death. Septimius was not concerned with legal niceties. It was enough for him that
the dead could not and, if force prevailed, the living would not dare
to protest. The army responded with enthusiasm, accepting him without question as legitimate heir to the Antonines. Not content with his
own elevation into the Imperial family, he announced that his elder
son, hitherto called Bassianus, would bear the name Marcus Aurelius
Antoninus.

The new dignity was not in itself a challenge to Albinus. Although
Septimius changed his son's name he conferred no title on him, and it
was still open to him in accordance with Antonine precedent to adopt
Albinus as his successor. Nevertheless Albinus might well take alarm.
He was in fact a year or so older than Septimius. His chance to enjoy
the right of succession, none too hopeful in any case, would be made
even more precarious by the rivalry of a seven-year-old boy growing
to manhood in the interval. There was great temptation to anticipate
his inheritance, especially when he had powerful friends at Rome urging
him and promising support. He was a favourite in the senate among
stalwarts of traditional outlook. Like Septimius he was born in Africa;
but not only were their birthplaces far apart, his own having been at
Hadrumetum to the south of Tunis, there was a wide difference
between them also in social standing. Albinus was of impeccable pedi-

gree, related to the best families in Rome. In a letter of recommendation the Emperor Marcus Aurelius describes him as 'a native of Africa, but with little of the African about him'. His rank in society and air of well-bred gentility were valuable assets to the new régime while he and Septimius worked in alliance.

Albinus also had behind him a career of unblemished worth, including distinguished service in command of an army on the Rhine and culminating in his present office of governor of Britain. It is not known how far these achievements contented, how far they whetted, his ambition. He was a man of cultivated tastes with interests transcending war and politics, author of a didactic poem on agriculture in the manner of Virgil and of a collection of 'Milesian tales', a literary genre taken over from the Greeks which combined the erotic and the humorous. It is recorded of him that even in his youth he was fond of quoting the Virgilian tag, *Arma amens capio nec sat rationis in armis*: 'Madly I take arms, but arms make no sense.' Nevertheless, having chosen arms for his profession, he contrived to become a skilful general.

There were rumours during the reign of Pertinax that he was involved in the abortive conspiracy led by Falco. Events moved too quickly for his part to be brought to light, and Septimius discreetly overlooked it when he appointed him Emperor designate. Many of his friends, however, were among the conspirators, and these were active now in inviting him to Rome to seize the purple for himself while Septimius was absent in the East. As news of their intentions came to his ears, Septimius made haste to cut short his Mesopotamian campaign and lead his army back into Europe. On his way messengers met him with information that increased his anxiety, confirming his suspicions of Albinus, and when he reached Viminacium on the Danube, some fifty miles downstream from Belgrade, he issued what amounted to a declaration of war. In the presence of his army and the local dignitaries he announced that his son, recently given the name of Antoninus, was to bear also the title of Caesar, Emperor designate. It is said that he made the decision with reluctance, foreseeing that civil war would follow, but that Julia persuaded him, determined that her son should inherit.

There could not be two Emperors designate. Albinus knew that he was deposed in favour of a child, and any hesitation restraining him hitherto was banished. He gathered all the forces at his disposal to transport them to Gaul, where allies were ready to join him. When Septimius led his army from the Danube to march on Rome he left sufficient garrison on the frontier to deter aggressors; but Albinus removed every legion stationed in Britain, stripping the defences of the Wall which, from the Tyne to the Solway, guarded the province from incursions of savage Caledonians. For the next few years the northern part of the province was devastated by ceaseless raids, murder and pillage.

The renewed outbreak of civil war provoked dismay, not only in Britain. The year 195 was drawing to an end, and it was the custom in Rome in the last days of December to hold chariot races in the Circus Maximus before the feast of the Saturnalia. A great crowd assembled for the event, but instead of applauding the winning teams the spectators sat silent and morose. At last the moment came for the chief race of the day, and the charioteers waited ready to start. Before the signal could be given the crowd interrupted with arms raised in prayer, invoking the divine genius of Rome to avert misfortune. Then all began to clap their hands in slow rhythm, shouting in unison: 'How much longer? When will the war stop?'

It was a long time before they were quiet and allowed the race to go on.

The friends of Albinus blamed Septimius for the strife, accusing him of double-dealing in giving his son the title of Caesar when it was already bestowed. Each side had arguments to prove its cause in the right. Public opinion, less concerned to lay blame than appalled by the prospect of anarchy, was ready to support whichever emerged victor, strong enough to restore peace. Septimius thought it advisable to pay a visit to Rome in person to show himself as lawful Emperor and re-establish his authority. He sent his army on from Viminacium without him to follow the frontier of the Danube and the Rhine, where the journey lay through friendly country and reinforcements could be picked up for the conflict with Albinus in Gaul. Meanwhile he himself rode off to Rome with a small escort.

When he addressed the senate he made no effort any longer to restrain his anger. He reminded his hearers of the forbearance that he had shown them when they submitted to Didius from fear of the Praetorian Guard. Even Niger's adherents were let off lightly enough. It was a fair fight between Niger and himself, but the present circumstances were different. Niger was an open enemy, Albinus a lapsed colleague who intrigued behind his Emperor's back, frustrating hopes of peace so nearly attained and condemning the Roman Empire to a renewed bout of civil war. The senators received clear warning of the retribution in store for those on the wrong side if Septimius won.

The war, however, was by no means won yet. Albinus was advancing through Gaul with his army from Britain strengthened with reinforcements from provinces as far away as Spain. He had already inflicted a heavy defeat on one of the generals whom Septimius left in charge. When Septimius himself arrived he took over the command, but it is evidence of the prevailing confusion that he was thankful for the help even of small bands of guerrillas. Dio has a story of a schoolteacher from Rome, who, happening to be in Gaul at the time on holiday, pretended that he was a Roman senator with a commission to raise troops. He collected a body of armed volunteers whom he led against Albinus on a number of daring exploits, even raiding a legionary camp and seizing the funds stored in the treasury. Septimius himself was deceived by the claim to senatorial rank and commended him in suitably honorific terms; but when the war was over the pretender revealed that he exercised no authority in Rome except over schoolchildren. Pleased by his boldness, Septimius offered him a seat in the senate to put things straight; but all that the former pedagogue and guerrilla leader would accept was a quiet house in which to live at ease in the country, with a sufficient allowance from the Emperor for his needs.

The civil war dragged on in Gaul through the summer and autumn, and it was not till February 197 that the contending armies met for the decisive battle at Lugdunum, a town familiar to Septimius as the scene of his early married life. Albinus came near to victory. His tactics were those used more than a thousand years later by Robert Bruce against the English at Bannockburn. He had pits dug in front of the battleline, screened with leaves, turf and light timber, and his men, advancing beyond them a short way and then retreating, lured the pursuing enemy into the trap. The thin covering broke and men and horses floundered, stuck fast in the depths. Septimius himself was unhorsed and fled on foot, stripping off his Imperial cloak to escape recognition.

The issue seemed no longer in doubt. A report spread that Septimius was dead; but as the British legions surged forward in heedless confidence a fresh force attacked them on the flank. It was said that the officer in command had been waiting aloof on purpose for Septimius to be killed, so that he might usurp his place. His sudden intervention turned the tide of battle. The victors, taken by surprise, became the vanquished, while the fugitives recovered their spirit and returned to fight. Among them was Septimius without horse or cloak. His soldiers supplied him with both, and he rode in triumph at their head as they galloped into Lugdunum. The double-dealing officer watched in dismay.

There was immense slaughter on both sides, and the plain outside the town was strewn with dead bodies; but Albinus escaped with his life and hid in a cottage on the bank of the Rhône. He was not left in safety for long: an informer betrayed him, and when soldiers came to arrest him he followed the example set by Cato and other noble Romans of the past and committed suicide, dying with his favourite motto on his lips, 'Arms make no sense'. Septimius ordered his head to be cut off and sent it to Rome to be exposed in public, stuck on a pole outside the senate-house.

The victory won at Lugdunum gave an answer at last to the question asked so insistently at the racecourse, 'When will the war stop?' Septimius received an enthusiastic welcome when he returned victorious to Rome. The cheers of the crowd were for peace, for an Emperor strong enough to reign without a rival, and they would have been equally loud for Albinus if he had brought the same blessings. Septimius however was content and responded with generous largess. He was anxious to keep the people's loyalty, knowing how little he could depend on that of the senate.

He was in a mood for ruthless vengeance on his enemies. Among the spoils taken at Lugdunum when the headquarters occupied by Albinus were sacked was a mass of letters from Roman senators and other dignitaries, revealing the extent to which they were implicated in the adventure. Many were condemned to death on this evidence, including Sulpicianus, father-in-law of Pertinax, the unsuccessful bidder against Didius when the purple was put up to auction. Niger's wife and children were also among the victims, for undisclosed reasons. Although Septimius was fierce in his anger, its action was not indiscriminate. It is recorded that out of a group of leading senators put on trial twenty-nine suffered capital punishment, thirty-five were acquitted and released.

Ever since Augustus reshaped the constitution, causing Republican to yield to Imperial government, the Roman senate had exerted dwindling influence in politics. Its dream of restored dignity under an Emperor of noble birth was shattered when Albinus met his end on the Rhône. Septimius, securely established by force of arms, had little to fear any longer from the antiquated claims of the senate-house. As soon as the first wave of executions was past, eliminating the most dangerous of his enemies, he was content to punish insubordination with a heavy fine. Nevertheless he took care to encourage a healthy state of apprehension in high places and went out of his way to re-habilitate the memory of his predecessor Commodus, under whom senators endured a reign of terror. He reminded them that he and Commodus were brothers since his posthumous adoption by Marcus Aurelius.

Four years had passed since Commodus was murdered, not long enough for people to forget that their new Emperor had been a party to the conspiracy, a friend of Eclectus and Marcia. There was an inconsistency in his changed attitude of which critics could take sly advantage. When the deification of Commodus was proposed in the senate, an orator denounced him for putting Imperial dignity to shame by appearing in person in the arena to kill wild beasts with his own hands. Septimius, having often expressed a similar opinion himself, could not plausibly deny it, but he had his repartee ready for the occasion: 'The beasts with which Commodus fought succumbed to a spear, not a phallus.'

He alluded to a scandal reported only the day before from Ostia, where an elderly senator, an ex-consul, was seen romping in public with a girl disguised as a panther. The remark was quoted gleefully for long afterwards by the common people, with imitation of the Emperor's African accent.

4

Peace Re-established

Augustus, having founded the Roman Empire, encouraged literary genius to flourish at his court; the poets Virgil and Horace, the historian Livy, a golden age of Latin literature whose lustre has outlasted the political achievements. No similar gathering of talent under Imperial patronage can be found in subsequent reigns till the last dynasty came to power, the last before the Empire was engulfed in chaos from which it emerged so changed that Augustus would not have recognized it. Septimius Severus staved off political collapse. His wife, Julia Domna, presided over the sunset of the arts and sciences.

The sciences fared better than the arts. The literary output of the writers frequenting Julia's circle was of an altogether lower quality than that of the Augustans. Latin literature had declined from the golden to the silver age, and even the latter was already superseded, replaced by standards of baser metal still. Most of Julia's friends wrote in Greek, but their level of achievement was no higher. It was an age preoccupied above all with literary style, in which honour was paid to the 'sophist'. The name was free at the time from pejorative meaning. The sophist was a professor of eloquence, admired for his skill in putting words together into effective phrases and the feeling with which he declaimed them. Those who excelled in the art earned praise, no matter whether they had anything worth saying. It was a common practice indeed to propose a theme to a group of sophists on which they were invited to exercise their skill in competition.

A leading sophist of the day, one of Julia's closest friends, was Flavius Philostratus, a Greek-speaking native of the island of Lemnos. His reputation rests mainly on a work that he composed at her request, the *Life of Apollonius*, to give expression to her ideas on ethics and religion. It tells the story of a certain Apollonius, sage and magician, who travelled in distant parts of the world—Parthia, India and Ethiopia

—preaching, observing and setting an example of righteous behaviour. The material is not wholly fictitious. Apollonius was a real person who lived in the latter part of the first century, and many of the details of his life seem to be founded on genuine tradition; but to Philostratus historical accuracy was less important than lively incident, literary grace and high-minded teaching. The book has interest as a record of the principles by which Julia was animated, no matter whether or not it draws a true portrait of a long-forgotten wonder-worker.

In later times attempts were made to treat the book as a counterblast to the Christian Gospels, and Apollonius himself as a pagan Christ; but Philostratus himself offers no support for this. There is no trace in him of sectarian jealousy. While he makes no specific mention of Christianity, he insists that all religions deserve respect. The Christian Gospels, already in wide circulation, were quite certainly known to him, and he has passages that echo them. When Apollonius raises from the dead a girl who had died on her wedding-day, the circumstances recall the miracle performed by Jesus on the daughter of Jairus. A similar echo can be detected in the scene where Apollonius, who is on trial for his life before the Emperor Domitian, comes by magic to join his disciples in the cave of the nymphs and tells them to take hold and feel him to prove that he is no ghost. His words recall those of the risen Christ: 'Handle me and see; for a spirit hath not flesh and bones, as ye see me have.' There is no need, however, to ascribe ulterior motives to Philostratus. He intends it as a compliment when he borrows from Christian tradition. The literary artist of his day looked on other men's ideas as an open garden, in which he was free to pick any flowers that pleased him to adorn his work.

The *Life of Apollonius* is written to entertain as well as to instruct. The Roman public enjoyed reading of marvels like the piebald girl found in India, black in the upper part of her body, her face and breasts, white below from her waist to her feet. Indian girls like this, Philostratus explains, are sacred to Aphrodite. In a more scientific spirit he describes a herd of elephants crossing a river with the smallest in front and the biggest in the rear, so that if the water proved too deep for the calves the whole herd could turn back in time and look for a better fording-place. He cannot resist a good story, even at his hero's expense. Apollonius, about to enter Parthia by a bridge over the Euphrates, is asked by the customs officer what he has in his luggage, and he replies with a string of abstract nouns: Temperance, Justice, Virtue, Patience, all feminine in Greek. 'You must apply for a permit for these girls,' the officer tells him.

Stories of this sort are the jam with which Philostratus lures the reader to digest his teaching. Much of it is too verbose for easy digestion, a heavy suet of conventional exhortations to piety; but from time to time ideas appear which are less commonplace and seem to owe their origin to Julia's inspiration. Her breadth of mind is reflected in the doctrine that divinity has its place in the human soul rather than in temples. Even the ascetic principles which tradition demanded of the pious are modified to suit her tolerant and pleasure-loving nature. When Apollonius and his disciples sit down for a picnic beside a stream and some passing nomads offer them palm wine, he refuses it for himself, but encourages the rest to drink it, declaring that as they are not philosophers there is no need for them to practise abstinence. He makes the point still more strongly on another occasion, when he tells the King of Parthia that rigorous austerity 'looks vulgar in a king and lowers his dignity'. Among common desires there is only one that earns unqualified disapproval: a man 'can be forgiven for yielding to laziness, anger, sexuality or drunkenness, but to let possessions be your master is unforgivable and loathsome, all vices rolled into one'. When a rich upstart boasts to Apollonius of his new house at Rhodes and the money spent on it, he is told: 'It seems to me, young man, it isn't you who own the house, but the house that owns you.'

Although Julia died before the book was finished and published, Philostratus himself declares that it was written in consultation with her and enjoyed her encouragement. It makes up for its lack of literary value by affording glimpses available nowhere else into the mind of a woman who played a dominant part in a crucial period of Roman history, and whose efforts, if they had borne fruit, could have fostered religious unity, forestalling the triumph of Christianity. She was not a Christian herself. There were even outbreaks of persecution during her husband's reign, arising from the prejudice of officers in the provinces whom the Emperor was unwilling or unable to check. Such prejudice, however, found no sympathy with Julia. The nurse engaged at Lugdunum for her elder son was the first of many Christians taken into her household. She followed the example set by Marcia in the reign of Commodus, a pagan protector of the followers of Christ. It would have been inconsistent with her character, ever curious of intellectual novelty, not to study their teaching and choose from it what she liked.

A story told in the *Life of Apollonius* illustrates far better than the borrowed phrases and episodes the debt that the work owes to the spirit of the New Testament. When Apollonius visits the Parthian court, the King sends a servant to his lodging to tell him that he is to receive ten presents, to be chosen by himself. The servant warns him that the King is anxious to show off his bounty and will be offended if the choice is insufficiently costly. This puts Apollonius into a difficulty. Having renounced material wealth, he is unwilling to accept anything at all, but no less unwilling to give offence, which could bring his visit to an uncomfortable end.

The presentation is due to be made on the following day, and as he turns the problem over in his mind during the night he remembers that, on his way from the frontier to the capital, he passed through some villages whose inhabitants were Greeks, descendants of prisoners captured by Darius in the ancient wars of the Greeks and the Persians, and that they described to him the hardship of their lives, scraping a bare subsistence from soil noisome with petroleum, and bullied and robbed by their neighbours, who still after all these centuries despised them as foreigners. Next morning he goes to see the King, who asks if he has chosen his gifts.

'I choose one,' he replies, 'worth more than many tens of gifts.'

Then he tells the King about the Greeks and asks for them to be resettled on good land, safe from interference. The request pleases the King, who sees in it an opportunity to display not only his wealth and power but also magnanimity to ancient and no longer dangerous enemies; but he reminds Apollonius that there are still nine more gifts to choose.

'Wait,' Apollonius replies, 'till I've been longer in your country. I haven't had time yet to make enough friends.'

Philostratus has first place in the literary circle over which Julia presided; but he owes it to values outside literature, to the ideas reflecting Julia's own which find expression in the *Life of Apollonius*, and to the portraits that he draws of his predecessors and contemporaries in the *Lives of the Sophists*. Other writers whose work has survived offer less to reward attention. Creative impulse flagged, and its place was taken by imitation of the achievements of the past. The long poem, whether epic or didactic, was a pattern that had inspired the genius of Homer and Hesiod in Greek and the *Aeneid* and *Georgics* of Virgil in Latin. It was less successful when it came to be handled by Oppian, son of the opinionated philosopher who annoyed Septimius by refusing to attend the victory celebration after Niger's defeat at Issus. Oppian wrote two immensely long poems in Greek, the one, in five books, on fishing, the other in four on hunting. Contemporary fashion applauded them, especially that on hunting, and when Julia's son became Emperor he rewarded the poet with a piece of gold for every line, a total of more than two thousand; but although the poems still exist to be read today, so are more fortunate than many less dispensable products of classical antiquity, they attract few readers.

More entertainment can be derived from Aelian, a Latin-speaking sophist born in Italy who insisted on writing in Greek and performed the feat in a manner that Greek politeness described as 'honey-tongued'. His collection of stories, *On the nature of animals*, introduces many as unfamiliar today as they were then: the mantichore, a shaggy red beast the size of a lion with a human face and a sting at the tip of its tail; the gryphon of Bactria, a quadruped with eagle's beak and feathered body, black above and red below, and white wings, which builds itself a nest of gold-dust; dog-faced men whose speech is a squeal, and the amphisbaena, a snake with a head at each end, able to move simultaneously in opposite directions. Julia and her friends loved to hear of marvels, and they had less reason to withhold belief when so much of the world was unexplored.

Not all Aelian's stories, however, strain credulity. He tells of a dolphin caught in a net and brought to land on the island of Paros to be sold with the rest of the catch. An islander intervened, paid the price that was asked and set it free. A short time afterwards this man was in a ship that foundered. He was sucked down into the depths and about to drown when the dolphin approached, racing and leaping towards him from far out at sea. It dived beneath him, hoisted him up and carried him on its back safely to the shore. Similar incidents as remarkable have been recorded in later times of these creatures, described in a poem that Aelian quotes as 'pets of the sea-nymphs'.

None of the writers named is conspicuous for literary talent; but anyone tempted to dismiss the age as the nadir of Greek and Latin letters should remember that Apuleius, whose picaresque romance, the *Metamorphoses*, better known by its later title of *The Golden Ass*, has been acclaimed ever since as a work of genius, was a near contemporary and may even have still been alive in his early seventies in North Africa. His book, founded like the literary experiments of Albinus on the old tradition of 'Milesian tales', combines a series of episodes, eventful, comic and salacious, into a story inhabited by living characters and inspired with deeply felt religious purpose, a distant ancestor of the modern novel. The age that produced it has no need to be ashamed of its achievement. Although Septimius himself was an African, there is no record that he and Apuleius were acquainted. It is even less likely that Julia ever met the ageing writer, sophist and philosopher, who spent the last years of his life at Carthage; but it can be assumed without doubt that she read his works and found support in them for her hope of a literary revival.

Literature however was far from being the only interest that engaged her attention: she and her friends paid as much, if not more, respect to questions of philosophy and natural science. Most people living then, everyone over twenty or so years old, could remember the days when a philosopher, Marcus Aurelius, reigned as Emperor over the Roman world. The Stoic principles professed by Marcus Aurelius, concerned above all with discipline of the will, lay remote from the field of religious speculation that attracted Syrian Julia; but the example set by the Imperial Stoic established a fashion, and philosophers of every school flourished in the following years. The most eminent of them, Galen, was already an old man when Septimius became Emperor, and he died in the last year of the century; but his name is proof that Julia was not content to be a patron only of mediocrity.

Galen has earned a lasting place in medical history for his accurate knowledge of anatomy and of the functions performed by the organs of the body. He was a student of philosophy as well as of medicine, who based his thought and practice on the principle that nothing can be accepted as true till it is tested by reason and experience. A story told of him illustrates his unwillingness to be bound by traditional authority. A friend, who was not his patient, fell ill and called in his own doctor, who prescribed the treatment recommended in the text-books, kept him in bed and warned him to eat as little as possible. Galen, calling on his friend to ask after his health, found him in an alarming state of weakness. Overriding the other doctor's advice with a high-handedness that medical etiquette today would deplore, Galen insisted that the patient should get up and come out with him into the fresh air, where they sat down to a hearty meal. The man made a rapid recovery. Not enough is known of the symptoms to show what prompted Galen's recommendation, but its success confirmed him in the belief that he records: 'Whoever wishes to understand the works of nature must put his trust, not in books on anatomy, but in his own eyes.'

A time was approaching when standards the very reverse of this would govern every field of research. From the fourth century onwards through the best part of a millennium the quest for truth came to rely more and more on hallowed precedent, pronouncements of time-honoured, if not supernatural, infallibility. Galen's voice is among the last in classical antiquity to ask how and why, and seek an answer from observation and reason, no matter what anyone however prestigious

said before. His surviving works range over many fields as well
as medicine, and when he applies his methods to religion it is evident
how closely his views and Julia's accord, insisting that there is nothing
final in a name or a cult, and that God remains the same whether he is
addressed as Zeus by the Greeks or as Jehovah by the Jews. He is
interested, as Julia was also, in Jewish and Christian teaching, but he
parts company with both when they demand unquestioning acceptance
of a sacred text. The miracles recorded of Christ seem to him evidence
less of divine revelation than of the operation of forces of nature not
yet explored. A younger contemporary, Alexander of Aphrodisias,
put this argument succinctly when he gives examples of events that
would be truly miraculous—if God, for instance, could make the
diagonal of a parallelogram equal in length to its side, or twice two
make five.

Among the learned who frequented the court those whose achievement is most noteworthy were the lawyers. The reign of Septimius
was the heyday of Roman jurisprudence as that of Augustus had been
of Latin literature. Ever since the foundation of the Empire it had been
the custom to appoint suitable members of the legal profession as
urists, to whom questions of law were submitted by judges and magis-
rates, an d whose answers carried Imperial authority. Long afterwards
under the Emperor Justinian a collection was made of these authoritative
pronouncements, known commonly as the *Digest of Roman law*, and
among the most frequently quoted is Papinian, who was Julia's cousin
and one of her closest friends. The quality of his mind is revealed in
his learning and acumen, and of his character in his courteous deference
when he expresses disagreement with the opinion of others. He has
been described as 'the greatest jurisconsult of all time'.

The work for which Papinian and his scarcely less famous pupil,
Ulpian, are chiefly known, that of giving a more human face to Roman
law, was already in progress before their lifetime. They did not invent,
but they did much to extend and elucidate, the principle of *jus naturale*,
rights inherent in human nature and demanded by reason. The new
ideas which they expounded favoured protection of the underdog
from oppression, restriction of the power of a father over his children,
of a master over the life and property of his slaves, of the central
government over provincials. The change was effected less by fresh
legislation than by reinterpretation of the old, modifying its rigour in
the light of equity. The later Roman Empire was an age in which
humane values and personal feelings enjoyed more consideration than
perhaps ever before in the ancient world.

Many reasons can be found for the intellectual fertility of the reign of Septimius Severus. It can be regarded as the final harvest of the prosperity of the Age of the Antonines, and as an expression of the relief felt when the interlude of civil war following the murder of Pertinax came so quickly to an end and peace and order were restored. Nevertheless a large share of the credit is due to the example set by the Emperor's wife, the Augusta, the personal encouragement that she offered men of talent and her enjoyment of their society. It may be asked what were their own feelings for their Imperial patroness. Was she merely a dispenser of wealth and preferment, on whose favour they relied to attain the prizes of a successful career, or was she also a source of genuine inspiration, a Roman Gloriana, not only fitted by her rank to preside over the arts and sciences but able too to add her own contribution, the fruits of a mind steeped in the learning of the temple at Emesa and of a charm that owed much to the beauty of her face and figure, still more to the lively spirit, the sympathy and curiosity that animated her? Words written at a later date by her friend Philostratus may appropriately be quoted here. They are addressed to her son after he became Emperor and had been responsible for events to be described in due course, which darkened her life with tragedy: 'Storks will not fly back into a city that has been devastated, they avoid the echo of bygone crimes; but you still live in the house whose devastation is your own doing, and you pay lip service to the gods within it as if they did not exist, or as if existing they could forget that you possess what is theirs.'

The symbolism reflects the nostalgic sorrow with which the author contemplates his devastated paradise. The outraged gods are those of grace, wit and reason who inspired the conversation over dinner in Julia's rooms in the palace, or in the gardens of the country house to which the Imperial family loved to retire on the Campanian coast, where she herself sat wreathed with roses among congenial friends, poets and philosophers, in the cool shade of a marble portico fragrant with the scent of clipped bushes of box and bay above the sparkling blue of the sea.

Roman tradition insisted on masculine supremacy. Even her patronage of the arts earned disapproval from the bigot, and her enemies, alluding to the reputation borne by Syrian women, accused her of seeking erotic adventure under cover of intellectual interest. The prejudice gathered strength when she turned her attention to politics, and discretion was needed to disguise the part that she played in her son's reign, when he left much of the civil administration of the Empire in her hands. Content to exercise the reality without the appearance of power, she recalled nevertheless with regret the precedent native to her own country, the exploits of Semiramis, legendary Queen of Babylon.

While her husband lived, however, she avoided political activity. He had no wish to share the burden of State, and she seldom offered him advice. It was as wife and companion, for his pleasure and her own, that she travelled with him, when he left Rome in the autumn of 197 to resume his interrupted campaign in Mesopotamia. Only a few months had passed since his victory over Albinus; but already his power was so securely established that he had no need to remain in person to enforce it. All important offices in the State were filled with trusted adherents of his own, and the senate, purged and cowed, made humble obedience. The strongest foundation, however, on which his confidence rested was the ardent hope cherished by the people both in Rome and in the provinces of the restoration of orderly government. Anyone renewing the civil war had reason to fear popular execration.

This second campaign across the Euphrates met as little resistance as the first. The Parthian King was still occupied with rebellion among his Persian subjects and unwilling to spare forces for the defence of an outlying borderland. Septimius built a fleet of boats to transport most of his men and stores from the Euphrates to the Tigris by the ancient waterway known as the Royal Canal, attributed by legend to Nebuchadnezzar. Then he himself led the remainder down the Euphrates to Babylon, no longer Babylon the Great, mistress of the world, but its ghost, plundered for centuries as a quarry to supply stone for buildings elsewhere. The gates stood open, and he entered unopposed. The town was without military importance, but the relics of antiquity had appeal for him, as in his younger days when he was exiled to Athens by the Emperor Commodus and amused himself inspecting the Parthenon and other monuments of ancient Greece. For Julia there was especial interest in a visit to Babylon, the home of the Chaldean science of astrology to which her native religion owed so great a debt. She found it not wholly derelict; it was the seat of a local Parthian governor, and its famous temple of Jupiter Belus (the Romanized name of the chief of the Babylonian gods) still survived. Philostratus who kept her company was fascinated by the 'secret bridge' under the river, a subway linking palaces on opposite banks, which he describes in his *Life of Apollonius*.

From Babylon the Roman army crossed the strip of land intervening between the two rivers and came to Seleucia on the Tigris, the town founded by and named after Seleucus, Alexander's general, to be the capital of his share of Alexander's Empire. Septimius was joined and reinforced here by the boats bringing his main body into the Tigris through the Royal Canal. On the farther bank of the river opposite Seleucia stood the Parthian town of Ctesiphon, which the King used as his capital when he was in this part of his realm. It was characteristic of the Parthians that, when they conquered Mesopotamia from the Greeks, they preferred to set up a capital of their own, rather than take over that of the Greek ruler. They felt out of place among the magnificent buildings and civilized amenities of Seleucia, and they were aware that their own outlandish dress and manners would have an unfavourable effect on the commercial life of the town, on which its prosperity depended. Seleucia remained a Greek city, faced across the river by Ctesiphon, a Parthian camp. The contrast between them when Septimius arrived was less striking than it had been in former times. Much of Seleucia lay in ruin, devastated and burnt by the Romans some thirty years before, during the reign of Marcus Aurelius.

Hitherto there had been little fighting as Septimius advanced across Mesopotamia; but at Ctesiphon the Parthians made a determined effort at last to stop him. Their King, Vologaeses, was present in the town in person, diverted from subjugation of Persian rebels by the rapid approach of the Romans to his heartland. His forces however were outnumbered, and the Tigris was an inadequate defence when Septimius had a fleet of boats available to ferry his men across. Ctesiphon was taken by assault, and Vologaeses fled. Although the town was in origin little more than a nomads' camping-ground, a considerable settlement had grown up in the course of time within the fortifications to serve the needs of the Parthian court when it was in residence. This was looted by the Roman soldiers with indiscriminate slaughter of the civilian population. Septimius did nothing to restrain them. Their morale had suffered during the uneventful progress of the earlier stages of the campaign, and an epidemic of dysentery provoked by the unhealthy climate aggravated their discontent. The sack of Ctesiphon afforded an opportunity to restore their spirits, rather as a master of foxhounds chops a fox in cover at the end of an otherwise blank day to give his hounds a taste of blood.

Ctesiphon fell on 28 January 198, the anniversary of the accession of the Emperor Trajan. Septimius took pride in the fact that he was accomplishing a task, the conquest of Mesopotamia, in which Trajan was interrupted by death. To celebrate the occasion he invited the army to acclaim his elder son Antoninus by the title of Augustus, and his younger son Geta by that of Caesar. The elder boy was not quite ten years old, the younger eight. The ceremony made it clear to all that their father intended to found a dynasty with succession dependent on ties of blood, and that the Antonine precedent of inheritance by adoption would lapse.

In spite of the ease with which victory had been won no attempt was made to pursue Vologaeses and his defeated army deeper into Parthia. Septimius turned and led his men home, choosing the longer route up the Tigris as they had already eaten the country bare beside the Euphrates on their outward journey. It was no doubt a reason for his unwillingness to advance farther that the purpose of the expedition was to annex Mesopotamia, not to extend the Roman Empire into remoter regions of the East. Nevertheless he might have been tempted to deliver the weakened Parthians a crushing blow, if he had had more confidence in the fitness of his soldiers and his own competence to command them. There had been few opportunities in his career to gain military experience till he was appointed governor of Upper Pannonia, and even now he had much to learn before he became proficient in the art in which he excelled later in his reign, that of enforcing strict discipline and at the same time inspiring devoted allegiance in the army.

The Mesopotamian climate increased his difficulties. Ill-health strained the endurance of the soldiers, and efforts made to bring them to a more resolute frame of mind had little success. Dio has a story of a Greek called Antiochus who offered his services as spiritual coach, describing himself as a philosopher of the Cynic school, a sect that professed contempt for both pleasure and pain. When the soldiers complained of discomfort, he put them to shame by deliberately seeking it out to show off his fortitude. He earned a salary from Septimius in reward for his exertions, and even if they provoked less emulation than mockery it is evident that he retained his employment in later campaigns. The principal feat recorded of him, that of rolling naked in the snow, is unlikely to have taken place in the Mesopotamian desert. The appointment ended, however, in the following reign when, hopeful of better pay, he absconded with his Cynic principles to serve the Parthians.

The sullen mood prevailing in the army in Mesopotamia came to a head on the homeward journey when Septimius turned aside to besiege Hatra, a town occupying an oasis in the desert midway between the Tigris and Euphrates that had supported Niger while he lived and still persisted in defying the new Emperor. It was a protracted siege: the town was strongly fortified, and the defenders made effective use

not only of conventional weapons but also of locally produced petroleum, which they ignited and poured down in flaming streams on the
enemy. At last however the Romans made a breach in the wall and
rushed forward to scale the debris, inspired to greater enthusiasm when
they saw that the point at which the wall was breached abutted on the
temple of the sun-god, a storehouse rich in treasure.

Septimius stood watching from a platform close by. Suddenly he
ordered the buglers to sound the signal for retreat. The soldiers already
scaling the breach, convinced that they had the town at their mercy,
heard the signal in astonishment and obeyed with reluctance. They
climbed down from the wall, and the temple was saved.

The explanation given by Septimius was that he expected overtures
from Hatra offering surrender. He drew his army back to wait for
them; but a day passed, and still he waited. No envoys came from the
town, where the people were at work on the wall busily repairing the
breach. At last he gave orders to renew the assault; but the best of his
men, legionaries from the European provinces, infuriated by their
recent disappointment, refused to move. The only units willing to
obey were a few recruited from local tribes, hereditary enemies of
Hatra. These were no match for the defenders, who wiped them out.
An officer watching their abortive efforts offered to capture the town
on his own, if he were given only five hundred and fifty European
soldiers to back him.

'I'd be lucky,' the Emperor retorted, 'to find you five.'

There were angry meetings of protest in the camp, speeches denouncing the Emperor for intervening to thwart his soldiers in the moment
of victory and deprive them of the treasure in the temple. The indignation did not fall on him alone. A military tribune able to quote
Virgil recited the lines from the *Aeneid*, 'So that Turnus may run after
a Royal bride, are we, lives of no account, to fall scattered over the
field, riff-raff unburied and unwept?' It was not difficult for his hearers
to translate the allusion into contemporary terms. The sun-god worshipped at Hatra was closely akin to Julia's own Elagabal, and it was
known that she deplored the intention to plunder and desecrate his
shrine. Septimius, when the words were reported to him by an
informer, had no doubt who was meant by the 'Royal bride'. The
classical quotation cost the tribune his life.

The unsuccessful siege of Hatra was a blow to Roman prestige. An
unimportant fortress defied an army led by the Emperor in person
and survived intact. Nevertheless, apart from the student of Virgil, few
victims of note suffered punishment for the mutiny to which the

failure was due. Having avenged with hot-tempered ferocity the attack on his wife, Septimius allowed judgement to overrule passion. His humiliation at Hatra taught him to avoid direct conflict with the will of his soldiers until care for their welfare and skilful leadership had earned him their confidence and personal ascendancy was assured. Julia too had learnt her lesson. Although she accompanied her husband on many other expeditions, she never again interfered in his conduct of military operations. Even in her son's reign, when much of the administration of the state was left in her charge, she kept her hands off the army.

In spite of the ignominious episode with which it ended, the Meso-potamian campaign brought advantage to Rome, adding a province to the Empire and establishing the frontier on the Tigris. As long as Septimius reigned, the conquest remained secure with a garrison of two legions to protect it. There was no repetition of the indiscipline that prevailed among them earlier. Septimius had to yield at Hatra, but the soldiers were soon made aware that they would be rash to presume on the example. When need arose he was ruthless, and no entreaty could persuade him to relent. A servant guilty of breach of trust pleaded extenuating circumstances.

'What would you have done yourself in my place?' he asked the Emperor.

He received the grim answer: 'I'd have borne the consequences.' The man was put to death.

Septimius accompanied his army back as far as Antioch. There he left it and set off with a small party, including Julia, to visit Egypt. His journey had a political purpose. Egypt was among the provinces that supported Niger in the civil war, and although the Prefect's defection turned the issue in favour of Septimius there were malcontents still active there, a source of danger in a place so vital to Roman security, the granary on which Rome depended for imports of corn. A personal visit from the Emperor could be useful to enforce submission. It was also an opportunity to indulge his own tastes and his wife's by study of the by-ways of religion and the antiquities in which Egypt abounded.

He himself declared in later years that this trip was among the most enjoyable experiences of his life. He and Julia were indefatigable sightseers. At Alexandria, the greatest city in the Empire after Rome, he was shown the Mausoleum where the reputed body of Alexander the Great lay embalmed, exposed to view in a glass coffin. Alexander was his favourite of the heroes of the past, less because of his career of conquest than of the benefits that sprang from it, the dissemination of Greek culture in the East. After his visit to the tomb Septimius ordered it to be locked. It offended him that the priests made profit from exhibiting the sacred face, and he hoped to earn Alexander's blessing by keeping his privacy inviolate. He believed devoutly in the influence that spirits of the dead could exert for good or ill. Immediately on disembarkation at Pelusium on the Egyptian coast he offered propitiatory sacrifice to the ghost of Pompey, murdered there nearly two hundred and fifty years before. The murderer's name was Lucius Septimius, a member, however distantly related, of the Emperor's own family.

An occasion of especial interest to the Imperial visitors at Alexandria was their attendance at a celebration of the rites of Serapis. This was a god more or less invented by the first Ptolemy, Alexander's general, when he received Egypt as his share of the dead Alexander's domains. His purpose was to unite his Greek and Egyptian subjects in a common religion. Serapis had attributes borrowed from both Greek and Egyptian mythology. He is usually represented in Greek style as a bearded figure resembling Pluto; but his worship had more in common with that of the Egyptian Osiris, and an important part was played in it by Isis, who was retained as his consort. The prescribed liturgy began at dawn when the sacred effigy was unveiled, and invocations were chanted to wake the god from sleep. A priest lit a fire on the altar and offered a libation of water drawn from the Nile before the statue was dressed in gorgeous clothes and jewels. It was a daily re-enactment of the stages necessary to the god's continued life on earth.

For Julia, brought up in the temple of Elagabal, the elaborate ritual had no great novelty, except in so far as the proceedings were adapted to the human figure of Serapis instead of the black meteorite at Emesa; but there was much in the cult to deserve her attention when she studied the ideas underlying it, especially those relating to Isis. Well versed in contemporary literature, she could not fail to recall the spiritual meaning given to the rites by Apuleius in the last book of *The Golden Ass*, the sense of divine companionship that rewards the believer initiated into the mysteries, the words put into his mouth as he prays to Isis: 'I shall keep your divine face and most holy power stored among the secrets of my heart for everlasting contemplation.' When the ceremony in the temple was over, the last formula had been pronounced and the hymns had died away, it was a custom peculiar to Egypt that the congregation remained standing without sound or movement, worshipping in gathered silence. Such was the impression made on the Emperor and his wife by the experience that he collected as many books on esoteric doctrine as he could find. The priests regretted his zeal as he removed the books and took them away with him, even from the celebrated library founded in Alexandria by the Ptolemys.

Nevertheless the visit gave cause for satisfaction in Egypt. Its main purpose, of more urgent importance than the indulgence of religious and antiquarian tastes, was to reorganize the administration of this vital province. Ever since the foundation of the Empire the Roman governor of Egypt had exercised despotic authority. It was considered too dangerous, in view of the value of the country's exports, to allow the inhabitants any say in the management of their affairs. Septimius changed this by permitting the election of senatorial councils in Alexandria and other large towns, to whose jurisdiction he delegated responsibility for local government, and he removed the ban excluding Egyptians from the senate in Rome. He hoped by these conciliatory measures to earn gratitude that would eliminate the remnants of Niger's faction and promote loyal attachment to his own dynasty. As long as he reigned, his policy was successful.

In the early summer of 199 he set out with Julia on a long voyage up the Nile. This was an expedition combining the joys of exploration with all the amenities of civilized comfort. The barge in which the Imperial couple travelled was large enough to accommodate the friends whose company they desired and a sufficient retinue of servants for daily needs. Other attendants, secretaries and officers of State followed either by water or on the shore. As the ship was square-rigged the great sail of coloured papyrus depended on a following wind; but when the wind changed or sank, boats manned by oarsmen were ready to take the barge in tow, and it glided on without interruption between carefully irrigated fields of corn, the granary of Rome, banks adorned with the monuments of a civilization already ancient when Rome was built.

The travellers paused on their way for sightseeing excursions. They paid a visit to the Pyramids and, when they reached Thebes, the capital of Upper Egypt, they drove in a light carriage to inspect a colossal effigy that stood at some distance from the town. The figure in fact represented a Pharaoh of the eighteenth dynasty; but the Greeks insisted that it was their own legendary hero, Memnon, son of the goddess of the dawn, because when the rays of the rising sun touched the stone it gave off a musical note like the twang of a harp, said to be the son's greeting to his mother. The statue was more impressive for its unusual acoustics than as a work of sculpture. Some two hundred years before the arrival of the Imperial visitors it had suffered damage from an earthquake which left most of the upper part of Memnon's body in ruin. Septimius, an enthusiastic antiquary, was appalled by its dilapidated condition and gave orders for the employment of skilled craftsmen to carry out repairs. Memnon recovered human shape, but he lost his voice in the process. The first breeze of dawn caught the restored figure at a new angle, and the singing statue never sang again.

From Thebes they continued on upstream, while the belt of fertile land grew narrower and the bare hills of the desert encroached nearer on either shore. They saw great beasts in the water, crocodile and hippopotamus, reminding Julia of those described by Aelian in his tales of wonder. At last they reached Philae, the southernmost town in Egypt, standing on two islands above the first cataract of the Nile on a site lake-bound today since the building of the Aswan Dam. A custom was observed at Philae, dating from the ancient days of the Pharaohs, that every year at the end of May the ruler of Egypt threw an offering of gold and silver into a cave to propitiate the sacred river. When independent Egypt succumbed to Rome, the annual task was performed by the Prefect of Egypt as representative of the Roman Emperor. It gratified the Egyptians, who held the ceremony in veneration, and did much to further the conciliatory policy which Septimius pursued that in this year 199, for the first and only occasion, a Roman Emperor came to preside in person.

From Philae the party intended to travel on still farther upstream beyond the frontier of Egypt to visit Ethiopia. This was country so little known that imagination was free to people it with fables. Philostratus later chose it to be the home of the Gymnosophists, the naked sages among whom Apollonius studies wisdom; but if he was hoping now for first-hand experience on which to found his description he was disappointed. On the borders of the mysterious land the Emperor was taken suddenly ill, and the expedition had to be abandoned. There had been a severe epidemic of smallpox in the Empire in recent years, and these outlying parts, the last that it reached, were the last to be rid of it. Julia escaped infection, but Septimius suffered an acute attack of the disease. Medical skill was improving under the influence of the teaching of Galen, and his doctors were able to save his life; but his constitution was weakened, and he never entirely recovered his former vigour.

He lingered on for more than a year in Egypt, partly for convalescence, partly to complete his administrative reforms. Even when he was ready to depart he travelled in easy stages, sailing at first only as far as Antioch. The town was still in disgrace, deprived of the title of provincial capital to punish the citizens for their support of Niger. The arrival of Septimius for a protracted visit encouraged hope of clemency, which he confirmed when he announced that the punishment was revoked at the request of his son Antoninus. It is more likely that Antioch's champion was Julia than a boy of thirteen. She was very fond of the town and made it her headquarters later in her life. The statement, however, earned goodwill for the boy at a time when his father wished to bring him into the public eye. On New Year's Day 202 the names of the consuls for the coming year were published, the Emperor himself and his elder son.

As the office had become an honorific sinecure no longer carrying any practical responsibility, no difficulty was created by the appointment of Antoninus at so early an age. Marcus Aurelius indeed set a similar example when he chose his son Commodus for the consulship; but Commodus was two years older at the time and, unlike Antoninus, already wore the *toga virilis*, official emblem of adulthood. By promoting a child to the post Septimius advertised the privileged status of his own family. He defied tradition also in holding the ceremony not at Rome but at Antioch, an appropriate scene for the inauguration of a dynasty that would be dominated by the Syrian Princesses.

Soon afterwards he returned to Rome, where he celebrated with lavish festivities the victorious end of the Parthian war. It was proposed that he should be accorded a triumph in traditional style, a procession in which the conquering general, wearing the robes of Jupiter, rode in his chariot to the Capitoline hill, escorted by his soldiers shouting 'Io Triumphe'. He refused the honour because of the discomfort of standing upright in the triumphal chariot. He suffered— an after-effect, it was said, of his attack of smallpox—from a form of gout, intermittent bouts of pain in the joints of his limbs. There was no procession, therefore; but to commemorate the occasion he ordered a triumphal arch to be built, inscribed with scenes of his victories. The site chosen was that of which he dreamt at Carnuntum, when he saw Pertinax thrown from his horse and he himself mounted in his place. An equestrian statue marked the exact spot, and the new monument rose beside it, testifying to the rider's achievements. It is still to be seen in Rome today, known as the Arch of Septimius Severus.

5

The Last Years of Septimius

As the sons of Septimius and Julia grew to manhood a great difference in character became apparent between them. The elder, Antoninus, inherited his mother's charm, but not her beauty. He was puny in figure, sallow and sharp-featured; unfriendly observers described him as ugly. He made up for these disadvantages by the easy affability of his manners and his high spirits, especially when he was anxious to make a good impression. In his early boyhood he was capable of generous indignation, to judge from a story told of him when he was seven years old. Hearing that a playmate had been beaten by his father for attending Jewish rites, he ran off to his own father, the Emperor, to demand that the chastiser should be chastised and deprived of employment in the Imperial household. His concern for his friend testifies to a loyalty of which few traces are revealed in his subsequent history. The vindictive punishment demanded for the friend's father strikes a more characteristic note.

Geta, the younger brother, made friends less easily. He was shy, often brusque, and spoke with a slight stammer. In looks he took after his father, stocky in build with wide brow and blunt nose. Although both boys were quick scholars, Antoninus affected to despise learning; Geta however shared his mother's love of knowledge, her curiosity and zest to explore its by-ways. He combined intellectual tastes, according to his biographer, with a relish for good food, gaily-coloured clothes and, as he grew older, for pretty girls.

Geta was his mother's favourite. It has been suggested that his ideas betray Christian influence, but the evidence is inconclusive. It was not he but his brother who was suckled by a Christian nurse, even if a child at that age had been likely to imbibe her doctrine with her milk. Nevertheless there were many Christians in the household as the boys grew up. Julia, as has been said, studied their teaching with genuine if sceptical interest, and Septimius himself, on the testimony of the contemporary Christian writer Tertullian, showed goodwill in his private dealings with them, retaining them in his service even while his officers in the provinces persecuted without restraint. When Antoninus became Emperor, whatever else his enemies have accused him of, it is agreed that Christianity was left in peace. Geta however was nearer to it in spirit. An occasion is recorded when the two were present at a council of war to decide whether prisoners should be executed. Geta asked: 'Do we want more people to be sorry than glad that we won?'

Antoninus on the other hand was in favour of putting all to death, children included.

There was an incompatibility of temperament between the brothers which from their earliest days bred perpetual quarrels. As small boys they fought violently, wrestling with each other, and as they grew older the rivalry persisted, dividing them in everything that they did. Whatever the one liked, the other of necessity condemned. The effect of the feud was to split Roman society, as partisans ranged themselves on either side. The Emperor deplored the strife, seeing in it a danger to the survival of the dynasty that he was founding; but all his efforts to reconcile his sons were in vain. Julia's were less effective still. Antoninus was jealous, knowing that Geta was her favourite.

Anxious to provide them with the best education available, Septimius chose his own secretary to be their tutor, a leading sophist called Antipater. He was a man of more learning, however, than understanding. When his pedagogic duties were completed, the Emperor appointed him governor of Bithynia. He was soon relieved of his office because of the unpopularity that he earned there, relying on the drawn swords of his soldiers to cover his incompetence in the art of government.

His stubbornness and pride brought misfortune in domestic as well as public affairs. Seeking a husband for his daughter, he picked on a young man called Hermocrates, a rising sophist whose good looks and pleasing voice marked him out for a successful career. Hermocrates, however, declined the honour. The girl failed to attract him. Not even the prospect of being son-in-law to the Emperor's secretary could reconcile him to the sour expression of her face. His refusal gave offence to Antipater, who regarded it as an affront to his dignity and threatened to complain to the Emperor. Hermocrates, fearing Imperial disfavour, overcame his reluctance and yielded to save his career. Philostratus who tells the story adds that after the wedding, at the customary unveiling of the bride, the bridegroom muttered in his hearing: 'That face needs more veils, not less.'

Antipater's injured pride was avenged, but no one had reason to rejoice. Hermocrates, finding that his wife's disposition matched her face, consoled himself with drunken revels that exhausted both his health and his means. The marriage ended in divorce, followed soon afterwards by his early death.

Whether or not the influence of his tutor was to blame, Antoninus acquired habits of behaviour that aroused misgivings. His manners changed for the worse between childhood and adolescence. The boy whose good humour and high spirits charmed all who met him received more adulation than was wholesome in Roman society, eager to court the heir to the purple. He took less trouble to please when arrogance could get him what he wanted, and his temper flared up in resentment, no longer of wrongs inflicted on another, but of obstacles thwarting the gratification of his own will. He shared his father's veneration for Alexander the Great; but it took the dangerous form that he identified himself with the conqueror, modelling his behaviour on that which he believed appropriate to his hero.

An event that had a harmful effect on his character occurred shortly after his arrival in Rome from Antioch. The most powerful man in Rome after the Emperor himself was the Praetorian Prefect, Fulvius Plautianus, the old friend of the Emperor's boyhood to whom, as is described on an earlier page, the task was given of seizing Niger's wife and children during the civil war. Plautianus stood high in the Emperor's favour, linked to him by sentimental ties and shared memories of youthful days in Leptis. He made the most of the opportunity afforded him. His wealth was as enormous as his political influence, and he loved to dazzle Roman society by the magnificence of his style of living and the costly rarity of his possessions, including a herd of zebras stolen from a temple on an island in the Indian Ocean. His ambition achieved a coveted prize when he persuaded the Emperor that his daughter Plautilla would be a suitable wife for Antoninus. The wedding was celebrated with a splendour extravagant even by Roman standards. A guest attending the banquet, who saw the bride's trousseau carried into the palace, calculated that there was enough to clothe and adorn fifty women of royal rank.

The only blot on the festivities was the discontent shown by the bridegroom, Antoninus. He was not consulted when the marriage was arranged, and whether for that reason or because, like his tutor's daughter, the girl was no beauty, he took against her at once. He was fourteen, she probably older, as it was intended that the couple should start living together without delay; but he stubbornly refused to consummate the marriage, either then or later. He ignored and insulted his wife, and could not even endure her presence at meals.

In his hatred of the match he had his mother's sympathy. She disliked Plautianus and was jealous of his influence over her husband. Already he was known by the facetious nickname of the 'fourth Caesar', raised to the level of her husband and sons. The Emperor, however, paid no attention when she complained of the favourite's presumption. In his eyes Plautianus could do no wrong. He wrote in a letter: 'I love the man so much I only pray that I die before him.' Gossip attributed the origin of his feelings to a homosexual attachment in youth.

Dio has a number of stories to illustrate the ascendancy that Plautianus enjoyed. When he travelled in the Emperor's company he took for his own use the most sumptuous lodgings in any town where they stayed, and there was an occasion when the Emperor would have gone without mullet, of which he was fond, if he had not begged one from Plautianus for his table. A possible explanation is that Septimius, a man of simple tastes, was not interested enough in luxuries to compete for them with his favourite. Another story reveals that Septimius had a sense of humour. He was sitting in judgement in court, and having got through the cases sooner than he expected he told the usher to add another to the list. The man replied: 'That can't be done without orders from Plautianus.'

The Emperor treated it as a joke, much to the relief of Plautianus when the story was repeated to him.

It was clear to all that Plautianus had an inordinate hold on the Emperor's trust and affection. So confident was he of his power that, when Julia opposed him, he did not hesitate to attack her, accusing her of unchastity. Her reputation was vulnerable because of her Syrian origin, her association from earliest youth with the groves and high places of her native religion, the freedom encouraged there at seasonal festivals. Although notorious for his own indulgence in the pleasures of the flesh, frequenting the society of prostitutes of either sex, he demanded an inflexible standard of female propriety and prided himself on the strictness with which he guarded the purity of his wife and daughter, whom he debarred altogether from social intercourse except under his supervision. He even insisted that all male attendants employed in the women's quarters should be castrated. These included before his daughter's marriage her teachers in music and the arts, many of them middle-aged or elderly with wives of their own.

In his search for evidence against Julia he had her waiting women brought before him, no matter how exalted their rank, and interrogated them under torture. Julia protested in vain. Her husband's suspicion was aroused and his regard for her estranged by the favourite's influence. Nevertheless, in spite of the most rigorous inquiry, bribery, intimidation and violence, nothing more damaging could be extracted from the witnesses than an admission of her part in organizing a gymnastic contest, which provoked scandal by including girls competing naked in the tradition of ancient Sparta. Septimius issued an edict forbidding any repetition of the event, and Julia sought consolation and distraction in the company of her literary and philosophic friends.

A chance came soon afterwards to take her revenge when she travelled with Septimius on a visit to Africa. He himself, angry with Plautianus when so small an offence emerged from such a cloud of suspicion, was in a mood to be reconciled with his wife. He paid attention when she pointed out that there were more statues put up to Plautianus than to Septimius himself in their native town of Leptis. It aggravated the presumption that several of them represented him in a group with Septimius and his sons, as if he were indeed a 'fourth Caesar', adopted into the family. Septimius was enraged. He himself was the most famous son of Leptis, and he was unwilling to share the honour. In addition he was intent on founding a dynasty to be raised from the heirs of his body, and he foresaw trouble if any idea of adoption were allowed to intrude. In a stormy interview with Plautianus, who was with them on the expedition, he ordered the offending bronzes to be removed and melted down.

After that, as was his habit, he recovered his equanimity and forgot the incident. He had ambitious plans, which were the purpose of his journey, to create a separate administration in Numidia, the western part of the province, and extend the southern frontier to the edge of the desert. Plautianus, a fellow-African, was familiar with the details and useful in putting them into effect. They worked on them together in restored friendship.

Meanwhile the story of the destruction of the bronzes was carried to Sardinia, where the governor, assuming that Plautianus was disgraced, had all images and tablets bearing his name demolished. When Septimius heard of this he was both astonished and indignant. The too hasty governor was recalled and put on trial. Plautianus saw to it that he was severely punished, and others whose hopes had been aroused by news of the incident at Leptis made haste to cover their disappointment and pay respect to the still powerful favourite.

Julia remained unreconciled. A common hatred of Plautianus drew her into alliance with her elder son, who could forgive her for preferring Geta to himself when she sympathized with him in the troubles of his marriage. His father-in-law ordered him about, patronized him, interfered in his domestic affairs, scolding him for the insults and neglect of which Plautilla complained. Father and daughter joined forces against him as he persisted in his refusal of sexual intercourse. Plautianus was impatient for a grandson to inherit the purple. Antoninus, unwilling to oblige, relieved his feelings in private conversation with his mother.

The rift was disguised, however, and an appearance of harmony restored in the Imperial family in the summer of 204 for the celebration of the Secular Games, an event that proclaimed the triumph of the dynasty and the inauguration in the Roman Empire of a new era of prosperity and peace. The festival had its origin in the remote past, instituted according to tradition by the Etruscans to mark the transition from an old to a new epoch, a period estimated at 110 years covering the span of memory of two generations. The custom was kept up under both the Republic and the Empire. The best remembered occasion was in the reign of Augustus, when the poet Horace composed the processional hymn celebrating the foundation of the Empire, a new era indeed. Since then there had been other celebrations without strict observance of the traditional interval. It was convenient to hold Secular Games to enhance the prestige of the Emperor concerned. Septimius, however, was too zealous an antiquary to be guilty of fiddling in his calculation. He chose a date exactly 220 years, two epochs in the sense defined, after the Games held by Augustus.

Religious ceremonial held chief place in the programme, processions, sacrifice and prayer, with choirs of boys and girls singing the *Carmen Saeculare*, a hymn invoking Apollo and Diana. An example of the hymn survives, that composed by Horace in the reign of Augustus, but that sung in the presence of Septimius in the year 204 was the work of a lesser poet. When the claims of religion had been satisfied, entertainment followed of the sort customary on a Roman holiday: hunters pitted in the arena against savage beasts, gladiatorial combat and chariot-racing, with the addition of special features like the 'Troy game', a mock-battle fought by teams of boys of noble birth. No girls, either clothed or naked, were invited to compete in the athletics.

Julia performed her part as Augusta with appropriate dignity, presiding in the temple of Jupiter on the Capitoline hill over an elegant conclave of matrons drawn from the Imperial family and others of sufficient distinction.

Among them was her sister Julia Maesa, whose husband Julius Avitus had been promoted to senatorial rank and was shortly to be appointed governor of Asia. Although Maesa was the elder of the daughters of the high priest of Elagabal at Emesa, she remained in the background as long as her sister lived. Her self-effacement was due to no lack of spirit. When the opportunity came, she revealed a forceful personality and outstanding ability well equipped to play a leading part in public affairs. For the present, however, she was content to bask in the reflected glow of her sister's eminence, and her husband's career prospered, nourished by Imperial favour. Her dominant motive, it seems, was the pride and passionate loyalty which she cherished for those of her own blood. She did not envy her sister the title of Augusta; but when her sister was dead and a stranger usurped it she fought relentlessly to retrieve it for herself, to restore the glory of the family, the dynasty.

She had two daughters, Sohaemias and Mamaea, but apparently no son. Sohaemias, the elder, a girl now in her late teens, was married to Varius Marcellus, an ambitious young Syrian already climbing the ladder of official preferment, where he enjoyed advantage from the favour shown by this régime to anyone of Syrian birth. Sohaemias was among the matrons attending her aunt in the temple of Jupiter. Mamaea was still too young to be married.

The success of the Secular Games brought satisfaction to Septimius, crowning his recent achievements with traditional honour and exalting him to the status of the divine Augustus. His family shared his glory, presenting an appearance of decorous unity that inspired confidence. It seemed that his fear of domestic strife was dispelled. Before the end of the year, however, his peace of mind suffered a severe blow from the death of his brother, Septimius Geta (he bore the same cognomen as his younger nephew), who had always been his loyal supporter, an indispensable ally in 193 when, as governor of Lower Moesia, he sent legions from the lower Danube to reinforce the muster at Carnuntum. The loss of his brother was a great sorrow to the Emperor, and it was aggravated by the information that his brother confided on his deathbed.

Dio, who relates the incident, reveals only that the information carried a warning against the designs of Plautianus, of which Septimius

Geta had been afraid to speak earlier, fearing that his brother was too infatuated to listen to him, and that the sole result would be to draw reprisals from Plautianus on himself. Even now when a dying man, his own brother, warned him, the Emperor hesitated to believe evil of his lifelong friend. He imposed stricter limits on the powers entrusted to the Praetorian Prefect; but Plautianus retained the office, and no manifest sign of disfavour diminished his prestige. Nevertheless he was aware of a deterioration in his relations with the Emperor. People commented on his changed demeanour on public occasions. They were accustomed to his self-important manner, the arrogance with which he paced the street, flaunting his wealth and power in the magnificence of his clothes, and the insolence of his escort of retainers, who jostled passers-by out of his way and clouted anyone so rash as to stand and stare at him. It was out of keeping with his character and drew the more attention now that he had began to wear an expression of strained anxiety, that his face had lost its ruddy glow of good living, and that he looked round nervously, even trembling, if any movement or sound disconcerted him.

The evidence is inconclusive whether at this stage he was plotting a *coup d'état*. From many points of view it might seem that he had insufficient motive. He occupied a position inferior to no one in the State but the Emperor himself, who, as he had reason to suppose, was too completely dependent on him to shake off the habit. Any cloud of displeasure was likely to pass over quickly, as was shown by the affair of the offending images at Leptis. There was, however, another side to the picture: Septimius was already approaching his sixtieth birthday, and his health had not been good since his attack of small-pox. If he died suddenly and was succeeded by Antoninus, the prospect was gloomy. Plautianus knew his son-in-law too well, both from his own observation and from Plautilla's reports, to believe that his dignity and wealth or even his life would be secure. To wait for events could be as dangerous as to forestall them. The Praetorian Prefect command-ing the Emperor's bodyguard was excellently placed to direct a success-ful revolution. There was encouragement in the example set by Laetus when he overthrew Commodus, and no need to repeat his mistakes, his inability to keep the soldiers under control. A stronger man, Plautianus himself for instance, could succeed where Laetus failed.

If Plautianus felt alarm as he looked into the future, it suited Julia, who hated him, to fan his fears. Hitherto she had treated her daughter-in-law with little cordiality, but now she sought her company and sat and talked to her as if taking her into her confidence, knowing that whatever she said would be repeated by the girl to her father. In this way Plautianus was fed with disquieting stories, warning him of danger in store. The chief part in events was played by a Syrian officer of the Praetorian Guard called Saturninus, conspicuous for the deference that he showed to Plautianus who held him in high esteem. This man, it seems, acted as a double agent, employed by Antoninus and Julia to incite Plautianus to treason, and by Plautianus to put the plot into effect, murder Septimius and Antoninus and proclaim Plautianus Emperor.

Saturninus was in command of the detachment mounting guard in the palace on a night when both Septimius and Antoninus were in residence. As officer on duty, he had access to all the rooms. It was arranged that he should enter the Emperor's on the pretext of an urgent message, and that when he was alone with him he should kill him, then go on to look for Antoninus and kill him too. As soon as both were dead, he would send word secretly to Plautianus to summon him before anyone else knew of the deed. Those were the orders given to Saturninus, and he fulfilled them to the extent of entering the Emperor's room; but when he was there he informed him of the plot, revealing with many assurances of his own loyalty what Plautianus intended. The Emperor at first refused to believe it; he suspected not without reason that Antoninus was at the bottom of the story, and he sent for him. When Antoninus arrived and heard the news, he professed to be as surprised and shocked as his father; but he suggested that the best way to test the story was to let Saturninus send word as arranged, to announce that all had gone according to plan. If Plautianus was guilty, he would betray himself in his haste to reap the fruits of success.

The messenger was sent, and Plautianus behaved as Antoninus foretold. He left his house at once, taking the precaution to wear a coat of mail under his clothes, and came across in his carriage to the palace. It was a wet night in January, the paving stones were slippery from the rain. He drove the mules at so eager a pace that they stumbled and fell as they entered the yard.

Saturninus met him in the hall, saluted him as Emperor and offered to show him the dead bodies. He led the way, and Plautianus followed in jubilant satisfaction, bursting into the Emperor's room as soon as the door was opened. Septimius and Antoninus stood there alive.

Septimius addressed him gently and reproachfully, asking why he wanted to kill him. Plautianus had time to recover his wits; he denied that he had any such purpose and, recalling his loyal services in the past, insisted that this was a trap laid for him by his enemies, that he was the victim of a frame-up. His words made an impression on Septimius, who listened with earnest attention, till Antoninus suddenly clutched Plautianus by the tunic and tore it from his shoulder, exposing the mail beneath.

'Why do you wear armour,' he asked, 'to visit the Emperor?'

He struck him in the face and would have throttled him if his father had not restrained him. Saturninus and the attendants hurried forward and, as Antoninus gave the order, and the Emperor confirmed it with a reluctant nod, they drew their swords and stabbed Plautianus to death. Antoninus grabbed a handful of hairs from the beard and ran in glee to show them to his mother. Unaware of the progress of events, she was in her room still priming the gullible Plautilla. Finding them together, he brandished the hairs in his wife's face: 'Your father,' he told her. 'What's left of him.'

The body of Plautianus was thrown out into the public street, so that this time there could be no doubt that the powerful Prefect had fallen; but when Septimius saw it lying there he ordered it to be taken away and decently buried. In his speech the next morning to the senate he avoided recrimination and laid the blame chiefly on his own partiality, the excessive favour shown to Plautianus, encouraging ambitions beyond the strength of human nature to resist. Dio who was present records, however, that before the details of the plot were revealed several senators whose loyalty the Emperor suspected were made to leave the house.

The death of Plautianus was not the end of the affair. It was certain that he could not have acted without accomplices, and the Emperor no longer hesitated to follow up the information given him by his dying brother. In the purge that resulted many high officers of state were dismissed, a few put to death. Dio has a story that reveals the insecurity and alarm felt by all concerned, whether guilty or innocent. A high officer of State was accused in his absence of complicity in the plot, and the charge was added—as with Septimius himself in Sicily under Commodus—that he resorted for the purpose to rites of magic. Others as well took part in them, according to a witness who testified: 'I saw a bald senator creeping in.' Suspicion fell at once on everyone in the senate who even tended to baldness. No one was free from un-easiness except those with the bushiest heads. Dio describes how the senators present exchanged furtive glances, each comparing his neigh-bour's crop of hair with his own.

'I can't deny,' he adds, 'what I did myself, ridiculous as it was. I was so disconcerted that I kept raising my hand to my head to feel the hair there. Many others did the same.'

Much anxiety was allayed among those without official rank when the clerk who read out the evidence came to a statement that the bald senator in question wore a toga with a purple border, the badge of a magistrate. Accusing eyes were fixed on a certain Baebius Marcellinus, who held the office of aedile, a junior magistracy, at the time and was as bald as a coot. Marcellinus, putting a bold face on it, demanded that the informer should be brought in before them and told to pick him out if he could. This was done, and the man stood staring at the senators, unable for a time to recognize anyone; but then it seems, according to Dio, that he received a hidden wink directing him to Marcellinus, and he pointed to him and swore that he identified him.

Marcellinus was arrested at once and led out of the senate-house. In the Forum his four children were waiting for him, knowing that the lives of many senators were in danger and fearing for the outcome of the debate. When they saw their father under arrest their fears were confirmed. As he said good-bye he told them that his chief sorrow was to leave them behind alive, at the mercy of his enemies. Then his head was cut off, before the Emperor knew anything about it.

The impression is given that Septimius, shocked by the treachery of Plautianus, relaxed his customary standards of justice, and that private malice took advantage of the confusion to pursue its own ends. Much was done to restore order and confidence, however, by the appointment of Papinian, the great jurist, to the place left vacant by Plautianus as Praetorian Prefect. The Emperor's choice had the purpose, among others, of divesting the office of military associations. A civilian Prefect was never likely to become a dangerous rival in command of the Praetorian Guard. The effect was not to diminish the importance of the post but to change its sphere of influence, when it was held by a lawyer and statesman. The part played by Papinian in directing Imperial policy, promoting honesty and efficiency in the administration and an enlightened interpretation of the law, set an example from which benefit accrued as long as the dynasty lasted. Julia, his friend and kinswoman, proved herself an apt pupil in the next reign when she herself was in charge of the government.

For the present, however, her attention was fully occupied with her sons, whose conduct as they grew to manhood gave her cause for anxiety. There was no longer even the bond of a common hatred to draw the elder to confide in her. Antoninus obtained a divorce from Plautilla, who was banished to an island in the Lipari group with her brother to keep her company, and without wife or father-in-law to hinder him he launched himself into the pleasures available to youth, rank and wealth. A frequent companion on these occasions was his cousin Sohaemias, left a lively grass-widow in Rome while Varius, her husband, was away on duty as Imperial courier in Britain. It seems that intimate relations between the cousins were already established at the date of the Secular Games, to judge from the scandal that prevailed about the paternity of her son who was born in that year. Varius returned to Rome, promoted to the senatorial order and given charge of the military treasury; but he was a tolerant husband, too intent on a successful career to resent his wife's friendship with the heir to the purple. She was not the only woman, however, on whose favours Antoninus could rely. His escapades, both amorous and riotous, became the talk of the town. There were no signs yet of the sexual impotence which later afflicted him.

These exploits troubled Julia less than his quarrels with his brother Geta. Relations between the two grew ever more embittered as the years went by. Each had his band of cronies to abet him, mischief-makers who throve in spite of the Emperor's efforts to banish them. A favourite scene of the rivalry was at the chariot races at the public games, where the brothers vied in costly ostentation, equipping their own teams for victory. At last, not content with racing by proxy, they challenged each other to a match in which each would be his own charioteer. They had the sense, lacking skill, to choose ponies rather than horses for the contest, so that the vehicles and the speed at which they travelled were less formidable. Nevertheless they collided as they drove round the turning post, and Antoninus fell out and broke his leg.

When Septimius heard of the accident he judged it time to intervene. He was among the few people whom Antoninus feared and respected. He visited the patient therefore and argued and pleaded with him, warning him of the danger that disunity brought on the dynasty and the Empire, with the example of the civil war barely ten years past to point the moral. Antoninus, confined to bed, listened in chastened mood; but when his leg healed, and he was about again, he resumed his old habits. Septimius betrayed in his dealings with his son a weakness hard to reconcile with the sterner aspects of his character. He himself was accustomed to blame the Emperor Marcus Aurelius for paternal indulgence, which left the Empire after his death to an unbalanced and incapable successor. Yet he was guilty of the same fault where his own son was concerned. He often threatened to disinherit him unless he reformed, but the threat was never carried out. The name of Antoninus accompanied his own in all proclamations, rescripts and other official documents, establishing the continuity of the dynasty in the eyes of the world.

After the suppression of Plautianus and his accomplices most parts of the Empire enjoyed peace, except for such incidents as the exploits recorded of a brigand who preyed on travellers in Italy, earning a reputation for boldness worthy of Robin Hood. He was able to recruit a gang of six hundred from men left unemployed and destitute by the confiscation of estates. There is evidence here of distress bequeathed by the civil war; but the effects were confined to a limited area and of a sort that restoration of order and confidence was likely to cure. In the Empire as a whole the prevailing mood was one of thankful relief. It was easy to believe that, after a brief jolt of alarm, the golden Age of the Antonines was resuming its tranquil course. The assumption of the name by the new dynasty, its claim to posthumous adoption, reinforced the impression.

Septimius himself took the great Antonine Emperors of the past as his pattern. His efforts earned the more approval because they contrasted so notably with the ferocious caprices of Commodus. Even if the decisions attributed to him in the *Digest of Roman Law* owe their inspiration mainly to Papinian, he deserves credit for choosing so sane a counsellor and for following his advice. The boy who loved to play the part of judge in games of pretence had grown into a man able to pronounce judgement on everyone in the Roman world, but he had the strength of mind not to yield to the intoxication of power. There is a characteristic note in his comment on the principle that Emperors are above the law: 'Although Emperors are not bound by laws, it is by means of laws that they live.'

An account of his daily routine is given by Dio, an eye-witness: 'He got up at dawn or earlier, then went for a walk with someone to talk and hear about affairs of State. After that, except on days of festival, he sat in court giving judgement. His method of procedure was admirable, allowing the litigants plenty of time to speak and those of us who were his assessors the utmost freedom to express our views. He heard cases till mid-day, then took a ride on a horse when he was well enough. After that he had a bath, with some gymnastic exercise to follow. He made a good meal at lunch, which he ate either by himself or with his sons. Then usually he lay down to sleep, after which he rose to go on with his work, pacing to and fro as he discussed business in Greek or Latin. Towards evening he had a bath again, then dined with his household. It was rare for a guest to be invited, and an elaborate banquet was prepared only on occasions when it absolutely could not be avoided.'

With increasing age and failing health he liked to retire to his property on the Campanian coast near Naples. His purpose had nothing in common with the morose disillusionment which, early in the first century, prompted the Emperor Tiberius to spend the last years of his life self-exiled to the island of Capri. Septimius was not a recluse. He took his family with him, Julia and his sons, hoping to encourage the latter in rural pursuits to divert them from the temptations of Rome. He himself was not idle in the country. He continued while he was there to attend to judicial and administrative business.

News from Britain interrupted this way of life. When Albinus stripped the province of soldiers to support his ill-fated march on Rome, he left the northern parts at the mercy of the Caledonians, the unconquered tribes beyond the frontier. They attacked the Wall built from Tyne to Solway, overpowered the scanty garrison and streamed across to kill and plunder. Even when Albinus was dead, and Septimius established at Rome, the army in Britain remained below strength. The first governor appointed by Septimius could do no more than hold a line from York to Chester. To obtain a respite from fighting and the release of captives, he tried to buy the invaders off; but the undertaking that they gave was soon broken. His successor was little more fortunate, and at last he sent a message to Rome asking to be given the forces needed to restore order, or else that the Emperor should come and do it himself.

It is not clear why Septimius put off the pacification of Britain for so long. His first care after the civil war was for the wealthy provinces in the East, to establish his command over them and eliminate the last traces of the influence of Niger. To complete his work there he thrust the Parthians back to the Tigris, adding Mesopotamia to the Empire. All this was finished, however, by the end of 201 and the bulk of the army withdrawn. He had forces available to send if he wished to help the governor of Britain and expel the Caledonian marauders. He could not be ignorant of the damage that the province was suffering. In addition to dispatches from the governor, he could rely for information on the reports of his own courier, his niece's husband, Varius, who was present there for much of the time. It is possible that the latter warned him of the danger of putting too much power in the governor's hands. Albinus, the last governor of Britain to command an adequate army, used it to attempt to make himself Emperor.

In answer to the appeal Septimius decided to lead the expeditionary force in person, rather than entrust increased forces to the governor's control. He was in poor health, liable to crippling attacks of gout; but he was not a man to spare himself, and he looked forward with zest to a last adventure, a renewal of his youth. In particular he hoped that his sons accompanying him would learn from practical experience what the task meant of defending the bounds of the Empire, and that on active service they would forget their mutual jealousy and turn into soldiers and statesmen worthy to succeed him. He left Rome in the spring of 208, taking them both with him, also Julia and Papinian. Unable as in the old days to march with his soldiers on foot, he let himself be carried in a litter; but his spirit was as impetuous as ever, and he reached the coast of Gaul before the fleet was ready to convey him across the Channel. Impatient of delay, he pressed on in a solitary ship. His arrival took Britain by surprise, and the Caledonians, dismayed by the news that the Emperor was present in person, sent envoys south to meet him and plead for peace.

He refused to treat with them. His purpose, to which he clung with determination, was to lead a punitive expedition to invade them in their own territory. Having added a province in the East, carrying the frontier to the Tigris, he was hoping that the final fruit of his reign would be a similar achievement at the other end of the Empire, extending the Roman occupation of Britain to the northernmost limits of the island. For the rest of that year and the early months of the next he remained in his southern headquarters, probably Londinium, London, which, favoured by its convenient situation, had precedence over other cities in the province and was the usual centre of administration. He was busy there restoring stable government and making preparations for his coming campaign. During the winter he conferred the title of Augustus on Geta, the same already borne by Antoninus, giving the brothers equal rank, and to celebrate the occasion he struck a medal with the motto, *Concordia Augustorum*. It was evidence of his own fervent wish, but of little else. Antoninus regarded Geta's promotion with bitter jealousy. He consoled himself by courting the favour of the soldiers, bribing and flattering, using all his charm to win followers devoted to his interest. He had a taste for eccentricity in dress and was in the habit of wearing a long hooded cloak of a design native to Gaul, known in the Gaulish language as *caracal*. This earned him the nickname of Caracalla. He took it as a compliment, a sign of popularity, to be greeted as Caracalla by the soldiers.

In the summer of 209 Septimius set out for the north to meet the enemy, taking Antoninus with him. He left Geta in the south in

D

charge of the administration, with a council of able men to advise
him. Geta was only twenty years old, but his father had more confidence in him than in his elder brother and chose him to govern in his
absence. Julia stayed behind with her son for the time being, but she
joined her husband later when his expedition made progress in territory beyond the Wall.

Her influence can be detected in the conduct of affairs, while Geta
was in charge, from an incident recorded in the earliest account of the
martyrdom of Saint Alban, a Roman soldier converted to Christianity
and reputed to be the first martyr to suffer in Britain. According to
tradition he was a native of Verulamium, the modern Saint Albans
(the town is called after him), who returned after service in the army
to spend his retirement in his birthplace, where he was caught in a
persecution and put to death. His date is nowhere firmly defined; but
it is unlikely that it fell as late as the great persecution of which Christianity was the victim at the end of the third century, as the effect was
confined for the most part to the Eastern provinces of the Empire.
The events of the saint's life fit most easily into the reign of Septimius
Severus. Although Septimius himself was no persecutor, there were
occasions, as has been said, when Christians suffered under an unfriendly governor in a distant province without his interference.

It is clear from the account of the martyrdom that Alban was already
dead when the Emperor and his sons arrived. The author of the persecution was the governor who had hitherto been in charge, or possibly
a subordinate official. The account describes the distress with which
even *impiissimus Caesar*—the epithet means no more in the context
than 'non-Christian', 'pagan'—heard of the punishment inflicted, and
it adds that 'without consulting the Emperors he gave orders on his
own authority to stop the persecution, declaring that, far from eradi-
cating the Christian religion as was intended, it caused it to prosper'.
Although Geta by that time bore the title of Augustus, his promotion
was so recent that it would be natural for people still to refer to him as
Caesar. The Emperors whom he failed to consult were his father and
elder brother fighting in the north. He and his mother, left on their
own, were free to act in accordance with their religious convictions.

Meanwhile Septimius advanced with his army to the Wall, driving
the marauders before him. The people inhabiting the northern part of
the island at this date were not the Scots, who lived still in Ireland and
did not arrive in Scotland till nearly two hundred years later. Ancient
writers speak of the original population as Caledonians, or else as Picts,
a Latin word meaning 'painted men', which could be applied with

equal justice to the Britons south of the Wall as well. The use of woad for personal adornment was prevalent everywhere in the island, and if it was no longer needed as war-paint in territory where Roman authority preserved peace, it was retained none the less in sacred ritual, at festivals for instance, according to Pliny, the Roman encyclopaedist, where girls and young women danced naked with bodies painted blue in honour of their native goddess. There was little difference in fact in race and customs between Britons on either side of the Wall, which was an artificial barrier set up as the limit of Roman conquest. The raiders who broke through to plunder when Albinus withdrew the garrison were not foreigners making war; they were fellow-Britons covetous of the fruits of civilization enjoyed by their more fortunate kinsmen.

Septimius set men to work at once repairing the breaches, rebuilding the entire structure in many places from the foundations. He foresaw that the line of defence would be needed for a long time to come; but his purpose as he pressed on beyond it was to reduce the whole island to obedience, so to pacify and reorganize the inhabitants that the barrier would at last be superfluous. While his fleet kept pace at sea he advanced along the eastern coast, building bridges to cross the Tweed and Forth and naval bases at Cramond on the Firth of Forth and Carpow on the Firth of Tay. After crossing the Tay he turned inland, skirting the Grampians to reach the valley of the Dee, then pushing on still farther north into Banffshire. The line of camps that he established on the way has been traced as far as Muiryfold in the pass of Grange within a few miles of the Moray Firth. It is not known whether this was his farthest limit, but it is the farthest site of which remains have been discovered. All that Dio says is that Septimius approached the 'utmost part of the island', and took observations there to note how the length of day and night varied from that usual at this season of the year in Italy. Even if he turned back at the Moray Firth, he advanced deeper into the highlands than any Roman general before him except Agricola, whose invasion more than a hundred years earlier is described by the historian Tacitus.

This was country better suited to guerrillas than to an army encumbered with heavy baggage. Superior force was lost on an elusive enemy, who was never there to be hit when the blow was ready to fall. The Caledonians had the advantage of fighting on familiar ground, and they were skilled in tricks that brought confusion and dismay. A favourite plan was to turn cattle and sheep out to stray towards the Romans who, eager for fresh meat, sent parties to round them up;

but the beasts at once set off for home, and the Romans pursuing them were lured on till they floundered in a swamp, easy victims for spears waiting in ambush. Much of the picture drawn by ancient authors of this remote part of the world is founded on hearsay many times removed; but the frequent mention of swamps in which the Caledonians lived receives archaeological support from the remains of stockaded islands found in lakes in the mountains. The Caledonians, according to Dio, 'plunge into the water and are able to stay there for many days with only their heads above the surface'.

In spite of the difficulties to which the Romans were exposed, and the harassment that they endured, the sheer size of the army and the devastation left in its wake intimidated the population and ensured that the invasion would not be quickly forgotten. A number of chieftains made submission and ceded territory. An incident that took place on one of these occasions reveals another source of trouble with which Septimius had to contend. In response to a plea for a truce from the Caledonian leaders a meeting had been arranged to discuss terms. A rough platform was set up for the purpose in a field, and Septimius rode towards it with Antoninus and other officers in attendance, while the Caledonians advanced from the other side to meet them. As the parties met there was some confusion of ranks, Romans and Caledonians mixed together. Antoninus who rode close behind his father checked his horse suddenly, taking by surprise those who followed on his heels. While they jostled in disorder, he drew his sword to plunge it in his father's back.

His idea was to lay the blame on Caledonian treachery, to explain that his sword was drawn in his father's defence; but his action was less hidden from observation than he believed. A Roman officer shouted, leant across and gripped his arm, and the Emperor looked round to see what was the matter. Antoninus thrust his sword back sheepishly into its sheath.

The Emperor said nothing. He continued on his way to the platform, dismounted and joined the Caledonian leaders awaiting him there. When the negotiations were concluded he returned to the Roman camp. Then at last he summoned Antoninus, who arrived to find Papinian present too. A sword lay on the table, and his father pointed to it: 'If you want to kill me, you can do so here without putting Rome to shame in the sight of the barbarians.'

As Antoninus shrank back he taunted him: 'What are you afraid of? I'm old and feeble, you're young and strong; but if you don't want to soil your hands with blood, here's Papinian, the Praetorian Prefect.

He'll obey your orders, he'll have to. You'll be Emperor when the deed's done.'

Antoninus knew very well that there was no one less likely to obey him than Papinian, his father's devoted friend.

The rebuke closed the incident. No punishment was inflicted on the offender, who resumed his duties and retained his rank. An explanation lies perhaps in the ardour with which Septimius longed to found a dynasty, a line of Emperors rivalling in glory those descended from Augustus. In spite of discouragement he persisted in believing that Antoninus would mend his ways. It was not in his heart to condemn a son on whom his hopes depended. If the fear nagged him that in sparing Antoninus he endangered Geta, he banished it to his own satisfaction by placing the two on terms of equality. In the announcement of his victories in Britain that he caused to be published through the Empire he took care to give credit to his sons as well as himself, and to insist that Geta was an equal partner in Imperial power.

The promotion of a younger brother whom he hated to a rank equal with his own exasperated Antoninus beyond endurance, but he did not repeat his attempt on his father's life. It was an act of folly provoked by jealous brooding on his wrongs, and he had reason in fact to be thankful that he was stopped in time. The days were long past when Septimius, threatened with mutiny at the siege of Hatra, complained that he could not find five men to follow him. Since then his care of the army and the reforms that he introduced had borne fruit. The soldiers respected and loved him, and they would not have rested till his death was avenged. Antoninus turned from murder to subtler means to promote his interests, seeking popularity in his turn. He could not supplant his father in the affection of the soldiers, but he could build up his own party among them ready to support him against Geta when the chance came. With this end in view he distributed bribes and favours, encouraged all under his command from the highest to the lowest to address him with easy familiarity as Caracalla. It contributed to his success that he was himself an efficient soldier, with aptitude and enthusiasm for military operations. His conduct on active service earned approval.

As the months went by he had evidence to encourage him to patience. It began to seem that he would not have long to wait for the succession, if he allowed nature to take its course. The Emperor's health was rapidly failing under the strain of the campaign in spite of his efforts to overcome his weakness. The recurrent attacks crippling his limbs with excruciating pain became more frequent, aggravated by damp mists, incessant discomfort and fatigue. For most of the way he had to be carried in a litter up and down the steep sides of mountains, over bogs and streams, through tangled woods, a feat scarcely less exhausting to himself than to his bearers. Autumn brought welcome relief, putting an end to the fighting season, and he led his army back to the Wall into winter quarters.

By this time Julia was with him to look after him. A story is told of her when a Caledonian chieftain came to conclude a treaty, bringing his wife. The women were left to each other's company and Julia, ever curious, asked about the social customs in her visitor's country, especially if it were true as she had been told that the women were promiscuous, and children the common responsibility of the tribe. The Caledonian agreed that this was their habit. She compared it favourably with the custom prevalent at Rome: 'We give ourselves to the best men without shame, while you sneak off with the worst to commit adultery.'

Julia, no Roman herself, was amused by the retort and repeated it to her friends with approval. As the story passed from mouth to mouth in Rome it came to Dio's ears, and he recorded it in his history.

The soldiers stationed at the Wall made acquaintance at first hand with the marital customs of the people living beyond it. The policy conceived by Septimius had effect on this as on other frontiers of the Empire. An Imperial edict abolished the law that forbade intermarriage with native girls. The social barrier was removed between the garrison and its neighbours, and fraternization encouraged. No depopulated wilderness remained, like that which appalled Septimius and Julia when they looked across the Danube at Carnuntum. Tillage and pasture obliterated the line of demarcation, and Roman soldiers wooed the daughters of the families inhabiting the farms in non-Roman territory and founded a population of mixed descent. The Wall was no longer merely a military outpost: it was a rampart protecting the homes, the wives and children of the soldiers who guarded it. They could be trusted to defend it with resolution.

Rest and care in winter quarters improved the Emperor's health. He was soon active again, superintending the work in progress of repairing and rebuilding the fortifications of the Wall. In addition he kept in constant touch through the swift messengers of the Imperial post with the central government in Rome, giving decisions from utmost Britain to settle disputes and regulate the course of life in every part of the great Empire. He was determined to resume his campaign against the Caledonians in the spring, to complete his annexation of the territory which he invaded.

Others, remembering the hardships of the journey, were less confident of the outcome. To dissuade him, they drew attention to a number of omens foreboding disaster likely to make an impression on his superstitious habit of mind. The most remarkable occurred at Luguvallium, the modern Carlisle. A festival was at hand that demanded sacrifice to the gods, and the Emperor agreed to officiate in person. A local contractor was ordered to supply animals suitable for use as victims. Ignorant of Roman custom, and relying on that prescribed by British tradition at the winter solstice, he chose specimens entirely black. When Septimius, approaching the altar, saw what awaited him there, he cried out in horror. Black was a hue of the worst possible omen in Roman lore. Refusing to proceed with the sacrifice, he turned in indignation to go home.

As he walked away towards his house a hubbub behind him caught his ears, and he looked round. The gate of the pen had been inadvertently left open, and the sacrificial victims reprieved from slaughter bolted. They followed close on his heels, a bleating procession of black heifers and gimmers, as portentous in his eyes as Furies incarnate.

His obstinacy, however, was stronger than his superstition. He refused to be deterred by presentiment from carrying out his plans. When spring brought favourable weather he led his army again northward to attack the Caledonians in the mountains. At first he marched on foot, but he overrated his strength and was obliged to mount a horse. Soon he was unfit even to ride and was transferred to a litter, till at last he became so ill that his life was in danger. He had to admit defeat, and the army turned back. It is probable that, to spare him the agony of the jolting litter, he was put on board ship and conveyed by sea. His destination was Eboracum, the modern York, which was the nearest town large enough to provide the treatment that he needed. There was a harbour at Dunum Sinus at the mouth of the Esk at Whitby, a convenient point of disembarkation for the last stage of the journey by road.

Since his arrival in Britain he had rebuilt and extended the commanding officer's lodging at Eboracum, turning it into a palace whose foundations lie buried today under York Minster. He took up residence there for the rest of the year with Julia and Antoninus, and Geta came from London to join them. He declared his will that after his death his two sons should reign together as joint Emperors. Month by month his condition grew worse. The best doctors in the province attended him, others were summoned from Gaul; but all their skill and reputation, their study of the teaching of Galen, proved unavailing. Rumour had it that they were in the pay of Antoninus, who made it more worth while for them to fail than to succeed.

In the New Year hope was abandoned. The Emperor lingered on for another month; then he lay on his death-bed, and his sons stood on either side. His last words to them are recorded: 'Keep peace between yourselves. Take care of the soldiers. Pay no attention to anyone else.'

He died on 4 February 211.

6

Brother Against Brother

Gibbon condemns Septimius Severus as 'the principal author of the decline of the Roman Empire'. He means that the concern shown for the army, expressed in the dying Emperor's advice to his sons, contained the seed of the subsequent chaos, in which soldiers transformed into kingmakers treated Emperors as their puppets. Septimius, it is true, never forgot to whom he owed his elevation to the purple, but he was not the first in Roman history to depend for power on military support. The weakness was inherent in the Empire from its birth. The founder, Augustus, won his title in battle, and his example was followed by other commanders of armies before Septimius set off from Carnuntum to march on Rome. By improving the conditions of military service and increasing the pay Septimius created an efficient army devoted to himself, a useful instrument of defence for an Emperor strong enough to control it, dangerous only when it fell into less capable hands, like the demon slave in the old fairy-tale of the sorcerer's apprentice.

No such danger threatened when Septimius died at York. The army accepted the appointed succession without demur and swore allegiance to his sons as joint Emperors. To Antoninus the reverence shown for his father's memory was a source of annoyance. When he claimed precedence over his brother by right of primogeniture he gave such offence to the soldiers that he dared not persist. They knew that Septimius intended both his sons to succeed him, and they were determined that his will should have effect. They felt especial affection for Geta because he resembled his father in features and build. In any case dual control was no novelty in Roman tradition. From the earliest days of the Republic it had been the rule to elect two consuls to hold office together, and even under the Empire there had been an experiment not so long before in a joint principate, when Marcus Aurelius shared the title with his adoptive brother, Lucius Verus, an arrangement lasting several years till Verus died.

Geta could count on his mother to support his claim. The provision for a joint principate was indeed largely due to her influence over her husband and careful advocacy. She was too well aware of the jealousy between her sons and their incompatibility of temperament to believe that they could collaborate successfully in the government of the Empire; but she was content for the time that they stood on terms of equality. When the arrangement broke down, as it was sure to, her opportunity would come to intrigue against Antoninus on behalf of Geta with the same skill as she had intrigued with him in former days to overthrow Plautianus. She had a valuable ally in Papinian, who retained his post as Praetorian Prefect.

Finding both the army and his mother united against him, Antoninus reluctantly resigned himself to what he regarded as the loss of his birthright. He nourished a bitter grudge in secret, and all his mother's efforts and Papinian's to reconcile him to his brother were in vain; but in public he put up an appearance of harmony, and official announcements carried the names of both Emperors, Geta's as well as his own. They presided together over the rites when their father's body was laid on the funeral pyre and his ashes were collected and put into an urn of local porphyry to be taken to Rome. They were anxious to return to Rome as soon as possible, for fear that a usurper might forestall them while they were in Britain. This was the first occasion of a change of Emperors since the dynasty was established.

Meanwhile it was necessary to bring the war against the Caledonians to an end. The scheme cherished by Septimius of annexing the northern part of the island to the Roman Empire was abandoned. The joint Emperors came to terms with the Caledonian leaders; the conquered territory was restored and the garrison withdrawn from the long line of forts between the Tyne and the Moray Firth. The Wall became once more the frontier; but it was no longer, as in time past, a beleaguered outpost under perpetual threat of incursion from savage tribes. The campaigns led by Septimius left the Caledonians chastened and subdued, in no mood to invite reprisals from the Roman army. There was also a more lasting reason for the security that the Wall enjoyed. As the garrison intermarried with the population of the borderland on the farther side, a buffer grew of independent but partly Romanized territory, whose inhabitants had kinsmen on the ramparts of the fortifications and in the camps and villages behind. This widening belt of consanguinity protected the Roman province in the north and kept peace there for the best part of a hundred years, no matter what troubles disturbed the rest of the Empire.

When the treaty with the Caledonians was concluded the Imperial party left Britain to return to Rome. It was an uncomfortable journey for all concerned. The brothers refused to speak to each other or eat in each other's company, and at every stopping-place they insisted on occupying separate lodgings. Each accused the other of trying to poison him, and Julia was helpless to mediate as Antoninus regarded her as Geta's accomplice. When they reached Rome in May a huge crowd including most of the leading senators, assembled to greet them, waving branches of laurel. It was a reception to inspire confidence, encouraging hope of a peaceful transition from one reign to the next. In view of the importance of the occasion to the survival of the dynasty the brothers forced themselves to present an appearance of concord. Dressed in Imperial purple, they marched side by side at the head of a solemn procession to the mausoleum, where they deposited the urn containing their father's ashes. As soon as they returned to the palace, however, they dropped all pretence of fraternal love. They chose rooms at opposite ends of the building and had partitions put up to block the connecting passages. Anyone seeking access from one part to the other had to go outside, walk round the outer wall and re-enter by another door.

Roman society was split by the quarrel into contending parties. The effect was similar while Septimius lived, but it held greater danger now that the leader on either side was Emperor in his own right. Geta had the support of his mother's circle of friends, including Papinian, and it is evident from the sequel that many prominent senators were also among his adherents. His performance in the south of Britain when his father left him there in charge of the administrative council earned him a reputation for moderation and reason rare in a man so young, and he confirmed it now by the integrity and good humour of his dealings with those who came in contact with him. Antoninus on the other hand was more inclined to dictate than to listen to others, and he took little trouble to disguise his contempt for civil dignity. The only opinion whose favour he courted was that of the Praetorian Guard. Unlike the army in Britain, these men had little knowledge of the purpose that prompted Septimius to bequeath the Empire to joint heirs. They saw no inconsistency between loyalty to the dead Emperor and an acquiescent response to the liberality of his elder son.

Although the quarrel provoked gossip in Rome, it made little impression in the Empire in comparison with the relief felt everywhere when it became known that the danger of a disputed succession was averted, the new dynasty securely established. There is evidence of a rapid growth of prosperity during the later years of the reign of Septimius. Inscriptions record the completion of baths, aqueducts, roads and other works of public utility, and the phrases breathe more than conventional piety when they express the gratitude of the local community for Imperial encouragement and protection. Septimius took the utmost care in the appointment of provincial governors to choose men qualified by ability and character, and he punished inexorably any found guilty of oppression. Among other reforms he made it a rule to appoint men of Greek origin to Greek-speaking provinces and Romans or the like to those that spoke or understood Latin, so that governor and governed might talk the same language. To the common people of the Empire, whose chief desire was to live their lives in peace, his reign was a worthy continuation of the Age of the Antonines, and they assumed that his sons as joint Emperors would persist in his policy.

Observers closer to the centre of government were less confident of the outcome, seeing the confusion wrought by fraternal strife. When a civil or military appointment fell vacant each Emperor wished to fill it with a friend of his own. In courts of law when a case was on trial inevitably they ranged themselves on opposite sides, less concerned to uphold the justice of a litigant's cause than to put each other in the wrong. They backed rival teams on the racecourse, and there were frequent brawls in the street where their factions came into conflict. Julia watched in growing dismay, helpless to achieve the solution that would best please her, to remove the elder brother and leave the younger alone and supreme.

At last she persuaded the two to attend a meeting with their father's old advisers to discuss the deadlock. A scheme was proposed by some of those present to divide the administration of the Empire, to give Antoninus charge in Europe and Geta in Asia, with the Bosporus as boundary. Antoninus would retain Rome as his capital, and Geta was content to make his own at Alexandria or Antioch, preferring either of these centres of ancient culture to Rome in any case. The senate would also be divided, with senators of Eastern extraction allotted to Geta, the remainder to Antoninus. Although fewer fell to Geta's share, they were the cream of the senatorial order, including nearly everyone of intellectual eminence, all indeed who had supported him against his brother in recent months. Antoninus would obtain from the division the larger field of commercial exploitation, Geta of accumulated wealth.

It was a scheme much less drastic than that put into effect in the following century. There was no question as yet of formal separation, still less of independent Emperors of East and West. Nevertheless Julia rejected the proposal in horror. She saw in it no prospect of reconciliation, only a threat to the unity of the Roman world, a rift that would grow till it shattered the Roman peace. If Geta could not reign as sole Emperor, it was better to leave him to share jointly in the undivided Empire than to carve him out a private dominion. It was her duty to mankind to preserve its wholeness intact.

'You might as well try,' she exclaimed, 'to divide my living body between you.'

Her opposition had decisive effect, such was the influence that she enjoyed. The meeting ended in a scene of passionate emotion with Julia in tears, clasping her sons to draw them together. The distinguished counsellors present expressed sympathy, and the scheme was withdrawn; but neither she nor even Papinian could devise one more acceptable to take its place.

Public affairs resumed their troubled course. The brothers lived apart and avoided each other's company, meeting only to perform official duties, bedevilled by their consistent failure to agree. Antoninus however was busy with a plan of his own on which he relied to clear everything up. He increased his contact with the Praetorian Guard, combining ingratiating manners with promises of rich reward, gathering a body of adherents attached by ties of loyalty and advantage. When his efforts had made sufficient progress, he told his mother that he was anxious for a reconciliation with Geta. He suggested that the two of them should meet in private in her presence, unarmed and unattended, dispensing with their usual bodyguard.

She was delighted to hear of his change of heart and willingly agreed to co-operate. Her ardour was such that she was able to overcome Geta's doubts and persuade him to attend the rendezvous. The three met late in the evening in her room in the palace. They were alone in the room together, in accordance with the condition agreed; but outside in the darkness Antoninus had a couple of armed centurions waiting in hiding. The brothers greeted each other with polite restraint, and Julia smiled at them to give them her blessing. Suddenly the door burst open, and the centurions rushed in with drawn swords. Geta, seeing that he was trapped, ran to his mother, hoping that his enemies would respect the dignity and authority of the Augusta and shrink from attack. He put his arms round her neck, and she clasped him to her breast, interposing her own body to protect him; but the murderers advanced on her fiercely, undeterred. She herself was wounded in the arm by one of them, while the sword of the other pierced Geta to the heart. Her dress was soaked in his blood.

As soon as Antoninus saw that his brother was dead, he ran through the palace shouting to the soldiers on guard that he had barely escaped with his life from a dangerous plot. He ordered them to escort him for safety to the Praetorian barracks. Believing what he said, they followed him out with brandished torches into the darkness of the street, where his appearance at so late an hour in frantic flight through the city spread alarm and confusion. At the barracks his arrival took the soldiers by surprise. Many were in the baths or about to go to bed, and they listened in bewilderment to his incoherent story, to which he added a few details about a desperate duel from which he had emerged victor, with a hint that his antagonist was Geta. Interest was aroused, however, when he announced that in gratitude for his deliverance he proposed to distribute a huge sum in largess, and to prove that this was no idle promise he sent messengers at once to the treasury to collect it. By this gesture he retained the support of the Praetorian Guard even when rumours arrived from the palace with a more accurate account of events. He spent the night in the barracks in the shrine sacred to Mars.

On the following morning he visited a legionary camp some thirty miles away at Albanum, the nearest military force of any consequence in the country round Rome. The garrison, loyal to Geta, shut the gates in his face, and he was kept fuming for many hours in baffled impatience, haggling over the bribe to earn him admittance. At last a sum was agreed, and the legion, surly but acquiescent, swore allegiance and acclaimed him sole Emperor. By now it was well past mid-day. He rode back in haste to Rome and entered the senate-house in the late afternoon, accompanied by a heavy bodyguard and wearing for precaution a coat of mail under his robes. The senators were still sitting.

He interrupted an anxious debate. All day Rome had been in a state of agitation and suspense as the full story of the night's events leaked out from the palace, that one of the Imperial brothers lay dead and the other, guilty of his murder, was riding into the country to gather military support. The situation was similar in some respects to that which followed the murder of Commodus; but on this occasion there was no suitable successor like Pertinax, acceptable to the majority of the senators. Even those who were not of Geta's party were appalled by the manner of his death and unwilling to condone the crime of fratricide. They hushed their denunciations, however, when the murderer himself strode in among them and his bodyguard lined the gangway between the benches, threatening the occupants with drawn swords.

In spite of this display of force his words were conciliatory. His throat was sore after all the shouting of the night and morning, and he began by apologizing for his hoarseness. The mildness of his tone disconcerted his audience, and he took advantage of the relaxation of tension to offer his own version of the night's events in his mother's room, insisting that Geta was the aggressor and his own part limited to self-defence. The senators were too well informed by this time to believe him, nor were they impressed when, in justification of his conduct, he quoted the example of Romulus, founder of Rome, who put his brother Remus to death. The presence of the armed bodyguard restrained them from open derision, but when he finished speaking he found few obsequious enough to applaud. He rose at last to leave the house; then, as he reached the door, an idea came to him, and he turned back to announce that to inaugurate his sole principate he intended to grant an amnesty covering all those banished or otherwise punished by his father for supporting Albinus in the civil war.

It was a cunning stroke, immediately winning him favour among the nobility. There were few families of note without kinsmen who had suffered either in person or in property for preferring the high-born Albinus to Septimius, the middle-class African. A quarrel between the heirs of the reigning dynasty, even if it culminated in fratricide, weighed less than the restitution of their friends and their forfeited rights. A senator of distinction rose to propose a resolution recognizing Antoninus as sole Emperor and denouncing the dead Geta as a public enemy. It was put to the vote and carried.

Antoninus spent the night at the Praetorian barracks; but on the next day, as the news spread in Rome that he had been acknowledged Emperor both by the army and by the senate, he grew more confident of the success of his enterprise and attended a ceremony for his formal investiture on the Capitol. He returned from it to the palace leaning on Papinian's arm. Although Papinian was his mother's friend and Geta's and never his own, his unrivalled knowledge of the law could be useful in the present emergency. As they walked together across the Forum, Antoninus asked what precedents could be found to set the seal of legal approval on his accession to power. Receiving no answer, he repeated the question, and at last Papinian replied: 'Fratricide is easier to commit than to defend.'

Antoninus had his father's hot temper. He called to the guards to arrest their Prefect and stood watching while they dragged him away.

They were men who had a grudge against Papinian for the discipline that he enforced. One of them grabbed an axe from a neighbouring shop and butchered him. Antoninus rebuked them: 'A sword would have been more decent.'

In the palace he found his mother weeping, surrounded by her women friends. He shouted to her to dry her tears and smile at him, warning her that she was guilty of treason in mourning a son condemned by the senate as a public enemy. The other women received still harsher treatment. All were arrested, several put to death, among them the aged Cornificia, daughter of Marcus Aurelius, one of the last survivors of his line. Told that she might choose how to die, she removed her jewellery, lay down in her simplest dress and herself took a knife to sever her own artery.

'Go, my soul,' she cried. 'Show them, whether they like it or not, that you're a daughter of Marcus.'

She was among Julia's closest friends.

Another who suffered was Antipater, tutor to the two boys when they were young. On hearing of Geta's death he composed a poem and sent it to Antoninus, comparing the Roman State to a body left with only one eye and hand. It was an elegant threnody written in classical style; but if he trusted to its literary merit to protect him, his self-esteem misled him to his doom. Antoninus was enraged by his former tutor's interference and banished him in disgrace to his native city of Hierapolis on the upper Euphrates. Lamenting the ruin of his career, Antipater starved himself to death.

Everywhere a rigorous purge of Geta's supporters was carried out, extending to the highest and lowest in his household, all the artists and dancers whose performance had delighted him, every girl pretty enough to have deserved his caresses. Punishment no less harsh fell on the companions who had shared his intellectual pursuits. It was a favourite pose of Antoninus, adopted in reaction against his mother, to represent himself as a man of action contemptuous of scholarship. The discovery among Geta's possessions of a well-thumbed copy of a learned treatise, *Rerum Reconditarum Libri*, earned sentence of death for the author, Sammonicus Serenus. The officers of justice interrupted him at dinner and dragged him off for execution.

The terror spread into the provinces, claiming among its victims dignitaries of the topmost rank. Dio compiled a list afterwards of their names running into thousands; but it is omitted from the surviving abridgement of his work, in which only a few are recorded who owe the distinction either to personal eminence or to the circumstances in which they met their fate. Helvius Pertinax, for instance, son of the former Emperor—the same who was sent from the palace as a boy to be brought up in quiet in his grandfather's house—had enjoyed a successful but uneventful career in the service of the State. He was too young to play any part at the time of his grandfather's abortive bid for the Empire at the Praetorian barracks, and the unassuming style in which he lived subsequently saved him from suspicion of complicity when his grandfather was condemned for intriguing on behalf of Albinus. The younger Pertinax was a public servant of blameless character, except that he was unable to resist the temptation of a witty tongue. His wittiest jest cost him his life when it came to the ears of Antoninus. It was the custom for a Roman Emperor after a victorious campaign to assume a title derived from the name of the people sub-jugated. Claudius took the title of Britannicus after the conquest of Britain, Trajan that of Dacicus after the conquest of Dacia. Pertinax suggested that Antoninus should entitle himself Germanicus. The Latin word *germanus* means 'brother'.

Most of the names of victims of the purge are drawn from families of noble lineage. There is a seeming inconsistency in their opposition to Antoninus, in view of the promise that he gave the senate to grant an amnesty to the exiles and others who supported Albinus against his father. The promise, however, was no more than a brainwave to extract him from an awkward predicament. It ceased to bind him as soon as his power was restored, and disaffected nobles became the more embittered against him, finding themselves deceived. Many who cared nothing for Geta while he was alive professed devotion to him after his death, using his name as a symbol of resistance, the means to stir up hatred against his brother left sole Emperor. The issue was no longer that of a quarrel within the family, but of an upheaval spreading through the Empire, in which the Emperor was opposed by forces of vested interest and inherited wealth, the same with which his father had to contend at the beginning of his reign. The 'best people', *omnes boni*—they borrowed the description from Cicero—despised the Im-perial house as upstarts of provincial origin and feared and hated it for its cosmopolitan sympathies.

This development of the conflict helps to explain much that would otherwise be hard to understand in the attitude adopted by Julia. Geta was her favourite son, and there is no doubt that, if she could have achieved her purpose without danger to the dynasty, she would gladly have installed him in his brother's place. She was not given the time, however. After he was murdered she herself was threatened with punishment for daring even to weep for him. Yet after his death she retained her title of Augusta and lived on terms of respect with her elder son, accepting him as Emperor. During his frequent absence in distant parts of the Empire she acted in all but name as regent, administering the Imperial economy on his behalf with the same talent that she devoted to philosophy and the arts. If the dynasty survived the shock of fratricide, and the Empire prospered in the new reign as in the old, the credit was hers.

Contemporary gossip, greedy for scandal, accused her of an incestuous passion for her son. Although Syrian religion sanctified concupiscence, there is no evidence that its permissiveness stretched to incest, and in any case the accusation is in conflict with recorded fact. Dio, who knew mother and son well, declares that she always hated, never forgave Geta's murderer. She was a woman, however, of great strength of mind, who refused to let personal feeling impair her political judgement. During her husband's reign she had seen and shared in his work of restoring peace and unity to the Roman Empire, and her heart was set on bringing it to fruition. The leader whom she would have chosen for the task was Geta; but he was dead, and those who professed to be of his party were less concerned to avenge him than to seek their own advantage. Antoninus alone remained to carry on the dynasty. She accepted him for lack of anyone better, and having made up her mind she accepted the consequence, the need to serve him to the best of her power. It helped to reconcile her to the duty that he came more and more to depend on her, and her political genius found scope denied it while her husband ruled. In twenty-five years the Syrian bride of a magistrate at Lugdunum had grown to be effective ruler of the Roman Empire.

Her achievement is the more remarkable in view of the jealousy with which Roman tradition cherished government as a male preserve. Her task was to govern without the appearance of governing, and even if in time as opinion grew accustomed to her her part needed less disguise, no orders were issued in the name of the Augusta, the fount of authority remaining the Emperor. It was a feature, however, of the administrative system of the Empire that the controlling centre for the direction of policy and day-to-day conduct of affairs was a bureaucracy manned by freedmen and slaves. Julia's dealings in her immediate work of administration were not with ministers of independent mind, but with a class born to servitude and accustomed to obey. Many indeed were slaves from her own household or freedmen who owed emancipation to herself. She could impose her will on them without provoking resentment, and her decisions were published to the world translated into Imperial decrees. The voice lost its feminine note in the impersonal formula of officialdom.

In her rooms at the palace and the gardens of her country house the meetings of her circle of friends were saddened by the absence of many familiar faces. Philostratus has described in words already quoted the desolation of the shrine haunted by the ghosts of Geta and Papinian; but unlike the storks of whose habit he speaks the Muses returned to rebuild and live again in their ruined home. When she herself made peace with her elder son her court had every reason to follow her example. Philostratus lived on for two more reigns, undeterred from creative work. His *Life of Apollonius* was not completed till after her death. In other fields too the active growth of ideas was resumed and flourished. Papinian's efforts to give a human face to Roman law were carried on by his scarcely less famous pupil, Ulpian. The poet Oppian enjoyed such favour with the new Emperor that he obtained pardon at last for his father, whose highbrow disdain for the merrymaking to celebrate the victory at Issus had earned the displeasure of Septimius and exile to a distant island.

For the next five years Antoninus reigned alone. He is better known to posterity as the Emperor Caracalla. The nickname given him by the soldiers accompanied him to Rome. He himself took no offence; on the contrary, he was flattered to see the *caracal*, the Gaulish cloak, worn by his imitators in the Roman streets. In official documents and inscriptions, however, his name is always given as Antoninus, more befitting his Imperial dignity. The substitution and exclusive use of the nickname did not come into general practice till a time long after he and his immediate successors were dead, when it suited the policy of Emperors of a later dynasty, founders of a new style of Empire, to belittle and deride the past. They succeeded so well that the undignified nickname has found a permanent place in Roman history. It may help to avoid confusion, therefore, to follow the custom of most historians and refer to him no longer as Antoninus but Caracalla.

Soon after the murder of Geta he sent an executioner to the island where his wife Plautilla and her brother remained banished since their father's disgrace and death. Septimius, while he lived, provided her with a small allowance sufficient to keep her from destitution; but she feared with reason that her condition would change for the worse when her husband succeeded as Emperor. She knew how eager he was to become a widower. It can have been no surprise for her now when orders were brought for her execution. She and her brother were both put to death.

Caracalla, however, did not use his freedom to marry again. Except for a proposal (which will be discussed later) for the hand of a Parthian princess, he showed no desire for a consort. Dio insists that he loved only himself, but there were physical symptoms also predisposing him to celibacy. His contemporaries attributed them to supernatural causes, divine retribution for fratricide, and he himself, sharing the belief, held a séance to invoke spirits to advise him. The ghost of Septimius answered the summons; but Geta unsummoned accompanied him, and neither spoke a word. He dismissed them in terror, and the more congenial spirit of Commodus took their place; but when Commodus spoke his words brought no comfort, warning him of a curse laid on him, 'an incurable disease of the privy parts'.

Although any mention of his infirmity was forbidden, an occasion is recorded when it received publicity through his own fault. He accused certain Vestal Virgins, celibate priestesses, of unchastity, on one of whom he himself had attempted rape. The girl protested that her maidenhead was intact.

'The Emperor ought to know,' she declared. 'He tried hard enough.'

The defence did not spare her the punishment incurred for breach of her vows. She was buried alive.

Much that is told of Caracalla comes from his enemies. Their evidence is that of contemporaries who knew him personally; but it has the weakness inevitable from the circumstances of distortion by political prejudice. In spite of his professed contempt for intellectual and artistic pursuits, he cannot have been entirely the boor that these sources present. Dio, who disliked him, admits that he played the lyre with skill and feeling, and that even after he became Emperor he went to teachers to study philosophy. It can be regarded perhaps as a sign of grace that he admired the interminable poems of Oppian, and he had some knowledge too of classical authors retained from his early education. Dio describes a conversation when the Emperor drew him aside after a banquet to discuss current events, concluding his remarks with an apposite quotation from Euripides. They were hackneyed lines that he quoted, a formula that Euripides repeats at the end of several of his plays; but they were no more likely than is a tag from Shakespeare today to be heard on the lips of an oaf.

In the right mood he could perform his judicial and adminstrative duties efficiently enough.

'He was not without merit,' Dio records, 'either as a speaker or in his judgement. He had a keen grasp of affairs and a ready tongue. His position of authority, combined with natural impulsiveness, encouraged a habit of blurting out on the spur of the moment whatever came into his head, exposing his thoughts without shame, and as often as not he stumbled in this way on a bright idea.'

Philostratus presents a less favourable picture in his account of the Emperor's conduct of an action in which a sophist called Philiscus claimed exemption from public service. Under the prevailing system of local government in the Roman Empire leading citizens were liable to be called up for official duties demanding heavy expenditure of both time and money, as they had to meet the costs out of their own purse. When Philiscus, a native of Thessaly, was summoned by his fellow-citizens to take his turn, he went off to Rome, sought an interview with the Augusta Julia and obtained through her influence the chair of rhetoric in the schools at Athens. He argued when the case came to court that his new post gave him immunity.

There was precedent on which he could rely. Rhetoric enjoyed such esteem that it was customary to exempt those who excelled in it from burdensome impositions. He was unlucky, however, in the mood in which he caught the Emperor, who resented his mother's meddling in the affair, circumventing his own authority. In addition, he took a dis-like to Philiscus at first sight, to the way in which he walked and stood, his peculiar clothes, long hair and effeminate voice. As Philiscus pleaded his cause the long-winded irrelevance of his speech with its flowery digressions soon exhausted what little was left of the Emperor's never abundant patience. Continual interruptions from the bench, abrupt questions demanding an answer and breaking the thread of the argu-ment, encroached on the limited time allotted to the defence, and as the water-clock emptied Philiscus made haste to conclude with an appeal to Imperial tradition, a reminder of the privilege due to the occupant of a chair at Athens.

'A man with hair like that,' Caracalla retorted, 'an orator with a squeak. Why should I deprive your city of your services to condemn pupils at Athens to listen to such piffle?'

Philostratus adds that he granted immunity without question to another applicant, younger than Philiscus, in reward for a successful oration. Caracalla was no enemy of rhetoric, but he liked orators to cut their hair and cultivate the deeper notes of the keyboard.

The bad moods became more frequent than the good as the reign went on. Dio describes him at his worst on a visit to Nicomedia, near Dio's own home in Bithynia: 'He used to send word that he would hold court or transact other business immediately after dawn; but when we came he kept us waiting till mid-day or often till evening, not even allowing us into the entrance hall, but making us stand outside, then as likely as not when it grew late he would decide not to receive us at all. Meanwhile he was poking and prying as I have said, or else he was driving chariots or killing wild beasts or fighting a match or drinking and befuddling himself, and he had bowls of wine poured out, in addition to the rest of their keep, for the soldiers on guard inside and sent round cups of it, while we stood and watched. After that sometimes he consented to hold court.'

The 'poking and prying' to which Dio objects encouraged informers, who throve on blackmail. Caracalla gave offence to official representatives of authority by his reliance in the conduct of affairs on private information gathered from his secretaries or even tittle-tattle from the soldiers.

He preferred the company of soldiers to that of polite society, of whose hatred he was painfully aware. He was vain by nature, eager for praise. When he was a boy he took trouble to exert charm to earn it; but he considered the effort beneath his dignity, and admiration his due, when he grew up to be heir to the Empire, then Emperor in person, and he resented it that his behaviour bred execration instead. Wounded vanity provoked him to persist in outrageous action, alienating him further from educated opinion. With the soldiers alone he was at ease. They honoured him as their Emperor and had a short memory for scandal, even for fratricide. He was never so happy as on active service with the army, sharing the manners and comradeship of military life.

For the greater part of his reign he was absent on one or other of the frontiers, where the only threat of war lay for the Roman Empire. The motive was choice rather than necessity. There were few troubles of sufficient importance to demand the personal attention of the Emperor. Nevertheless he was far from idle. His interests and his talents alike found scope in military operations. When hostilities broke out he showed himself a capable commander, profiting from experience gained under his father during the campaigns in Britain. His principal achievement lay, however, in organization of the defences, completing the work begun by his father to pacify and assimilate unsubjugated tribes. Inscriptions testify to his activity on the Rhine and reconstruction of the wall of turf defending the province of Rhaetia, where the frontier passed through the Alps. Similar industry is recorded on the Danube and beyond the river in Dacia, the province added to the Empire by Trajan and destined to be lost when the dynasty founded by Septimius no longer survived to preserve it.

Caracalla owed much of his success to the popularity that he enjoyed with the army. It can be attributed in part to his liberality in pay and largess and his care for the soldiers' welfare; but he took pains in addition to earn their affection by the affability of his manners, presenting a very different face to them from that whose scowls appalled the senate in Rome. He adopted his fathers' custom of marching with them on foot, refusing to ride on horseback or in a carriage. He carried it indeed to lengths beyond anything that his fathers' dignity allowed, when he insisted on hoisting the legionary standard on to his own shoulder. It was enormously long and heavy, encrusted with gold, a weight fit to tire the most powerfully built. He himself was short and puny.

There was something of a clown in his make-up. It flattered his vanity to overact the part that he played. If there was a ditch to be dug or a stream to be bridged, he liked to seize a spade and toil with the men. His food had to be exactly the same as theirs, served in wooden utensils, and there were occasions when the whim took him to be his own cook, to grind corn with his own hands and bake it over a fire of charcoal into a cake which he ate. If these histrionics provoked laughter they also endeared him to his men as evidence of his wish to be accepted as one of themselves. When his charioteer saved his life in battle, he wrote to the senate demanding a public vote of thanks, declaring that a man pre-eminent among soldiers deserved honour far outshining any mere senator's.

His preference for life on the frontier suited Julia very well. While he occupied himself with military affairs he left her in charge of the civil administration, free to pursue her own policy. The division of powers was of benefit to the Empire, which flourished under her careful housekeeping. In spite of her son's lavish expenditure on the pay and maintenance of the army she was able to find the money needed for public works and other business of state, relying for the purpose, not on an oppressive increase of taxation, but on the vigilance with which she directed the flow into the treasury, thwarting the dishonest and corrupt. She left the state solvent at her death.

An outstanding reform which she carried out is that known as the *Constitutio Antoniniana*, an act extending Roman citizenship to all the inhabitants of the Empire except slaves and a few others. Hitherto the citizenship had been a right reserved for those who were either born to it or granted it as a mark of special favour, often for a large sum of money. The principal advantage that it originally conferred was the franchise entitling citizens to vote at the election of magistrates and other officers of central and local government; but this lost much of its importance when the Republic was replaced by the Empire, and the power of the Emperors encroached on that of the elected authorities and came to supersede them. Nevertheless, useful privileges remained, many rights of property, for instance, denied to those lacking citizenship, and the ability to contract marriage in a form that carried legal recognition. In addition, the citizen enjoyed immunity from corporal or capital punishment, unless the sentence was confirmed by the Emperor himself. A famous example is afforded by Saint Paul claiming at his trial before the procurator of Judaea, 'I appeal unto Caesar.'

The honour involved duties as well as rights. The citizen was compelled to take his turn in the performance of public services, receiving no payment for the time spent on them and no compensation for the out-of-pocket expenses that they imposed. He had to provide labour, either in person or by his servants, for the repair of roads and bridges and similar purposes necessary to the community, horses for the Imperial post and accommodation for itinerant officials and their train, including detachments of soldiers. If he was of sufficient rank and wealth to be appointed a decurion, a member of the local council, he was expected to maintain the dignity of his position by contribution to public funds and lavish entertainment. A further burden was laid on the council in that it was responsible for collection of taxes, and the councillors were personally liable for any default. Among the few excused from such duties were men eminent in learning and the arts, the occupant for instance of a chair of rhetoric, unless like Philiscus, the Thessalian sophist, he irritated the Emperor by his curled hair and squeaky voice.

The *Constitutio Antoniniana*, by increasing the number of Roman citizens, brought relief to those already qualified. The more numerous they were from whom public service was demanded, the less often the turn of each came round. Dio, who takes a jaundiced view of the measure, insists that its purpose was to replenish the treasury by imposing fiscal burdens on people formerly exempt. He offers as example the taxes due on inheritance of property and the manumission of slaves, to which only citizens were liable. The non-citizen was excused from these, however, for the reason that he was unable to inherit with legal security or to enfranchise the slave whom he manumitted. Julia's ordinance took away his exemption from taxation, but it gave him in return the benefits to which those who paid the tax were entitled. There is no need to assume that he was dissatisfied. In any case, if the treasury was short of money, means were available to extract it from the taxpayer without so radical a change in Roman society.

The spirit animating the change had more importance than any financial profit that accrued. It was Julia's ambition to transform the Empire from a domain conquered by Rome into a commonwealth shared by the greater part of mankind. Roman citizenship was a distinction that gave prestige, but when all were citizens it lost its social value. Those who prided themselves on the purity of their Roman blood were distinguished no longer from the lesser breeds. This was what rankled with Dio and his cronies in the senate.

Another field in which Julia was active was that of religion. There have been few periods in history in which it has claimed wider attention and offered greater variety. A reason can be found in the expansion of the Roman Empire to cover most of the known world. As local frontiers were absorbed, and men could no longer identify themselves with a nation or tribe, they turned inwards to seek meaning for their lives. The quest led them to explore many spiritual by-ways.

There was no satisfaction of the sort desired in the official religion of Rome, whose concern was with rules to be observed, ceremonies to be performed to promote the welfare of the state. Its most appropriate expression was the cult of the deified Emperor. His worship commanded obedience, but the motive was political rather than religious. The gods and goddesses of the traditional pantheon were similar to him, demanding public observance rather than private devotion. They retained their temples and sacrifices, their seasonal festivals; but they were of less account than the Emperor, lacking the material weapons at his disposal to reward and punish. The prevailing state of mind of their worshippers was a pious conformity with time-honoured custom, not inconsistent on occasions with irreverent mirth. The old myths were mocked on the stage in ribald mimes, such as *Diana Castigata*, a Homeric brawl on Olympus, in which Diana is bent across Juno's knee and caned with the shafts of her own arrows. There was nothing to affront pagan tradition in so undignified a posture for a goddess, nothing that would have been strange to an audience watching a play by Aristophanes in ancient Athens.

A vital myth, as the medieval Church knew, can reconcile without incongruity the serious and the comic. Roman religion would have taken no harm from these mimes if it had been able to satisfy the worshipper, who desired neither a code of rules nor sanctified folklore but spiritual comfort. The age thirsted for a personal message, and the foreign cults flowing in from the East owed their success to the extent to which they provided it. In some of them the chief appeal lay to the senses, in the rites of the Great Mother imported from Asia Minor for instance, which mourned the death of Attis with frenzied lamentation, devotees flogging, slashing, even castrating themselves, and culminating on 25 March in the feast of his resurrection celebrated by holiday-making crowds with food and drink and dances.

Such revels offered little comfort, however, to those troubled by personal cares and sorrows, and no solution to the problem of the purpose of life. A growing number of people in every class of society demanded that religion should teach rather than excite, and the cults adapted themselves to the mood. They shifted the stress from orgy to 'mystery', a term of very ancient origin denoting a dramatic representation of inward truth. As secrecy was of the essence of the proceedings no record survives of the details; but it is known that a central feature was the performance of a scene drawn from sacred tradition, enriching familiar myth with symbolic meaning. The worshipper attained knowledge, not from sermons or books, but by taking part himself in the story in which it was enacted. Each cult, whether Syrian, Persian or Egyptian, retained its own flavour, using the divine names and mythological incidents to which it was accustomed; but all alike carried a message addressed personally to the worshipper, and in all of them a predominant theme was the fate of the human soul after death. Among the chief motives inspiring the devout was the hope that initiation into the mysteries would earn them a fortunate place in the afterlife.

This was a theme familiar to the 'philosophic Julia', as Philostratus calls her. The doctrines of Chaldean astrology, in which she was brought up at Emesa, were closely concerned with the journey of the soul towards interstellar felicity. There was much in common between them and those taught to devotees of the mysteries; but the cults had other ideas also to offer that spoke to the condition of the times. Men not only looked to the future, anxious to survive death; they longed too for reassurance in their present life, for a god to whom they could talk in quiet in their hearts. It was an impulse denied satisfaction by Jupiter Optimus Maximus, Best and Greatest, propitiated with solemn ceremonial; it sought companionship rather than majesty from the divine. In his novel, *The Golden Ass*, Apuleius shows how nearly the Egyptian cult of Isis came to satisfy the demand. The book ends with an outburst of gratitude to the goddess for her care and love. Lucius, the hero of the story, concludes his prayer to her with the words: 'I will keep your divine features and most holy spirit present for ever in my heart for my secret contemplation.'

Perhaps Julia had them in mind when she worshipped in the temple of Serapis on her visit to Egypt. They recall those of Christ: 'Pray to thy Father which is in secret.'

She had many Christians working in her household and on her staff with whom to discuss Christian teaching. There was no persecution while she was in charge of affairs, not even, as in her husband's reign, fitful outbreaks of spleen from a governor in a distant province. She doubted the truth of Christianity, but she had no doubt of her hatred of intolerance. There were difficulties nevertheless that hindered relations between the Roman State and the Christian Church. It shocked Roman opinion that the Founder of Christianity died on the cross. Crucifixion, like the gallows in later times, was a punishment reserved for the lowest criminals. For this reason the early Christians were reluctant to display the crucifix, preferring an emblem with less shameful associations. Graver disadvantage arose from the custom that made it obligatory on public occasions to cast a grain or two of incense on the altar dedicated to the Emperor. No more was intended than a gesture of respect, as when an audience today rises to its feet for the National Anthem; but the Christians condemned it as idolatrous and refused to conform, incurring thereby a charge of disloyalty. When the authorities were in a lenient mood, a blind eye could be turned on the offence; but in other circumstances, when prejudice was inflamed, the punishment might be imprisonment, slavery or death.

Neither of these difficulties was of a sort to deter Julia's curiosity. It is more probable that her sympathy was estranged by Christian insistence on uncritical acceptance of evidence, the subjection of reason to revelation. No scope was left for the speculative argument that interested her and her friends, the philosophers. The Christian writer Tertullian, who was her contemporary, shows what answer a sceptic received: 'We have no need to be eager for knowledge, having Jesus Christ, or to ask questions, having the Gospel. If we believe, we desire no further belief. For this is the first principle of our faith, that we owe faith to nothing else.'

It is not an attitude that could satisfy the 'philosophic Julia'.

The dogmatic certainty of the Christians was matched by the fierce intransigence with which they rejected every religion but their own. All pagan creeds in their opinion were the work of the Devil, all pagan deities his children. There could be no accommodation between this point of view and that which sought in every manifestation of religious impulse a glimmer, however faint, of the truth, an expression of man's perpetual striving for the divine. Julia's philosophy is summed up by Philostratus in the words put into the mouth of his missionary sage, when a young man consults him about the merits of celibacy: 'I do not call it wisdom to defy any of the gods, as Hippolytus defied Aphrodite, for it is wiser to live on good terms with them all.'

Julia could offer hospitality to the God of the Christians, but He refused to share it with hers.

7

Julia's Eldest Son

During most of the year 213 Caracalla was on the Rhine, busy with operations against the German tribes beyond the frontier. A victory won near the head-waters of the Main towards the end of the summer broke their resistance, and he completed his work of pacification by a distribution of large sums of money to the principal leaders, extending his influence deep into the hinterland as far as the Elbe. A combination of coercion and bribery was the accustomed method favoured by the Romans to maintain peace and order on the bounds of the Empire, and as long as Rome remained formidable it had satisfactory results, persuading the tribesmen of the advantage of Roman friendship. The gold coins distributed on this occasion gave especial pleasure. They were of pure gold, unlike those in circulation in Rome which, according to Dio, were more often gilded copper. The Emperor was unwilling to affront the Germans on the frontier; he cared less for the effect of debased money on Roman bankers.

The success of the negotiations owed much to his own efforts. He was at ease among the tribesmen as in the company of his soldiers, able to behave with freedom and enjoying the applause earned by his histrionic talent. The Germans were delighted when he came to meet them dressed up in German clothes with a long wig of blond hair. As the story was carried to remote villages his popularity grew into a legend. The treaty that he made preserved peace for twenty years.

The strain of the campaign, aggravated by the unnecessary exertions that he imposed on himself, was too much for his never robust health. A visit paid to the shrine of the local god of healing, Apollo Grannus, at Aurelia Aquensis, the modern Baden-Baden, failed to afford relief, and he was obliged to return to Rome for medical treatment. He consoled himself with a triumph to celebrate his German victories and with the construction of public works to adorn his reign, including the building whose ruins still bear witness in Rome to his name, the Baths of Caracalla. It was begun at this date but not completed till after his death.

His health improved in the course of the winter, and with the approach of spring he grew restless as usual in the city and longed to resume military life. Events in Parthia brought the opportunity: King Vologaeses IV was dead, and his sons, Vologaeses and Artabanus, fought each other for the succession. Caracalla, who had plenty of effrontery, announced the news to the senate in a letter written with his tongue in his cheek, deploring the strife between the brothers and predicting that it would bring great harm to the Parthian State. He regarded Parthia's misfortune as a piece of luck for himself, a chance to fulfil his ambition to model his own career on that of his favourite hero of the past, Alexander the Great.

The excuse he needed to intervene came when one of the Parthian brothers, Vologaeses, gave refuge to an Armenian rebel, Tiridates, a pretender to the Armenian throne. Armenia, lying between the Parthian and Roman Empires, was a territory sensitive to the influence of both. The Parthians claimed suzerainty, but the Romans kept a jealous eye to protect their interests. As the reigning King of Armenia at the time was well disposed to Rome, any threat to his security was discouraged. Parthian support for Tiridates could be denounced as an act of hostility. It was convenient for Roman propaganda, tending to bring the cause of Tiridates into derision and contempt, that he had as right-hand man the Cynic philosopher Antiochus employed by Septimius in the old days to set an example of hardihood to the soldiers by rolling naked in the snow on Scottish mountains. The feats of which he boasted were still remembered with ribald laughter, and the scorn that he provoked was increased when he deserted from the Roman army to earn promotion in the service of the enemy.

Caracalla invited the Armenian King to Rome to concert plans with him against the pretender. The King arrived as a guest, but stayed on as a hostage, detained in comfortable and honourable but strict custody. Although he was an ally, Roman policy was unwilling to take risks. Held securely at Rome, he was out of the way of any temptation to change sides in the course of the war. Meanwhile diplomatic approaches were made to Artabanus, recognizing him as King of Kings of Parthia and assuring him of Roman sympathy in his struggle with his brother Vologaeses. The favour shown him was dictated by circumstances, but Caracalla had reason to be satisfied with his choice. Artabanus had his headquarters at Ctesiphon, with only the width of the Tigris to keep him from the Roman province of Mesopotamia, and was therefore to be feared as an enemy. Vologaeses on the other hand, established in Media on the southern shore of the Caspian Sea, was too far off to forestall the Romans before they themselves were ready to attack him.

Elaborate preparations were needed for an expedition on the scale that Caracalla had in mind, an enterprise worthy to be compared with Alexander's conquest of the East. Fresh levies were raised to bring the army up to strength, and the reinforced legions were assembled in camps conveniently situated for the coming campaign. In addition, parties of engineers and workmen were sent in advance to construct *mansiones*, stopping-places where the expeditionary force could enjoy rest and shelter on its long journey across desert and mountains. Caracalla himself was unwilling to sit idle till all was complete. Having time to spare and work to fill it, he set off by a roundabout route, visiting the Danube on his way and inspecting and strengthening the defences there. Many inscriptions bear witness to his reorganization of the military establishment in Dacia.

Turning south at last, he travelled down the Balkan peninsula to cross the narrow seas into Asia. The journey led him through Macedonia, Alexander's homeland, and he responded to its associations with characteristic enthusiasm, wearing Macedonian dress, a wide-brimmed hat and laced boots covering the calves, and enrolling young Macedonians into a body modelled on Alexander's phalanx, equipped with armour and weapons of a style already more than five hundred years old. If these antics gave offence to elder statesmen, they earned him popularity among the soldiers and local country people, who shared his veneration for the cult of the ancient hero. His exuberant enjoyment of his own play-acting endeared him to his humbler subjects.

As he approached the sea he was eager to sail across to the site of Troy and pay his respects to the tomb of Achilles, another hero of the past in whom he recognized a soul twin to his own; but a renewed attack of the illness from which he suffered on the Rhine persuaded him to change course and sail on down the coast to a port within easy reach of Pergamum, where the temple of Aesculapius, god of healing, enjoyed a high reputation for miraculous cures, higher even than that of Apollo Grannus at Baden-Baden. It was a trying voyage for an invalid. A sudden gale struck the ship, shattering its yard-arm, and as it plunged, likely to sink, in the heavy swell he was lowered into a boat in charge of a few retainers, who rowed him with difficulty to the safety of a trireme of the naval escort. When at last the fleet put into port he had to be transferred to another boat to reach Pergamum, which lay some fifteen miles up the river. He arrived at the temple more in need of the god's curative efforts than when he had set out. Nevertheless he composed a hymn of gratitude to Aesculapius, to whose power exerted from a distance he attributed his salvation.

Not enough is known to attempt a diagnosis of the disease that troubled him, except that the failure of his virility was among its symptoms. Aesculapius was less successful in curing it than in saving him from a watery grave. The traditional routine for a patient in the temple was to spend a succession of nights there in a cubicle allotted for the purpose, till the god appeared in a dream and revealed what should be done to restore health. A detailed account of the proceedings survives in a treatise written about seventy years earlier by a travelling sophist called Aelius Aristides, who visited the temple himself to be cured of his many ailments. Much of the treatment prescribed was of a sort as likely, it seems, to kill as to cure: a plunge in cold water, for instance, or a barefoot walk in the depths of winter for a patient suffering from fever and catarrh. Even Galen, however, whose attitude to medicine was based on exact study of anatomy, speaks with approval of the god's understanding, and Aristides bears witness from his own experience that he went to the temple sick and returned healthy.

There is an ardour in the devotion expressed by Aristides which suggests that faith played an important part in the cure. The atmosphere of the place fostered by venerable tradition favoured release from neurosis. An affinity can be traced with some of the methods in use in modern psychotherapy, especially in the attention paid to dreams and the preference shown by the god for a language of symbols, whose interpretation was left to the priests. The effect was successful on patients like Aristides who gave willing co-operation, but the god was unable to overcome the resistance of ingrown fears. In the darkness of his cubicle Caracalla was visited, not by the kindly Aesculapius, but by the ghost of his brother Geta haunting his conscience. He ordered the priests, much against their will, to perform forbidden rites of blood sacrifice; but the ghost remained unexorcised, his bodily functions inhibited.

While he stayed in the town verses were circulated which purported to be from an ancient oracle foretelling the coming to Pergamum of an 'Ausonian Beast'. Although 'Ausonian', a poetical synonym for 'Italian', was inappropriate to Caracalla whose father was African and mother Syrian, there was no doubt whom the oracle-mongers had in mind, and all Pergamum laughed at the description applied to his puny frame. He himself however took it as a compliment, a tribute to his ferocity and brutality, and he was indignant when an officious scholar revealed that the oracle was spurious, a *jeu d'esprit* composed on the spot by a local wit. He refused to be deprived of his glory, the title of 'Ausonian Beast', and flatterers who sought his favour took care to insist on it.

Although Aesculapius disappointed him, he recovered sufficient health to pay his deferred visit to Ilium, the town rebuilt on the site of ancient Troy. His mother and many of her friends including Philostratus accompanied him. During the last few years since her return from Britain she had been living at Rome, attending to the cares of State which her son left in her hands. Even if she could have spared the time to travel with him, as was her custom with her husband, the prospect had no attraction for her. She preferred to keep her distance from Geta's murderer. She made an exception, however, of the present occasion. The campaign in the East was no ordinary enterprise; it was the realization of a dream that appealed to her own imagination too to re-enact the conquests of Alexander the Great in the East. The exploits of the Macedonian hero retained a legendary prestige in the countries once subject to him, not least her native Syria. She had in addition the motive tempting her to follow the army to Asia Minor with her court, that she felt at home in the Eastern provinces of the Empire as she never could in Italy. Having arrived in the East, she stayed there and did not return to Rome for the rest of her life.

Philostratus wrote an account of the heroes of the Trojan War to celebrate the visit that he paid with the Imperial party to Ilium. The reputed tomb of Achilles, a lonely barrow on the promontory of Sigeum overlooking the sea, made such an impression on him that he reverts to it in his *Life of Apollonius*, conducting his itinerant sage there to spend the night in the open and describing how the earth shook and a radiant vision of Achilles emerged, who complained that his worship was neglected, and no Muses sang, only the Nereids beneath on the rocks. Caracalla made up for past neglect by the magnificence of the ceremonies that he held in the sacred precincts. It happened that while he was at Ilium a cherished freedman, his personal secretary, was taken ill and died. Fuel for the pyre was carried out to the promontory, and the funeral was celebrated there with rites imitating those described in the *Iliad* when Achilles mourned the death of his friend Patroclus. Determined to be exact to the last detail, Caracalla insisted on throwing a lock of his own hair into the flames. The gesture lost dignity as he wore his hair crew-cut. The clipping was so minute that it floated away on the wind.

These and similar activities recall the antiquarian sightseeing for which Septimius found time in the intervals of war and politics, when he travelled with Julia. Among Caracalla's motives was the hope that his relations with his mother would improve if he kept her amused. Knowing of her interest in Apollonius, the historical or partly historical wizard out of whom Philostratus created his eponymous sage, he had a shrine set up in his honour at Tyana, his birthplace, to please her. Whatever their private feelings towards each other, the Emperor and the Augusta took care to maintain an appearance of harmony when they established their winter quarters at Nicomedia on the Sea of Marmara. Each was too dependent on the other to afford a quarrel, he on her to administer the Empire loyally and capably in his absence, she on him to preserve the dynasty.

The arrival of the Imperial court to spend the winter at Nicomedia was a heavy burden on the citizens. Dio who, as has been said, knew this part of the world well, having been born and still holding property in the neighbouring town of Nicaea, describes the trouble and expense that the community suffered. His account of a day's business in court with Caracalla has already been quoted, but there were worse hardships to be borne than loss of time and patience. The cost of entertaining the visitors included not only the provision of sumptuous board and lodging, but also of amphitheatres, racecourses and similar places of amusement put up for their temporary enjoyment and pulled down again when they left. As public funds were insufficient for the purpose, the wealthy were obliged to contribute from their private means.

The Emperor's behaviour did nothing to reconcile his hosts to the strain that he put on their resources. He preferred the conversation of a regimental mess to that of the local worthies. It was his habit therefore, when he was invited to a banquet, to demand that his escort of soldiers should be admitted to share it, and he was careful when they took their place at table to have his military cronies round him, crowding out and ignoring the master of the house, whose costly food they devoured.

In the spring of 215 he launched his attack on Vologaeses, who was already in Armenia supporting the claim of the pretender Tiridates to the throne. The Roman army advanced to oppose him in the name of the rival King held as hostage in Rome. Contrary to his habit, Caracalla did not take command of the expedition in person. Grave news had arrived from Egypt of riots in Alexandria, and he dared not lose touch with events in a province vital to Roman security. He delegated the command in Armenia to a general called Theocritus, a freedman employed in his boyhood to teach him to dance. The promotion of a former dancing-master to be commander-in-chief provoked anger and mockery among those who believed that their own qualifications entitled them to the appointment. Dio accuses Theocritus of peculation, dishonest sale of army stores, and of presuming on the Emperor's favour to get rid of anyone who stood in his way. Many unscrupulous adventurers rose to power under Caracalla, who preferred to choose men of low birth for positions of responsibility on the ground that, as they owed their careers to him, he could count on their loyalty. His opinion of the upper classes is revealed in a letter to the senate: 'I know that my behaviour displeases you, but that's what I keep arms and soldiers for, so that I need not care what you say.'

Nevertheless, in view of the importance that he attached to victory in the East, it is unlikely that he would have committed his army into incompetent hands. The faults attributed to Theocritus are not of a sort incompatible with military ability. Although he suffered a heavy defeat at the outset of the campaign, the subsequent course of the war vindicated his generalship.

Meanwhile the news from Egypt became more disquieting. The trouble had its origin two years or so earlier when the legion stationed in the province was transferred to the Rhine to take part in operations against the Germans. The success of the reforms carried out by Septimius on his visit to Alexandria at the beginning of his reign encouraged confidence in the ability of the government to maintain its authority without reliance on military force, and the complacency persisted in spite of disturbing incidents. Dio has a story of an occasion at Alexandria when Theocritus was present, and a quarrel arose with a junior officer who taunted him with his dancing days. Theocritus ordered the man to be put to death. Nothing more is known of the circumstances, except that the author of the sneer was a kinsman of the younger Pertinax, whose own tongue, punning on the title Germanicus, cost him his life in the purge following the murder of Geta. It is possible in the light of events that Theocritus had other motives as well as injured pride to prompt him to deal severely with insubordination. Subversive influences were active again in Egypt, remnants of the party that once owed allegiance to Niger, and the government was without armed force adequate to control them.

Disaffection was at last kindled to revolt by a group of wealthy citizens of Alexandria, contractors employed to erect statues of Caracalla in the streets in the likeness of Alexander, who complained that their bills remained unpaid or were paid in depreciated money. They had no difficulty in recruiting followers ripe for violence from the mob of displaced countrymen who crowded into the town, seeking escape from the heavy taxation imposed on farmers in the villages. Riots provoked an orgy of sacrilege and arson, sparing neither temples nor private property, and the Roman governor Heraclitus, Prefect of Egypt, looked on helplessly and failed to restore order. It was alleged that he was himself a party to the conspiracy, and he was later charged with sedition and put on trial. These events were sufficiently alarming to demand the Emperor's intervention, even without the reports that reached him of derisive jokes circulating at his expense. The Alexandrians were notorious for ribald wit. They published caricatures of him, short, puny and ugly, posing as Alexander or Achilles, and with insidious malice sang lampoons describing his mother as Jocasta, who, in Greek legend, was both mother and wife to Oedipus and bore two sons whose internecine strife brought ruin to Thebes.

The Imperial court had already travelled south to Antioch. The disgrace imposed on the city by Septimius for its support of Niger was long forgotten, its splendour restored. Julia made it her headquarters for the rest of the reign, receiving envoys and correspondence there from every part of the Empire and spending her leisure with her friends discussing philosophy and lterature beside the streams of the wooded valley of Daphne, a gardein sacred to the nymph loved by Apollo, renowned for its pleasures both spiritual and carnal and its beauty throughout the Roman world. There was happiness at Antioch, and she had little time left to enjoy it. A pain from which she suffered was diagnosed as cancer of the breast, and her doctors were unable to offer hope of recovery. She allowed no weakness, however, to interfere with the eager activity of her mind or with her diligent attention to the cares of State. Her son left her in supreme charge of the Imperial government when he set off to deal with the troublemakers in Egypt.

For the time being he kept his purpose to himself, giving out that he was going to Alexandria, following his father's example, to pay his respects to the tomb of Alexander and take part in the festival of Serapis. The Alexandrians believed him and exerted themselves to greet him with honour, all the more effusively as they were anxious to banish suspicion of their loyalty. Flowers were scattered as he passed through the gate, clouds of incense filled the streets, sacred music rang in his ears. When night fell a great procession lit by torches escorted him to the temple of Serapis, where he made sacrifice, then to the tomb of Alexander on which he laid with appropriate reverence the purple cloak and the rings and other jewels that he wore. The citizens kept up the festivities till dawn, much relieved to see everything going so well. The Emperor seemed to be in the best of humours, and if he was accompanied by a formidable army it was only to maintain his dignity on a scale befitting Imperial majesty.

His own headquarters where he lodged were in the temple of Serapis, as if to advertise that he had the god on his side. On the following morning he gave orders for all young men of consequence to muster on open ground in front of the temple, so that he might pick the most eligible for a phalanx to be enrolled in Alexander's memory. The proclamation was eagerly obeyed. A multitude of young men assembled from the chief families in the city, all aspiring to the honour of being chosen for the select troop. Proud parents flocked there too to watch their sons drawn up smartly on parade in their best clothes, the Emperor himself strolling between the ranks, pausing for a gracious question here, a word of praise there, raising high hopes in each whom he addressed. Having completed the inspection, he withdrew as if to consider his choice.

The proceedings resembled and were probably modelled on his father's treatment of the mutinous Praetorians, who sold the Empire to Didius. While attention was fixed on himself, armed soldiers were closing in unobtrusively from every side, and his departure was the signal for the plan to take effect. The sequel, however, was very different from the precedent set in Rome. Septimius won a bloodless victory, but Caracalla's orders to his soldiers were to kill everyone present. The young Alexandrians, caught unaware and unarmed, fell easy victims, and their parents and friends were included in the slaughter. In a few minutes Alexandria was deprived of the flower of its youth, the chief of its citizens.

As the news spread through the city, all were aghast. There was some attempt to express indignation in organized riot, but soldiers stood posted in readiness at strategic points to deal with the demonstrators. Indiscriminate massacre followed. Soldiers were everywhere, soldiers lusting for blood, murdering everyone in reach without distinction of rank, sex or age. As the heaps of bodies mounted in the streets, pits were dug into which they were thrown, not only the dead but also many still breathing. On occasions a victim retained enough strength as he was dragged to burial to clutch his captor, hold fast and pull him after him over the brink of the pit, so that they fell in together like wasps into a jam-jar, and both were buried alive.

To complete his victory and forestall any revolt Caracalla built a wall across the city, cutting it in two, with guards posted at intervals to stop people from passing to and fro, a barrier such as that which in modern times divides Berlin. In addition he expelled all strangers except for visiting merchants, closed places of entertainment and forbade public assembly. Alexandria was the second greatest city of the Empire, with a population little below that of Rome. The example set by its fate aroused dismay, promoting a sense of insecurity in weaker communities less fitted to resist military violence. An official version of the massacre was put about, that the soldiers had got out of hand and exceeded their instructions; but Caracalla's own behaviour contributed nothing to its plausibility. He gloried in the notoriety that he earned, a reputation worthy of the 'Ausonian Beast', and he celebrated his triumph with a ceremony in the temple of Serapis, at which he dedicated a sword to the god, describing it as the one with which Geta was murdered.

There is no reason to suppose that he retained the sword belonging to the centurion who committed the crime, or that after all this time he even knew where it was; but the defiant gesture gratified his histrionic instinct, a deliberate affront to public sentiment and a retort to the nagging of his own conscience. If he fell short of Achilles and Alexander in looks, he could outdo them in bloodthirsty exploits.

He was now free to devote attention again to the Parthian war; but he left Theocritus in command against Vologaeses in Armenia, while he pursued plans of his own to strengthen his alliance with the other brother, Artabanus. To the surprise of all who knew of his reluctance to fill the place left vacant by the unlamented death of Plautilla, and of the reasons prompting him to celibacy, he sent envoys to Artabanus to ask for one of his daughters in marriage. Apart from diplomatic motives, he had the example of Alexander to inspire him, who took to wife the Persian princess, Roxana. Artabanus, however, was unwilling to commit himself too irrevocably to the Roman cause, and his lack of enthusiasm for the match was shared by his daughters, who had heard reports of the suitor's shortcomings. He replied that the Roman Emperor would do better to choose a bride from his own dominions, more likely to please him than a Parthian girl, who spoke no word of his language and whose customs in food and dress were so different.

At this stage in the negotiations the news came from Armenia that Theocritus had brought the campaign to a successful conclusion, and that Vologaeses agreed to withdraw from the territory, surrendering the pretender Tiridates to the Romans, and with him the Cynic philosopher Antiochus, who would be lucky as a recaptured renegade to be spared to practise hardihood in a Roman gaol. The new state of affairs produced a reversal of the attitudes adopted by Artabanus and Caracalla. The former, fearing that his brother was about to usurp his place in Roman favour, made haste to agree to the wedding, heedless of his daughter's nuptial bliss. Caracalla, however, was no longer inclined to reveal his embarrassing inadequacy to a Parthian princess. It suited him better to keep the brothers bidding against each other, till the opportunity came to outwit them both and emerge as a second Alexander, conqueror of the East.

Nevertheless he had to be careful not to offend Artabanus, who was all impatience now for the marriage to be completed and who accepted without further argument the terms that the Romans demanded. At last, when no excuse could be found for delay, Caracalla announced that he would come in person to claim his bride. A large army escorted him on his journey across Mesopotamia, and he was greeted with enthusiasm in the towns and villages through which he travelled. All were delighted at the prospect of a bond of kinship linking the reigning houses of Rome and Parthia, to put an end to the long series of wars that had devastated the country in the past.

Artabanus awaited his guest at Arbela in the hills beyond the upper Tigris, a stronghold of ancient sanctity venerated for its necropolis where the Kings of Parthia of the Royal line of the Arsacidae lay buried. As the Roman soldiers approached, he rode out to meet his future son-in-law and embrace him. Crowds followed from the town, all dressed in their best clothes and wreathed with wild flowers. Those on horseback dismounted and turned their horses loose to graze, leaving their bows and quivers in the grass. The field in front of the town was filled with people drinking and merrymaking, clustering in inquisitive groups to peer at the bridegroom. Wine flowed, and men and girls danced to the accompaniment of flutes and drums.

Caracalla waited till the revellers were too drunk to pay attention. Then he gave the signal to his soldiers, who suddenly drew their swords and attacked those around them. Caught without arms and on foot, the Parthians fled in terror, and many of them, hampered as they ran by the flowing skirts of their gala dress, were killed before they could get their horses. Artabanus himself barely escaped with his life. His servants found him a mount, and he swung his daughter up in front of him on to the horse's withers and galloped to safety.

Arbela, left defenceless, was looted and burnt by the Romans, and to add supreme indignity the Royal tombs were broken open and the bones scattered. Alexander was guilty of a similar act of vandalism after his defeat of Darius. Caracalla could not resist the urge to follow the example of his hero, no matter how inexpedient to his own policy in the contemporary world.

His decision to pick a quarrel with Artabanus was inspired by the successful outcome of negotiations with the other brother, Vologaeses, which persuaded him that the time had come to swap allies; but when Vologaeses heard of the desecration of the ancestral shrine he was so gravely offended that he came to terms with his brother to present a united front against the Romans. Both built up their forces to take revenge together on the common enemy. Threatened by their combined opposition, Caracalla did not dare to penetrate deeper into Parthian territory. He contented himself with desultory plunder, then withdrew into Mesopotamia to make adequate preparation for invasion on a massive scale. In a letter to the senate in Rome he claimed that he had won a great victory and was awarded triumphal honours; but the senators, noting that the letter came from Edessa in the corner of the Roman province farthest from the Parthian frontier, suspected that the conquest of the East was not proceeding as fast as he hoped.

Edessa was famous for the quality of its spring-water sacred to the Syrian nymph Atargatis; it was also the home of a flourishing community of Christians, influential in ruling circles in the town. Caracalla, like his mother, treated Christians with benevolent tolerance. He chose the town for his winter quarters, establishing himself there in the autumn of 216. It was the custom when the Emperor travelled abroad for a detachment of Praetorians, his bodyguard, to accompany him, together with the Prefect. Septimius took Papinian with him on his visit to Britain, and Caracalla followed the example, except that he had both the Prefects appointed after Papinian's death, Adventus and Macrinus, in attendance on him at Edessa. The former was an old soldier who had risen from humblest duties in the ranks, including, so gossip hinted, those of regimental executioner. His military career was without reproach, but he was by now well advanced in years, with failing eyesight. He was overshadowed in importance by his younger colleague, Macrinus.

There was great contrast between Adventus and Macrinus, the former a rough soldier, the latter a polished lawyer of fastidious tastes. Macrinus came of a middle-class family in Mauretania, the westernmost province of Africa, where his talent caught the attention of a fellow-African, Plautianus, the all-powerful minister under Septimius at the beginning of his reign. It happened that Plautianus heard Macrinus argue in court and was so favourably impressed by his knowledge of the law that he offered him employment in the legal department of the Imperial treasury. When Plautianus fell into disgrace, and anyone associated with him stood in danger, Macrinus was saved by the intervention of Junius Cilo, an elderly statesman to whom Septimius entrusted the guardianship of his sons till they came of age, and who still enjoyed considerable influence. Cilo took Macrinus under his protection, pleased by his civil manners and efficiency, and got him appointed to supervise traffic and maintenance on the Flaminian Way, the busy road leading from Rome to Rimini across the Apennines.

The death of Septimius threatened Macrinus with fresh disruption to his career. It seemed that his new protector was as little able as Plautianus to afford him lasting security. During the purge following the murder of Geta, when many took advantage of the confusion to satisfy a private grudge, Cilo's enemies sent a party of soldiers to plunder his house and arrest him. Cilo was about to have a bath, all but naked in slippers and a short vest. The intruders dragged him as he was into the street to bring him to the palace for judgement, never doubting that in the prevailing frenzy of slaughter the Emperor would condemn him to death.

The outcome, however, was not what they expected. Cilo was popular in Rome, and the violence and indignity to which he was exposed provoked public outcry. The disturbance was such that Caracalla himself came out into the forecourt of the palace to see what was happening. Whether it was that the sight of the angry crowd alarmed him, or that he was moved by genuine pity and affection for his old guardian, he strode forward in haste and threw his own cloak over him to cover his nakedness.

'How dare you insult him,' he shouted, 'my guardian, my father?'

It was typical of Caracalla that, having assumed the part of champion of the oppressed, he played it with exaggerated zeal to earn applause for his dutiful piety. The soldiers guilty of the raid were put to death, and everything possible was done to make up to Cilo for the outrage. He exerted more powerful patronage than ever before, and anyone dependent on him prospered. Among these was Macrinus, raised to sudden eminence as Prefect of the Praetorian Guard.

He was a useful servant to Caracalla, fulfilling his duties with tact and diligence; but there was an incompatibility of temperament between the two that impaired their relations. Macrinus loved the amenities of social life. He dressed with care, priding himself on his elegance, and even at Edessa he contrived to find delicacies for his table, refusing to share the common food provided for the soldiers. His behaviour provoked scorn from the Emperor, whose own inclinations were in the opposite direction, to fraternize with the soldiers and pose as one of themselves. He jeered at Macrinus for his unmilitary habits and described him as effeminate and a catamite. Nevertheless he kept him in charge of affairs, knowing into what disorder they would fall in the hands of Adventus.

Macrinus bitterly resented the contempt with which he was treated. Beneath his decorous manners he cherished restless ambition, and he listened with avidity when fortune-tellers promised him a glorious destiny leading even to the purple. Although the details are obscure, it seems that these predictions were inspired by a group of senators in Rome, who saw Macrinus as a handy tool, and hired soothsayers to play on his vanity, to help to rid them of an Emperor whom they hated. Caracalla had spies of his own in Rome, from whom he learnt that conspiracy was in the air; but as the names of the conspirators were unknown he had nothing against Macrinus. He sent word to the Prefect of the City, Maternianus, telling him to investigate the rumours and report what truth, if any, lay behind them. Meanwhile at Edessa he took the precaution of surrounding himself with picked men, natives of unsubjugated territory beyond the Rhine and the Danube, attached to him by personal loyalty and unconcerned with Roman politics. He called them his 'lions', a term of high praise. He was very fond of lions and kept several as pets.

As Macrinus was in charge of the Imperial correspondence he was well aware of the orders sent to Maternianus; but, unable to prevent the inquiry, he could only hope it would fail to elicit the facts. This hope was dispelled by a private letter from a friend in Rome, warning him that he was betrayed. It was by chance that the letter reached Edessa before the report from Maternianus himself. Both were dispatched at the same time; but the report addressed to the Emperor was diverted to Antioch in accordance with instructions to refer all official communications to the Augusta, so that she might sort out the unimportant to save troubling the Emperor with matters of routine.

When Julia read what Maternianus had to say, she lost no time in posting the news on to Edessa; but again luck intervened to save Macrinus from exposure. Caracalla was changing his clothes for a chariot-race when the post arrived. He told Macrinus impatiently to take the letters to his room and read them through, and if there was anything urgent he could let him know. Meanwhile he hurried out of doors and drove off to the racecourse to take part in his favourite sport. Needless to say, on his return from the race, he was informed by Macrinus that the letters contained nothing of importance.

Nevertheless Macrinus was in panic. He knew that Julia would not rest till she heard that those named in the report were punished. He was not even sure that he was not already under suspicion. Several of his friends had been removed on the pretext of promoting them to higher office. His guilty conscience suggested that the true reason was to put them out of reach when he needed their help. He was convinced that the choice lay between the Emperor's life and his own, and he made haste not to be the victim.

There was a soldier in the army at Edessa who owed him gratitude for past favours, and who bore the Emperor a grudge for denying him the rank of centurion, to which he was entitled as a veteran serving an extended term. His name was Martialis, and Macrinus, summoning him secretly, won him over to his cause, together with two accomplices, military tribunes in the Praetorian Guard, who agreed for a price to do what was wanted. The occasion chosen was a pilgrimage that the Emperor was about to make to Carrhae, a town some forty miles off, known in the Bible as Haran, famous for its temple of the moon and revered in Jewish lore as the early home of Abraham. Caracalla, whose piety like his mother's could embrace a variety of creeds, wished to invoke divine blessing on his efforts before launching his campaign against Parthia. The small escort of cavalry that he took with him included Martialis and the two tribunes.

An unforeseen event at Carrhae played into the hands of the conspirators. The temple stood at a short distance from the town, and on the way there the Emperor was suddenly taken short by an attack of diarrhoea. He halted the escort and retired out of sight into the bushes, while the soldiers waited, discreetly turning their backs. Martialis grasped the opportunity. Pretending that the Emperor called him, he ran after him and found him pulling down his breeches. The posture restricted his movements. Martialis, ready with his dagger, stabbed him in the ribs.

Caracalla had no chance to defend himself, but he was able to shout for help. As soldiers came running Martialis made haste to slip away, and he might have escaped in the confusion if he had not kept the fatal dagger in his hand. The German bodyguard, the devoted 'lions', led the rescue, and when they saw the weapon they knew that this was the murderer, and one of them hurled a spear and killed him. While attention had been diverted to the pursuit of Martialis, the two tribunes ran straight to the spot where Caracalla lay. They drew their swords and finished him off.

Macrinus himself soon arrived. With exclamations of horror he raised the body in his arms and examined it. Much to his relief Caracalla was dead. He died on the 8 April 217, four days after his twenty-ninth birthday.

His death was lamented with overwhelming sorrow by the soldiers, who loved him both for his free-handedness and for the easy familiarity with which he consorted with them, sharing their work and conditions of life. Macrinus was careful to attune himself to their mood and denounced the crime as angrily as any of them. He presided over the ceremony when a pyre was built and the body cremated. The urn containing the ashes was sent to Julia at Antioch, and from there for burial to Rome.

Julia was appalled by the course of events. It was not the loss of a son that she mourned, a son for whom she felt no affection. Her tears were for the death of an Emperor, who left no heir, either natural or adopted, to carry on the dynasty. Everything achieved by her husband and after his reign by herself to hold the Empire together was threatened with destruction. The danger was greater even than on the occasion of the murder of Commodus. There was no Pertinax to take immediate charge of the State, no Septimius Severus ready to succeed him. News reached her from Edessa that the army, left leaderless, wished, or was persuaded, to acclaim one of the Praetorian Prefects as Emperor, that Adventus refused the honour on grounds of age and lack of qualification and that Macrinus in consequence had been chosen. She knew from the report received from Maternianus that Macrinus was in league with conspirators at Rome, and although she could not have known how the report was intercepted it was easy to guess that he was responsible for her son's murder so soon after. She had good reason to regard his accession to power with dismay. In her despair she beat her breast, a gesture traditional in Syria as in other parts of the East when women expressed their grief. The cancerous growth had been quiescent in recent months, but the blows awakened it to renewed virulence. She was without hope, tormented with pain.

Then a message came from Macrinus, respectful in tone, addressing her by her title of Augusta and giving her permission to retain her guard of Praetorians. She was quick to read weakness into his words, evidence that he felt his position insecure, and her naturally sanguine temperament responded with exultation. Leaving the letter unanswered, she sounded the soldiers with her in Antioch to assure herself of their support. At the same time she sent emissaries to inform her of the state of feeling elsewhere in the Empire. The reports that they brought back were encouraging. Macrinus was unpopular in the army, despised for his unmilitary appearance and background, and already suspected of complicity in Caracalla's death. Similar opinions prevailed among the population at large, combined with angry disapproval of an action interrupting the prosperity and peace of the Roman world. There was abundant evidence of continued loyalty to the dynasty, gratitude for its success, due largely to Julia herself, in preserving and extending the golden afternoon of the Age of the Antonines. Her hopes revived and she was able to forget the pain in her body as she devoted herself to the task of building a party to overthrow the usurper. The dynasty was not yet extinct, it persisted as long as she herself lived. What did it matter that Rome was unaccustomed to a female sovereign? Ancient Babylon throve under the great Queen Semiramis.

Macrinus was alarmed when he received no reply to his letter. He interpreted her silence rightly as an act of defiance, and as information reached him of her doings he decided that there could be no safety for him while she was free. Exchanging diplomacy for force, he sent an armed detachment to Antioch to arrest her and escort her to her old home at Emesa, to live there in enforced seclusion with her sister Maesa. The arrival of the men took her by surprise. Her preparations were incomplete, her own supporters not yet organized for resistance. Perhaps too, never free from pain, she lacked the strength when the moment came to make the effort. None the less she refused to accept orders signed by Macrinus. She shut herself up in her room whose windows overlooked the shady walks and sun-flecked water of the gardens of Daphne, scene of happy days in the past when she held court, presiding as Augusta over a verbal duel between rival sophists or a recitation of poetry.

The officer in charge of her arrest hesitated, not daring to break in and carry her off by violence. He laid siege to the house to prevent her from escaping, till she herself relieved him of his difficulty. Worn out by pain and disappointment, she refused any food that was offered her, and died of starvation, weakness and a broken heart. She was only in her middle forties.

After cremation her ashes were carried to Rome and buried there. Later, her sister Maesa, when she came to power, gave orders for them to be exhumed and taken with the urn containing those of Geta to be buried in the Imperial tomb of the Antonines. Julia and her favourite son lay side by side.

8
The Usurper's Plight

When Julia died, her sister Maesa was already a widow. Her husband, Julius Avitus, was older than herself and, having filled a number of eminent posts in the public service, where he enjoyed the favour of Caracalla as of Septimius, he was appointed to the advisory council in Cyprus and died there, leaving Maesa with two daughters, Sohaemias and Mamaea. The elder was married, as has already been said, to Varius Marcellus, whose career prospered from the complaisance with which he connived at his wife's dalliance with the heir to the purple. When Caracalla became Emperor and was absent on the frontier on the Rhine, he left Varius as his vice-gerent in command of the forces in Italy. Further promotion followed from the division of the province of Africa into two administrative units. Varius was made governor of the western half, Numidia; but he died there soon after his arrival, while Caracalla was alive. A tablet put up to his memory: 'dearest husband and father', by Sohaemias and her children at Velitrae survives on the outskirts of Rome. The suburban site was chosen perhaps so as not to attract too much attention to him, when the eldest boy, Bassianus, was claiming to be Caracalla's natural son. Of the other children nothing more is known.

Maesa's younger daughter, Mamaea, was of a different character from her sister, less lively, more studious. She shared her aunt's interest in philosophy and religion and inherited much of the practical ability which both the Syrian Princesses of the older generation possessed. Her first husband died young, and as her second, Gessius Marcianus, was of humbler birth, she applied for permission to retain the senatorial rank to which the first was entitled, and Caracalla granted her the privilege. Gessius himself had been married before, and he was evidently a man of advanced years as he had a daughter by his first marriage who was already married herself. He played no part in the events following the murder of Caracalla, and it is probable that he was no longer alive. He left Mamaea with two children, a boy called Alexianus five years younger than her sister's son, Bassianus, and a girl called Theoclia.

On the death of the high priest of Elagabal, father of Julia and Maesa, the title followed the elder branch of his family and passed to Maesa's eldest grandson, Bassianus, son of Sohaemias. As he was still a child, his grandmother controlled the great wealth stored in the temple at Emesa. When Macrinus, acting promptly, rounded the family up—Maesa herself, her two daughters and her grandchildren—and confined them at Emesa, he put them unwisely where they could do him most harm. Emesa was no backwater remote from the course of events; it was a busy centre of commerce and goal of religious pilgrimage in one of the wealthiest parts of the Empire, and Maesa enjoyed prestige as head of the high-priestly family with the sacred treasure of the temple at her disposal. There was in addition a legionary camp situated at a distance outside the town, and the officers stationed there were little inclined to acquiesce in the elevation of the Praetorian Prefect to be Emperor, which the army in Mesopotamia imposed on them. The camp and the temple were soon on friendly terms.

The political talent and ambition which Maesa held in check while her sister lived had the chance now of fruitful outlet. Whether or not she was yet aware of the part played by Macrinus in Caracalla's murder, he incurred her fierce resentment as a usurper stealing the purple, to which in her opinion her family alone was entitled. Neither Caracalla nor Geta, her sister's sons, left an heir; but she herself had grandsons, Bassianus and Alexianus, to carry on the dynasty. Even if they were unrelated to Septimius Severus by blood, his great-nephews only by marriage, much could be made of the doubt attached to the paternity of Bassianus, the rumours of a liaison between his mother, Sohaemias, and Caracalla just before he was born. He himself, thirteen years old, was already a conspicuous figure in the town, performing the duties of hereditary high priest and much admired for his good looks when he appeared on ceremonial occasions in the gorgeous clothes appropriate to his office. Although later she was to regret the choice, there could be no question in Maesa's mind at this stage that he was a more eligible candidate for the purple than his cousin Alexianus, who was only eight.

She set to work with vigour, undeterred by the difficulty of proposing an heir for the Empire who was of immature years and whose claim rested on illegitimate birth. Encouraged by the sympathy that she found in the neighbouring camp, she extended her efforts farther afield and resumed contact with leaders of the civil and military establishment in other provinces, from whom her sister had obtained assurance of support. Her argument spoke to the condition of the times when she declared that her grandson, as heir of the dynasty founded by Septimius, stood for continuity, for the tradition of orderly succession that had kept peace in the Empire through the Age of the Antonines. She had the resources too to reinforce the argument with financial reward.

Macrinus ignored these doings with contempt. He had, as he thought, more important matters to occupy his attention than a bevy of women and a child. Almost immediately after the murder of Caracalla and his own elevation to the purple the news arrived that Artabanus, without waiting for the Roman army to invade, was advancing in force to avenge the affront to himself and his daughter at the abortive marriage feast, the sack of Arbela and desecration of the tombs of his ancestors. He was already across the Tigris, penetrating deep into Mesopotamia. Macrinus, a lawyer by profession and no soldier, tried to bring him to terms, informing him that the Emperor guilty of the outrage was dead, and that he himself succeeding to the title was ready to make amends. The soft answer had the opposite effect to that intended. When Artabanus understood that Caracalla had been murdered, and that the new Emperor was not yet secure in the seat of power, he was encouraged to put up his price. He demanded not only that the towns destroyed by the Romans should be rebuilt and a huge sum paid in reparation for the sacrilege to the tombs, but also that the Roman army should retreat across the Euphrates, leaving all Mesopotamia to revert to the Parthian Empire.

This was more than even Macrinus could accept. He led his army eastwards and came on the Parthians and joined battle with them at Nisibis. Accounts of the battle are conflicting; but it is clear that Artabanus was disappointed in his hope that the Roman soldiers, uncertain in their allegiance to the new Emperor, would allow him an easy victory. The outcome of the fighting was inconclusive, and the armies encamped opposite each other in the desert while a further attempt was made to settle the dispute by negotiation. They remained like this for months, unable to reach agreement and too evenly matched to renew hostilities, till at last, as autumn drew on, the Parthians grew restless. A Parthian King had no professional army on which to rely. When he went to war he called on his vassals to support him, each with a contingent of retainers raised for the immediate purpose from the local countryside, who were obliged to leave their homes and fields neglected while they followed their overlord. The ill-assorted horde lacked patience to endure prolonged inactivity. Tired of waiting in the desert, suffering shortage of food and water, the unprofessional soldiers began to melt away to resume their lives as farmers and herdsmen.

The Roman army was in scarcely better plight. Idle and uncomfortable in the desert, the men had nothing to do except grumble while they compared the new Emperor unfavourably with the old. Macrinus was able neither to inspire loyalty nor to enforce discipline. He craved as eagerly as the men themselves to return to civilized surroundings. When at last Artabanus offered to withdraw beyond the Tigris in exchange for full payment of the compensation demanded, Macrinus accepted with relief. The amount was enormous and, at the same time, to appease Vologaeses in the north, Rome submitted to ignominious defeat in Armenia, where the pretender Tiridates, taken prisoner by Caracalla's general, was restored to his throne to reign under Parthian suzerainty. All that Artabanus conceded in return was to leave Mesopotamia for the time being unmolested. There was no knowing how long his forbearance or his brother's would last. Macrinus disposed his army in a string of garrisons to guard the frontier, while he retired to spend the winter in comfort himself at Antioch.

Meanwhile Rome still waited to greet the new Emperor. There had been remarkable scenes in the senate when his letter was read announcing Caracalla's death. At first no one dared to believe that the news could be true. Senators privy to the conspiracy feared a trap set by Caracalla himself to lure them into betraying their feelings; but when Adventus, who delivered the letter, described in detail the incident at Carrhae and confirmed that on his own proposal the army had acclaimed his colleague Macrinus as Emperor, doubt yielded to unrestrained jubilation. Caracalla had many enemies in the senate who hated him, apart from those whom he offended by outrageous behaviour in his role of 'Ausonian beast'. The 'best people', as they still called themselves, were bitterly opposed to the policy of the Imperial House that deprived them of their privileges, extending rights of citizenship to the uttermost provincials. Even if they had little love for Macrinus, whom they despised as a parvenu, they were in a mood to welcome anyone in Caracalla's place. In spite of their strict insistence on correct procedure they forgave Macrinus even his precipitancy in assuming the title of Emperor before it had been confirmed by a vote of the senate. A vote was promptly taken to correct the oversight.

Outside the senate-house, however, they were careful to keep their feelings to themselves. They knew what devotion Caracalla inspired in the army, and there were enough soldiers present in Rome to provoke a riot if his memory was insulted. His ashes, which Adventus brought with him, were buried with solemn rites in the tomb of his ancestors, and in due course the senate passed the customary decree exalting him to divine status in company with the deified Emperors of the past. Some who voted for the decree declared in private that the honour was better suited to Martialis, the tyrant's murderer.

Among the working population, including freedmen and slaves, the far from 'best' people in the city, there was neither exultation nor sorrow, but great uneasiness. Caracalla's misbehaviour, even the murder of his brother, had little effect on the immediate interests of his humbler subjects. The impression left by his reign was that it carried on his father's work, providing strong government under which men could live in peace and prosper. The violent interruption created by his assassination recalled events vivid in the memory of anyone past middle age, the civil war and anarchy that followed the death of Commodus. Many still alive were present in the crowd at the Saturnalia in the year 195, shouting: 'How much longer? When will the war stop?' They feared that they would soon have to shout the same words again.

A scene resembling it took place in fact in September when Macrinus gave the title of Caesar to his nine-year-old son, and horse-races were held in Rome to celebrate the boy's birthday. There was no enthusiasm felt for the new Emperor, an absentee ruler who had not presented himself in Rome since he took office, and public anxiety was aggravated by his choice of a mere boy to be Emperor designate at a time when the State needed capable hands to save it from danger. When cheerleaders tried to elicit applause for the happy event, the crowd gathered for the races listened in gloomy silence, till suddenly arms were raised pointing to the sky, and voices called in unison on Jupiter: 'He alone is our Augustus. Him we need, no one else.'

The growing despair of human leadership, and the urge to seek comfort in divine, found expression in a story that attracted popular belief. It was said that before the news arrived of Caracalla's death a man was seen leading a donkey up the Capitoline hill, who replied when he was asked his business that he was taking it to its master, that the Emperor was dead and Jupiter reigned in his place. The Prefect Maternianus had him arrested, meaning to send him to Caracalla for trial, but on the way the prisoner vanished; he was not, it seems, a man but a spirit. The details of the story varied with repetition, but a point on which all were agreed was that the donkey represented Macrinus.

Among the senators too Macrinus was losing favour. As the first flush of joy wore off, they became increasingly aware of his shortcomings.

It was especially harmful to his reputation that, not being present in person, he was judged by the example of Adventus, whom he had sent to act on his behalf. The choice of Adventus was a reward to the old man for his obliging attitude in the confusion at Edessa, when he told the leaderless army that Macrinus, although junior to himself, was better fitted to wear the purple. He was, however, no less unfit for the duties with which Macrinus now entrusted him. These included the post of Prefect of the City, in which he superseded Maternianus, the officer whose report to Caracalla so nearly cost Macrinus his life. Maternianus was not only dismissed, he was put to death. He was greatly respected in Rome for his integrity and the loyalty with which he had served the late Emperor, and the vengeance taken on him earned Macrinus disapproval and contempt.

His loss was felt the more because his successor cut so poor a figure. Adventus was out of his depth in Roman society, and he had neither the education nor the talent to deal adequately with official business. Even if he had ever known how to read, his eyesight by now was too dim to distinguish written words. The derision provoked by his incompetence mounted when he was appointed to share the consulship for the coming year with Macrinus himself. As Macrinus was unable or unwilling to leave Syria, it was left to Adventus alone to attend the ceremony of inauguration on New Year's Day 218. Adventus was appalled by the prospect. He was at his worst on social occasions. His bearing lacked dignity, and he had no small talk. When the time came, he pleaded illness and retired to bed.

Hearing what a bad impression Adventus made, Macrinus removed him from the post of Prefect of the City; but it was too late to restore confidence in the government. There were many grounds for dissatisfaction: senators were aggrieved because they failed to obtain the profits and advancement that they expected, others because they suffered disgrace for their compliance with policy in the previous reign. At the same time Macrinus was accused of shielding the informers who served Caracalla, and with whom he himself had close contact while he was Praetorian Prefect. Nevertheless in spite of these complaints an appearance of loyalty was preserved in the senate, if only because Macrinus was believed to command the allegiance of the army, and there was no one else yet available to set up as rival. When he wrote describing in as favourable a light as possible the terms of his agreement with Artabanus, the senate voted a public thanksgiving and conferred on him the title of Parthicus to celebrate the victory. He refused the title, knowing how little he deserved it. As a lawyer, he disliked inaccuracy.

If he had been present in Rome to meet the disaffected in person, he might have overcome their objections. He owed much of his success earlier in his life to a smooth tongue. As it was, however, he remained out of their sight in Syria, and his enemies took advantage of his absence to discredit him. They accused him of dallying in Antioch to enjoy the pleasures for which the town was famous, denounced him for dressing up in fine clothes to attend performances of mimes and dances and for aping the philosopher, cultivating a long beard and speaking with measured deliberation in imitation of Marcus Aurelius. The picture drawn was consistent with his habits. His taste for elegance and Malvolio-like pose of gravity were among the aspects of his character that had irritated Caracalla. Antioch was a pleasant place, and its way of life appealed to him. He had reasons, nevertheless, of greater importance that detained him there, preventing him from returning to Rome to establish his authority. He feared a renewed invasion from Parthia and believed that he must keep his army ready to repel it.

As events proved, his fear was groundless. The Parthian brothers were already resuming fraternal strife, and very soon both were fully occupied by the threat of a national uprising in Persia, the same that had hindered their father from opposing the Romans under Septimius when they occupied Mesopotamia, and which was growing more formidable now and spreading with fanatical resolution, destined a few years later to replace the Parthian with a Persian Empire. If Macrinus had foreseen this, he could have saved himself from an error fatal to his survival. His delay in Antioch was due to political misjudgement, not to self-indulgence.

The dissatisfaction provoked at Rome was not the worst of its consequences. There was greater danger to be feared from the demoralization that prolonged idleness fostered among the soldiers. If he could have disbanded them at once and sent them home, his lack of military qualification would have been less conspicuous; but keeping them under arms, without a battle to exercise them, he provided them with both cause and leisure to grumble, and exposed himself continually to unfavourable comparison with Caracalla. The stories of his doings in Antioch at which his enemies jeered in Rome aroused the bitterest resentment in the camps, where the army was quartered on the edge of the desert. The contrast between the hardships of the camp and the luxury that he himself enjoyed afforded an irresistible theme for agitators. The anger of the men was exasperated when he announced reforms in the course of the winter, cutting the rate of military pay back to the level that had prevailed in the reign of Septimius, and abolishing a number of costly privileges. He was in fact in a dilemma, urged by powerful interests in Rome to alleviate the burden of taxation, blame for which they laid on Caracalla's pampering of the army at the expense of the State. Nevertheless, in view of the ugly mood of the garrisons in Mesopotamia, a worse moment could scarcely have been chosen to break the news.

Accustomed to negotiation, he did his best to soften the blow by limiting the application of the new rate to recruits, leaving the pay untouched of men already serving. He hoped that the old soldiers, losing nothing themselves, would be content, and that the new intake would lack confidence and experience to oppose his decision. At any other time his hope might have been fulfilled, and the change accepted with resignation; but the circumstances were unfavourable when the army was mobilized for war, aware of its own power, and old and young were drawn together by ties of common interest and fellowship. The new Emperor was suspected of trickery, very capable, according to the gossip of the camp, of withdrawing the exemption as soon as the emergency was over and making the new rate of pay the standard for all.

As discontent spread through the ranks, discipline suffered. Macrinus was alarmed by reports reaching him of outrages committed by soldiers on the native population. This was territory constantly in dispute between Parthia and Rome, and the security of the Roman government depended on retaining the goodwill of the inhabitants. He sent word therefore ordering that the offenders be severely punished to deter others from following the example. Many incidents were recalled after his fall, illustrating the harshness with which his orders were obeyed. A story is told of a group of soldiers convicted of multiple rape on a girl employed at the house where they were billeted. They were sentenced to be sewn up alive, each in the carcass of a bullock emptied of its vitals. Only their heads were left protruding, so that they could talk to each other and listen to each other's groans, lying side by side in stinking bondage till their own flesh rotted with that which enclosed them. Their fate is recorded as evidence of the cruelty of Macrinus; but it is more probable that the method of punishment was chosen by an officer on the spot than by the Emperor himself far off at Antioch. In any case it was effective to protect local girls from molestation.

Meanwhile at Emesa, up the river from Antioch, Maesa and her daughters kept themselves informed of the progress of events, of the disfavour that Macrinus was earning at Rome by his delay in visiting the city, and the low morale of the army guarding the Tigris. They learnt too from their envoys travelling farther afield of the angry regret with which Caracalla was mourned by distant legions throughout the

Empire, and of the support that a candidate could attract who claimed the purple as his son. The truth was beginning to leak out about the part played by Macrinus in the murder at Carrhae. Although Martialis was killed on the spot, the two tribunes survived for a time, long enough to indulge in indiscreet boasting before means were found to shut their mouths for ever. The rumours which arose came to Maesa's ears, and she exerted herself to propagate them and foment indignation against the author of the treachery. If Macrinus, with much else on his hands, felt that he could safely ignore the activities of the women at Emesa, he soon had cause to change his mind.

The legionary camp on whose support Maesa counted lay some forty miles away at the foot of a range of low hills. There was frequent intercourse between the camp and the town, army vehicles travelling to and fro, and soldiers on leave flocked to the temple, attracted by the fame of its wealth and the pleasures associated with its rites. On such occasions they were favourably impressed by the appearance of the high priest, who already in spite of his youth played a leading part in the proceedings, gorgeously clothed. The pomp and ceremony made him look older than he was, and the interest aroused among the sightseers was enhanced when they were told that the late Emperor was his father. It needed little argument to persuade them, or their comrades to whom they spoke of it back in the camp, that he was better fitted to wear the purple than Macrinus. Any doubt was removed when the news spread that Macrinus was responsible for Caracalla's murder.

Among Maesa's friends at Emesa the most active on her behalf were Comazon and Gannys. The former was an old soldier whose background was not unlike that of Caracalla's general Theocritus, as he began life on the stage. The name Comazon is in fact a Greek word meaning a strolling player. A disreputable flavour clung to the profession, and his enemies seized on it to disparage him; but as he had already a long and successful career of military service to his credit, it is clear that his dramatic performances dated from a distant past. The disdain expressed in Roman society for his humble origin was not shared by his fellow-officers who set more store by his gift for leadership and skill in battle.

Gannys, the other ringleader, was less a soldier than a statesman. Little is known of his past except that Maesa employed him as her grandson's tutor, and that the boy's mother, Sohaemias, became so attached to him that she accepted him as her lover; but he seems to have been the brains of the movement to raise his pupil to be Emperor. In the early days after its success he was Maesa's principal adviser, and his loyalty and organizing ability were indispensable to convert a conspiracy in a Syrian temple into the working government of the Empire. Dio, who regards the adventure with disapproval, accords him reluctant praise: 'He did no harm to anyone and much good to many.'

The decisive step was taken late in the evening of 15 May 218. Gannys acted on his own, without informing Maesa and Sohaemias, fearing perhaps that they would not consent to the risk. He revealed his plan only to his pupil. There were clothes put away in the high priest's house at Emesa, stored there at some time by Julia, which Caracalla had worn as a child, easily recognizable by the Imperial emblem with which they were adorned. Gannys told the boy to put them on, and they set off together on horseback into the darkness with an escort of six soldiers, deserters from the army of Macrinus who had been hiding in the neighbourhood and were able to lead them by little-used paths. They reached the legionary camp just before dawn.

Although Gannys had made soundings to prepare the ground, winning over many of the garrison to his side, he could not be sure what reception to expect as his little party rode up to the gate. His boldness, however, was rewarded. The sight of the boy in clothes of Imperial splendour, combined with the rumours of his parentage, earned him an enthusiastic welcome from the soldiers. They opened the gate for him at once, and he rode into the camp greeted on all sides by eager cries of support. A purple cloak was brought and thrown over his shoulders, and the entire garrison acclaimed him Emperor by the name of Marcus Aurelius Antoninus.

A messenger carried the news to Emesa with the advice to Maesa and her family to take refuge in the camp before Macrinus could retaliate. She arrived with Sohaemias and Mamaea and the latter's small son, Alexianus. The accommodation within the walls suffered further strain when the soldiers brought their own wives and children in for safety from the villages in the surrounding countryside. There was reason for urgency. Julianus, the officer in command of the nearest forces loyal to Macrinus, did not wait even for orders from Antioch to move into action against the rebels. He advanced to reduce them to submission and showed no mercy to any of their dependants whom he caught. Mamaea's stepdaughter and her husband were among the victims. They put off their departure from Emesa till too late, and were intercepted and killed.

Having given his men this taste of blood, Julianus led them to the camp to take it by assault. His army contained recruits from Mauretania, fellow-countrymen of Macrinus, who fought for him with devotion and succeeded in forcing an entry at one of the gates; but the others showed no zeal to follow up the advantage, and at last as the hour was growing late Julianus withdrew them, hoping that the garrison would offer to surrender without further fighting. His hopes were disappointed; the garrison repaired the breach during the night, and in the morning the boy Emperor came up on the rampart to show himself and his supporters shouted to the enemy below: 'What are you doing, comrades? Why are you fighting against your benefactor's son?'

The words had immediate effect, increasing the unwillingness shown on the previous day by all except Mauretanian recruits to fight for Macrinus. The boy Emperor himself made a speech, praising his reputed father and promising to follow his example of liberality towards his soldiers. In addition Comazon, who was present in the camp and had many acquaintances on the other side, got in touch with them secretly and told them that anyone killing an officer would be rewarded with that officer's property and rank. Julianus, seeing that the battle was turning into a debate, urged his men on angrily to renew the assault; but he no longer commanded their obedience, his orders provoked open mutiny, and the soldiers turned on their officers, killing those who refused to change allegiance. The army that had come to attack the camp stayed to reinforce the defenders.

Julianus himself fled with the surviving remnant of the Mauretanian recruits and escaped down the river to Apamea. It was an ill-advised choice of refuge. The legion stationed there was that in which Comazon served, and he had many friends there. They fell on Julianus, overcame his escort and cut off his head.

News of the defeat of Julianus, but not of his death, reached Macrinus at Antioch, and he set off at once to Apamea to find out what was happening. His arrival at the head of a formidable army overawed the disaffected, and he was greeted with profuse expresssions of loyalty. No one revealed what had become of Julianus, for fear that he would take vengeance on guilty and innocent alike. Pleased by his reception and persuaded that Julianus was still active against the rebels, he exerted himself to strengthen his influence in Apamea, a town large enough to be a rival to Emesa on the upper Orontes. To add lustre to his visit, he announced that his son, already proclaimed Caesar on his birthday, was now, only eight months later, promoted to the rank of Emperor, co-equal with himself, and that in honour of the occasion he proposed to distribute a great sum in largess to the soldiers and to entertain the townspeople at a banquet. A magnificent dinner was prepared, to which everyone of note in the town was invited. As he presided over it, a soldier approached with a parcel wrapped in cloth and tied with cords, informing him that it came from Julianus and contained the head of the boy from Emesa. To confirm his words, he pointed to the wax with which the knots were sealed. They bore the imprint of the official signet-ring.

Macrinus was delighted by this stroke of good fortune. In his exultation he insisted on opening the parcel at once in front of all his guests. He seized a knife, slit the cords and removed the wrappings. As the last layer of cloth was unwound the soldier slipped unobtrusively away to rejoin his grinning comrades. A head fell from the cloth, rolled on the floor, the head of Julianus.

Haunted by treachery and not knowing whom to trust, Macrinus returned in haste to Antioch. On his departure the legion stationed at Apamea declared itself openly for the rising star of Emesa, and many others followed the example in Syria and the neighbouring provinces. An exception for a time was Egypt, where the name of Caracalla stank. The governor appointed by Macrinus seized Maesa's agents and put them to death; but when the people heard of the growing strength of the movement elsewhere, they thought less of the massacre at Alexandria than of the benefits to be earned from the winning side. They rose in revolt against the governor, who fled to Italy, where he lurked in hiding till a friend betrayed him to his enemies. In most parts of the Empire the change of allegiance provoked little opposition from either civil or military authorities. It is remarkable indeed with what ease they accepted a new ruler who was not only immature in years but was also high priest of a Syrian cult alien from Roman tradition. If his subjects could have seen him as he was, officiating in oriental robes with painted face at the altar of Elagabal, they might have been less eager to acclaim him Emperor; but in fact they knew little of him except that he claimed to be the son, no matter whether illegitimate, of Caracalla, able to carry on the dynasty founded by Septimius Severus. He was a symbol of continuity. The very name that he assumed, Marcus Aurelius Antoninus, associated him with the peace and prosperity of the Age of the Antonines.

Success could have been harder to achieve if his rival had controlled either military force or the support of public opinion. Macrinus could rely on neither. He was no governor of a province on the frontier enjoying the allegiance of a great army like Septimius at Carnuntum in 193. The army on the Tigris had come under his command more or less by accident, in the confusion of the emergency, when he was chosen to fill the gap left by the murder of Caracalla. The soldiers felt no personal loyalty, and he himself lacked the qualities to inspire it. A man of the eminence of Papinian could hold respect as Praetorian Prefect although he was a lawyer and no soldier; but Macrinus was of weaker character, and his legal background only earned him contempt. The allegiance, at best only perfunctory, which was paid him, fell away dangerously as the rumour spread that Caracalla was murdered at his instigation.

His influence was no less insecure at Rome. The people were without enthusiasm for an Emperor who had never shown himself in the city since he began to reign, and in the senate those who applauded his accession in the first joy of the news that Caracalla was dead regarded him with dwindling favour as they waited in vain for the benefits expected from him, promotion to remunerative office and relief from the burden of taxation. They spoke scornfully of his humble origin and lack of qualification to rule over them; at the same time, in their impatience for change, they were ready to overlook similar faults in his rival. They were in no mood for sympathy when a letter was read in the house, received from him at Antioch, in which, while professing contempt for an enemy led by a mad boy, he complained of the difficulty of enforcing military discipline and gave warning that he might be compelled to restore pay for recruits and veterans alike to the old level, in spite of the cost to the treasury. He concluded, with a touch of self-pity, that stern measures had no effect on men who cared less to preserve their own lives than to deprive an Emperor of his; then as if afraid that he had said too much, he added that the words were not to be taken personally, that no one wanted him dead. At that point, according to Dio who was present, an ex-consul notorious for his bluntness interrupted: 'We do, we're all praying for it.'

As news reached Macrinus of the rapid spread of disaffection he gathered his forces for a decisive effort, to lead an invasion into the enemy's country, take prisoner the boy who dared to defy him and nip the insurrection in the bud. Before his preparations were complete, however, the enemy forestalled him. Comazon, who was in command at Emesa, preferred to attack rather than wait to be attacked and, advancing down the river, he was already within twenty-four miles of Antioch before Macrinus was aware of his approach. Taken by surprise, Macrinus mustered the Praetorian Guard, the only reliable soldiers immediately available; but they were a defensive force armed with heavy breastplate of overlapping scales of metal and an enormous shield shaped like a pantile, and when he ordered them into battle they grumbled, asking, how they could fight under the weight of such a burden in the scorching heat of the open country. In exasperation he told them to strip off their armour and go out in the light equipment of auxiliaries. Whether to show that in spite of the change they remained Praetorians at heart, or because they enjoyed the unaccustomed freedom of movement, they charged into action with such vigour that the enemy's ranks broke and turned in flight.

Maesa and Sohaemias sat with the boy Emperor watching from a carriage in the rear. When they saw what was happening, the two women leapt to the ground and ran among the soldiers calling to them and imploring them to stand and fight. The boy himself seized a horse and mounted it, waving his drawn sword above his head and galloping to the front to charge the advancing Praetorians in person. The example set by the women and their bitter reproaches put the fugitives to shame, and the sight of the galloping boy with his flashing sword had the force of a divine portent. All turned to follow his lead and beat the Praetorians back.

Even so, the issue remained uncertain; but Macrinus, seeing the enemy rallying and thinking that the battle already was lost, left the field in alarm and made haste to return to Antioch. When the Praetorians, still fighting on stoutly, observed that the Imperial standard was no longer in position they were dismayed, not knowing what had become of their general, whether indeed he were dead. Then witnesses of his flight brought the news, and there was so indignant a revulsion of feeling among the men that they sent an envoy to Comazon offering to transfer their allegiance in return for an amnesty, which he willingly accorded. The combined forces bore down together on Antioch to take Macrinus prisoner.

He himself had arrived in the town announcing, to keep up his credit, that his army was victorious; but the story was quickly refuted by refugees straggling in from the surrounding farms and villages, and when he learnt the full extent of the disaster, that the Praetorians had gone over to the enemy, he was filled with despair. He had his son with him, the nine-year-old boy on whom he had conferred titles of honour, seeing him with pride as his successor one day at the head of the Roman Empire. His first care was to protect him, and he chose a party of trusted attendants to see him safely to the Parthian frontier and seek sanctuary with Artabanus. It would be a recommendation to Artabanus, he hoped, that his enemy was the reputed son of the Roman Emperor who defiled the wedding feast with blood and sacked the tombs of the Parthian Kings at Arbela. Meanwhile, as the attacking force drew near, panic bred chaos in Antioch. Citizens were murdered for favouring the enemy, murdered for opposing surrender. In the confusion Macrinus got a barber to crop his curled hair and shave off the philosophic beard with which in happier days he had modelled himself on Marcus Aurelius. Then with the further disguise of a cloak to hide his purple tunic, he mounted a horse and galloped northward with a few companions into Cilicia.

When he came to the road leading across Asia Minor from the southern sea to the Bosporus, he commandeered a carriage by posing as an Imperial courier, supporting the claim with documents signed with his own hand. Nothing was yet known here of events in Antioch. He hurried the horses on to outpace the news of his downfall, hoping to reach Byzantium and take ship from there to Rome, where he counted on the senate to favour his cause. His luck held out as far as Chalcedon on the Asian shore of the Bosporus; but there he ran short of money and had to apply for help to the municipal treasurer, pleading Imperial business. The officer's suspicions were aroused, and he referred the matter to the governor, who was a friend of Maesa's, a collaborator in her plans. He recognized Macrinus and held him in custody till an escort was sent from Antioch to bring him back under arrest.

On the way he suffered the last blow to his hopes. He learnt that his little son, betrayed by his guardian, had been caught trying to escape to Parthia and had been put to death. Macrinus had nothing left to live for. In deference to his former rank he was allowed to sit in the carriage unbound. He waited till the horses broke into a gallop and the vehicle gathered speed, then he threw himself out on to the road. The attempt failed to achieve suicide; he succeeded only in breaking his shoulder. He owed death to the centurion in charge who, unwilling to be burdened with a cripple, cut off his head to carry to Antioch and left the trunk behind. It lay unburied by the roadside, the nameless remains of a man not quite fifty-four years of age, who had reigned for a year and two months as Roman Emperor.

9

The Boy Emperor

Marcus Aurelius Antoninus is the name that the new Emperor assumed, following the example of Caracalla, and which he bears on
surviving coins and inscriptions; but it is not the name by which he
is known to posterity. More than a hundred years after his death the
author of the Augustan History, anxious for reasons of contemporary
politics to denigrate an earlier dynasty, invented for him the nickname
of Heliogabalus. The word is a deliberate monstrosity, a conflation
of Syriac and Greek, substituting for the Semitic 'El' in the name of
the god of Emesa the Greek 'Helios' meaning the sun. The purpose
was to sneer at the outlandishness of the name by distorting it into a
Greek mould. In fact the Emperor in his lifetime never bore the name
of his god, and the god was not called Heliogabalus. Nevertheless the
nickname has stuck, and the Emperor Heliogabalus has an established
place in Roman history except in the pages of Gibbon who prefers
to retain, but misapply, the god's correct name, Elagabalus. It will be
convenient therefore, in spite of the anachronism, to refer to him in
the following pages by the name that tradition has adopted, recalling
Gilbert's Major-General in *The Pirates of Penzance*: 'I recite in elegiacs
all the crimes of Heliogabalus.'

The crimes owe more to fiction than to fact. When he entered
Antioch in triumph in June 218 the Emperor was only fourteen years
old, and he died at the age of eighteen. There was more oddity than
wickedness in his short reign. It began with an act of clemency when
he stopped his soldiers plundering, murdering and raping, the customary privilege of conquerors in a conquered town. In compensation
for their restraint he paid them a handsome gratuity, to which the
citizens of Antioch had to contribute. The town none the less was
grateful, having expected a fate so much worse.

As the news spread of the defeat and death of Macrinus, governors of provinces made haste to send envoys to Antioch to assure the new Emperor of their support. He for his part wrote to the senate in Rome announcing his accession and demanding allegiance. To forestall adverse comment on his youth, he reminded the senators that they allowed Macrinus to invest his nine-year-old son with Imperial dignity. If the usurper's son could receive the title at so early an age, how could it be denied to the heir of the Antonines, descended from a long line of deified Emperors? His claim rested on disputable grounds, the unproved assumption that Caracalla was his father, the legal fiction of posthumous adoption which made Septimius a son of Marcus Aurelius; but it had the support of an impressive consensus of opinion armed with military force in many parts of the Empire, and no one was found in the senate bold enough to contest it. A reply was sent recognizing him as Emperor, meekly swallowing the insult that he had taken the title without waiting for it to be conferred. At the same time the stigma of public enemy, attached to him under pressure from Macrinus, was removed and transferred to the dead Macrinus instead.

Although the example of Macrinus taught the lesson that an Emperor should present himself in Rome as soon as possible, the new government was unable to leave the East till its influence was sufficiently consolidated there. To be within easier access of the capital the court moved northwards from Antioch to Nicomedia, the town near the Sea of Marmara where Caracalla had his headquarters two years earlier, while he prepared his invasion of Parthia. Far from mobilizing forces, however, Heliogabalus disbanded a large part of his army and sent the men home. His advisers were determined not to repeat the mistake made by Macrinus in keeping soldiers unemployed in camp with nothing to distract them from their discomforts and grievances. There was no danger on the frontier any longer to be feared. The Parthian Empire itself was breaking up, as the leader of the Persian rebels—whose name, Artaxerxes, recalled the glorious past when Persia was a great power in the world—fought not only for independence but also to restore Persian hegemony to its ancient bounds, to avenge the defeat inflicted by Alexander the Great and the incursion of Parthian barbarians. Artabanus and Vologaeses, occupied with their own quarrel, were threatened by an enemy eager to annihilate them both.

The government of Heliogabalus was free therefore from external troubles. Its main task at Nicomedia was to repair the damage done to u blic order by the recent unrest and to wipe out the last traces of resistance. Confidence was promoted by a decree announcing that no person or community would be punished for help given to Macrinus in the past. Those only had need to fear reprisal who persisted in hostility to the new Emperor's authority and were guilty of sedition. The promise of amnesty was kept, but officers in responsible positions who had shown zeal for Macrinus were replaced by more reliable successors. Some of those who lost office expressed their resentment in active conspiracy. There was an abortive plot to foment mutiny in the fleet in the Bosporus, and to intercept and subvert the allegiance of German soldiers on their way home after disbandment. The conspirators extended their activities to Rome, where a senator was found in possession of a private mint stamping coins with his own image. His plea that they were keepsakes for his girl-friends failed to carry conviction when a further hoard turned up in Cappadocia, ready to finance a rebellion.

Senators under suspicion were summoned from Rome to Nicomedia without being told what they were wanted for. When they failed to return, and the senate made inquiries, the answer came that there was no need of evidence against them as they were already dead.

The guiding spirit behind the government was Maesa's. She was ruthless but not vindictive, preferring to get her way by diplomacy. When the circumstances demanded it, however, she did not shrink from arbitrary justice, treating the Roman senate with Syrian disdain. Her principal adviser in the conduct of affairs was Gannys, and the rapid success achieved in eliminating opposition bore witness to his statesmanship. Unlike Comazon, promoted to be Praetorian Prefect, who was accused of abusing his position to pay off old scores, Gannys served with single-minded devotion the interests of the high-priestly family, in whose household at Emesa he was brought up. His loyalty was reinforced by passion for the attractive Sohaemias, who had accepted him as a lover and now promised to become his wife. It was agreed that after the marriage he would bear the rank of Caesar, Emperor designate, a title ensuring him eminence in the state even if it was never likely to be more than honorary, conferring on a man already in the prime of life the right to succeed a reigning Emperor who was still a child.

The plan had the approval of his pupil, the Emperor, with whom he was on terms of close friendship; but it led none the less to their estrangement. Recent events had had an intoxicating effect on the boy —the expedition by night to the legionary camp, his acclamation by the soldiers as Emperor, his own exploits finally on the field of battle outside Antioch. After these experiences he was unwilling to return to tutelage; he regarded himself as grown up and resented it when Gannys asserted the authority no longer merely of a tutor but also of a prospective stepfather to oppose his wishes. No conflict arose between them over affairs of State. Maesa had assumed the title of Augusta (so too had Sohaemias, but without corresponding effect), and her grandson was content to leave administrative decisions in her hands. The anxiety that he caused her and Gannys had its source, not in politics, but in his fanatical zeal for religion, his conviction that he became Emperor to promote the greater glory of the god of Emesa.

He insisted on appearing in public in the robes of a high priest of Elagabal. Even Nicomedia, a Greek city accustomed to eccentric cults, was astonished by the sight of the Emperor adorned with necklaces and bracelets, crowned with a golden head-dress and accompanied by an ecstatic din of flutes and drums. His conduct gave more serious offence on the occasion of his inauguration as consul to fill the place left vacant by the death of Macrinus. The ceremony was of importance in Maesa's eyes. She intended it to confirm the authority of the restored dynasty and had deliberately omitted to consult the senate in Rome over the appointment. The dignity of the proceedings necessary to her purpose was marred when her grandson defied tradition by refusing to wear the Roman toga, whose cumbrous folds he detested, and turned up instead in oriental finery. His love of dressing up recalls Caracalla and argues in favour of the belief that they were father and son. There was more of the visionary, however, than the clown in Heliogabalus. He sought effect less for his own sake than his god's.

There was another impulse too that inclined him to sartorial extravagance. He was an emotional invert, by nature a pathic, more feminine than masculine, and the robes in which he flaunted himself had a transvestite appeal. The Roman world was accustomed to regard such abnormality with tolerance. If he had behaved more discreetly, it is probable that his habits would have been accepted with little demur. Discretion, however, was not in his character. He had an impish desire to shock, and his efforts succeeded so well when he came to Rome that they earned him a scabrous immortality.

Maesa, who was well acquainted with Roman society, foresaw how unfavourable an impression he would produce there unless he mended his ways. She and Gannys did their best to persuade him that he could not behave in Rome as he did in Nicomedia. He was learning, however, to assert his own will, and his natural stubbornness was reinforced by religious conviction. Dissimulation was hateful to him. When his grandmother and tutor spoke of the need of tact to reconcile the Romans to an Emperor who was also high priest of Elagabal, he had his portrait painted in sacred vestments and sent it to Rome to be hung in the senate-house above the presidential seat, so that everyone would know what to expect when he arrived in person. Maesa was unable to prevent him. She feared to provoke an estrangement that would deprive her of her influences over him in the government of the Empire.

Nevertheless she persisted in remonstrance, as did Gannys also. There came an occasion when the latter was alone with the boy except for the soldiers on guard at the door. The argument between Gannys and his pupil became more and more heated, the former scolding, the latter defiant, till suddenly the boy lost his temper and struck Gannys in the face with his fist. Ganny, taken by surprise and in pain, drew his sword. The gesture was automatic, without conscious intent, but the guards, believing that he threatened the Emperor's life, came running and stabbed him to death.

Maesa was deprived of a wise counsellor, Sohaemias of her lover and promised husband. It is not known what the Emperor's own feelings were, but the incident created no rift between him and his mother. She was unlike the other women of her family, more interested in pleasure than politics; but she was devoted to her son and put his interests before her own.

The business needing attention in the East was completed before the end of the winter; but the Emperor fell ill and the journey to Rome was postponed. It was summer before he was well enough to travel, and the court set out and came to Rome in the middle of July. The most treasured article carried in the baggage was the black meteorite representing Elagabal, brought for the purpose from the temple at Emesa. The Emperor insisted on taking it with him. Maesa, whose views were more akin to her sister's, regarded it as a symbol deserving respect for its use in popular worship rather than for any inherent sanctity of its own; but she was unwilling to oppose her grandson in a plan on which his heart was set. Rome was full of shrines dedicated to foreign, mainly Eastern, gods. To add another could make little matter.

She underrated the ardour of his purpose. He brought Elagabal to Rome not to install him among a multitude of similar divinities, but to exalt him to the head of the Roman pantheon, supreme over Jupiter himself. A temple of suitable dignity was built on the Palatine hill and consecrated with unprecedented magnificence. Men and women danced in frenzy round the altar with rattle of drums and clash of cymbals,

F

and the Emperor himself danced among them, more gorgeously clad, more outlandish than any, epicene in silks and jewels. The Roman people had seen Syrian rites before, but never on such a scale, never with an Emperor cast as high priest. It was a scene to delight the populace, especially when a liberal distribution of money followed.

The senators however were appalled. Although the portrait hung in the senate-house had warned them, the reality seen in flesh and blood surpassed their wildest fears. They could not avoid seeing it. The front row of seats at the service was reserved for them, and everyone had to attend; no excuse was accepted. Worse still, the more eminent were expected to participate in the rites in person, to carry bowls of spices and steaming entrails of sacrificial victims on their heads and put on for the purpose a long-sleeved gown with vertical stripe of purple and linen slippers, the despised uniform of vagrant priests of Semitic cults. The Emperor believed that he honoured the solemn dignitaries by appointing them to such tasks. They themselves felt, and the spectators agreed, that he made them figures of fun.

It is not surprising perhaps that Dio, a spokesman of senatorial opinion, regards the reign of Heliogabalus with invincible prejudice, but it does not follow that it earned similar condemnation throughout the Empire. The frontiers were at peace, and the legions stationed there well contented to serve an Emperor who was Caracalla's son. If stories of his antics in Rome reached their ears, they were more likely to provoke laughter than offence. Civil life in the provinces was undisturbed. The amnesty granted after the death of Macrinus left capable and experienced men to continue in office, many of them appointed by Septimius, and Maesa like her sister before her was an efficient housekeeper in control of the Imperial economy. Her sister's example made her task easier. Rome was growing accustomed to feminine government, not too obtrusively exercised.

She did her best to conciliate the senate by arranging a marriage for her grandson with a girl of aristocratic lineage, Cornelia Paula. The wedding was celebrated with appropriate splendour in strictly Roman style with the Imperial bridegroom correctly dressed for once in a toga. The customary entertainment followed in the amphitheatre, matches of gladiators and slaughter of wild beasts, and there was a banquet for the commonalty and another for the soldiers, the latter on the more generous scale. Cornelia Paula received the title of Augusta, and the Emperor himself was in excellent humour, boasting that he would beget an heir. He was past his fifteenth birthday, mature enough in years to consummate the marriage; but Rome waited in vain for news that his wife was pregnant. At last he announced that she had a blemish on her body that displeased him, and the marriage was dissolved, having lasted little more than a year. The nature of the blemish was not revealed, and in view of his abnormality few doubted that he was more to blame than she for her failure to conceive. She retired without protest into private life, still a virgin.

Far from disguising his sexual tastes, he went out of his way to advertise them, exhibiting himself in public with painted face, often in female clothes, in the company of male lovers. No other Emperor in Roman history made their work so easy for the scandalmongers, and his enemies have recorded a glut of prurient detail. He was not effeminate, however, in his choice of recreation. He had a passion, possibly inherited from Caracalla, for chariot-racing, a sport demanding strength of body and nerves. So devoted was he to this exercise that he had a private course made on which to practise in the grounds of the palace, to which he invited his mother and grandmother as spectators. Later he added another for the same purpose in the Gardens of Ancient Hope in the suburbs.

His performance was often unconventional. He was unable to refrain from fantastic innovation. On occasions he had four huge dogs yoked to the chariot, at other times four stags. His most dangerous feat was a charade in which he impersonated the god Dionysus driving four tigers. A variation practised in the absence of his mother and grandmother was to drive a team of naked girls yoked abreast. The chariot was light, and the girls were strong. They suffered no hurt, except for the flick of his whip across their too vulnerable buttocks.

His humour was impish, but free from ill-will. When guests came to dinner he had the couches piled with cushions whose brocaded covers draped inflated balloons. During the meal a slave crept surreptitiously behind and pierced the cushions with a dagger. The air escaped with a flatulent gurgle, and the victim sank on to hard boards. Another joke of which he was fond was to offer a guest a voluptuous bedmate, lead him to a darkened room and turn the key on him, leaving him there to spend the night with an unwashed crone. Even so, the disappointed philanderer was luckier than those rash enough to drink themselves into a coma at his table. When they woke up they found themselves in a cage shared with a lion or a bear. They were not to know that the beast was the Emperor's pet and quite tame.

Little as his practical jokes endeared him to the victims, they gave amusement and earned him popularity in taverns and barracks. He ran graver risk of offending public opinion with a plan that he put forward in sober earnest. No Syrian Baal was content without a consort, and as Elagabal had left his own behind at Emesa a replacement was needed at Rome. The Emperor, seeking a bride worthy of his god, chose the goddess Pallas whose image known as the Palladium was kept in the temple of Vesta. This was a wooden figure of great antiquity, carved to represent a woman armed with spear and shield. It was among the most hallowed treasures of the Roman people, dropped from heaven according to legend into ancient Troy and brought from there to Rome by Aeneas. The fortune of the city depended on its preservation. The proposal to remove it from its shrine for nuptial intercourse with the Syrian immigrant was not only an outrage to piety but also a disturbing threat to Roman prosperity.

Another shock was in store for religious prejudice. The Emperor announced his intention of marrying a Vestal Virgin, Aquilia Severa, to reinforce the union between god and goddess with an earthly counterpart between priest and priestess. Having divorced Cornelia Paula, he was free to take a new wife, but not from the sacred college of Vestal Virgins, who were under a solemn vow of chastity. He defended his behaviour in a letter to the senate arguing that a child begotten by the high priest of Elagabal on a priestess of Vesta could be little short of divine; but he betrayed his true motive when he added that he was in love with her. She was, it seems, the one girl able to overcome his distaste for the opposite sex. The rare evidence of a natural passion in him failed, however, to reconcile the priesthood to the violation of a Vestal. Dio speaks for established opinion when he describes it as an act 'for which he ought to have been publicly scourged, thrown into gaol and put to death'. The indignation aroused was such that the Emperor yielded, and Aquilia had to go.

His grandmother found him a more suitable wife to take her place, the well-connected widow of a senator executed for sedition after the fall of Macrinus. It was a marriage of convenience intended as an overture to a powerful group in the senate; but it broke up in a few months, and other attempts of a similar kind were equally abortive. He put an end to them at last by bringing Aquilia back into the palace and remarrying her. This time there was no outcry. Her earlier escapade had deprived her of Vestal status.

The proposed marriage between Elagabal and the goddess of the Palladium was also given up in deference to public opinion. The Emperor saved face by announcing that Pallas was too warlike a harridan for a god of peace, and that Elagabal had changed his mind and was sending envoys to Carthage to woo Astarte, the Semitic moon-goddess. Astarte gave a favourable reply, and her image was embarked on a ship to be carried to Rome. It was of an antiquity scarcely less venerable than the Palladium, reputed to have been set up by Queen Dido when Carthage was founded. The Emperor was satisfied, and a temple was built for the convenience of the divine couple during their honeymoon in his favourite suburb, the Gardens of Ancient Hope, where he had his private racecourse. The Romans, untroubled by the fate of a foreign goddess, looked forward with pleasure to the celebrations, expecting from what they knew of the Emperor novelty and entertainment.

They were not disappointed. The bride was installed in the new temple as soon as she arrived, and on the wedding-day the chunk of black rock representing the bridegroom was propped in a chariot studded with gold and jewels to drive in state from the Palatine hill to join her. There was no charioteer. The reins were looped round the stone as if the god himself was driving. To hold the horses to their course, the Emperor kept pace with them with his hand on their bridles, running backwards so that his face was always turned to the god. The street was sprinkled with sand to save him from slipping, and he had men on either side to grasp him if he stumbled. The procession included divine wedding-guests, all the Roman pantheon, whose images were carried by their priests, and a military escort rode in front and behind. Packed crowds lined the way, scattering flowers and brandishing flaring torches. The hour chosen was after dark, so that the glow of torchlight enhanced the splendour and mystery of the equipage.

When the bridal pair had been wedded and bedded, the Emperor climbed to the top of a tower and threw down gifts on the waiting crowd, a shower of utensils of gold and silver, fine clothes, even domestic animals, except pigs whose meat Semitic cults forbade. All scrambled to grab what they could, and a few were hurt when missiles, animate or inanimate, fell on their heads. It was the sort of day Heliogabalus thoroughly enjoyed, a make-believe wedding of dolls and a hilarious romp pelting the crowd with livestock and tableware.

Maesa watched his eccentric behaviour with increasing concern. All through the best years of her life she had remained in the background, while her sister enjoyed power and fame; then suddenly, with the murder of her nephew, followed shortly afterwards by her sister's death, the call had come to her to put her own talents to constructive use, and she had responded with such success, playing the game with skill, that the dynasty was restored and her grandson reigned as Emperor. She was over fifty now, on the verge of old age, entitled to reap the fruits of her efforts. In some respects they fulfilled her expectations, gratifying her ambition and offering scope for the exercise of her ability. She was in a position not only of social eminence, saluted as Augusta, but also of powerful influence in the State, the first woman in Roman history to be admitted into the senate to take part in debates. Her grandson depended on her in the government of the Empire as much as Caracalla had on Julia, her sister, more so indeed as he was quite unfit to perform the work himself.

None the less his unfitness disturbed her, his indulgence in irresponsible whims heedless of consequences. Even at Nicomedia there had been ground for misgivings in the enthusiasm with which he played the part of high priest of Elagabal, and the exaggerated reverence which he lavished on the black stone, a relic of primitive superstition, could attract no sympathy from a mind accustomed to the enlightened ideas of Julia's philosophic circle. To Maesa the god of Emesa was too often a tiresome menace inspiring her grandson to extravagances offensive to Roman prejudice. She had been in time to avert the worst of them all, the desecration threatened to the Palladium; but she could never be sure what fresh folly he might not be cogitating, and she knew that he would keep it from her as long as possible and cling to it with fanatical obstinacy.

His religious antics had at least the merit that they afforded an opportunity for public merrymaking. From this point of view the wedding of Elagabal and Astarte was an outstanding success. No matter if the senators sneered, the people and the soldiers enjoyed themselves, and the Emperor earned their favour. That of the soldiers was especially important. Maesa was quite old enough to remember the events following the death of Pertinax, when the Empire was put up to auction by the Praetorian Guard. The present Emperor had started well with the Praetorians, who esteemed him as Caracalla's son and avenger and admired his courage shown in the battle at Antioch; but now that they were back in barracks in Rome she feared that his popularity was waning. She herself, anxious to curb expenditure, was largely responsible for the fact that, since the banquet given on the occasion of Cornelia Paula's wedding, no further distribution of largess to the soldiers is noted; but the Emperor too was neglectful himself of their interests. Unlike Caracalla, he had no taste for military activities. He insisted on the omission of references to warfare from an inscription put up in his honour:

'I need no titles of war and bloodshed. It is enough for me to be called god-fearing and a bringer of good fortune.'

It did not make his words any more palatable that he spoke with sincerity.

The grievance that rankled worst with the soldiers was his habit of appointing his favourites to lucrative positions of command. These were not men like Comazon, the victor in battle at Antioch, who, whether or not an actor in his youth, had many years of military service to his credit, and whose appointment to be Praetorian Prefect and later to be Prefect of the City was accepted without demur. The new favourites had neither military nor administrative qualifications. They included former charioteers and athletes, a barber, a cook, a mule-driver and a locksmith, all of the humblest birth. The only recommendation that they had in common, and to which they owed their preferment, lay in the success with which they indulged the Emperor's inverted desires.

The scandal provoked angry discontent disguised as virtuous indignation. Even if the soldiers themselves were seldom immaculate in their morals, a convenient target was offered at which to direct their taunts, while they denounced the upstarts whom they hated. Jealousy lay at the root of their resentment. It was galling to have to obey officers who lacked ability and training and were less qualified to command than those whom they commanded. It was more galling still to contrast the level of pay earned in the ranks with the wealth accumulated by these shady adventurers. Fortunately for the Empire, the trouble was confined to the garrison in Rome. The parasites of the Imperial court had no ambition for office, however exalted, far off in the provinces, and the official establishment there was left undisturbed. The Emperor, replying to an address from the senate, could declare with truth that he was sure of the loyalty of the legions on the frontiers. He added ruefully that he wished that he could say the same of the Praetorians.

Nevertheless, when Maesa tried to persuade him to purge his household, to rid it of the most glaring sources of offence, he refused indignantly to give up his friends, and when she persisted he lost his temper. Remembering the fate of Gannys, she let the matter drop. In any case a quarrel between them would benefit no one but their enemies. It was not in her character, however, to sit helpless while her work was undone. At the time of Caracalla's death her elder grandson was the only possible candidate to put forward as Emperor to carry on the dynasty. The younger, Alexianus, was still a child; but he was at an age when every year made a notable difference to his appearance, and the gap of five years between the boys began to lose importance. Alexianus, unlike his cousin, was docile and impressionable, and his mother, Mamaea, to whose control he responded with willing obedience, was the daughter most congenial to Maesa herself. Mamaea, serious-minded and interested in political and religious ideas, was better fitted to exert influence in public affairs than the gay and volatile Sohaemias.

It was a sign of the direction that Maesa's thoughts were taking when rumour hinted that Alexianus as well as his cousin was Caracalla's natural son. A lapse of this sort, not incongruous with the reputation enjoyed by Sohaemias, was hard to believe of the virtuous Mamaea, especially as Caracalla was known to be impotent at the date at which Alexianus was conceived; but Mamaea herself said nothing to refute the calumny, and the story throve on the lips of scandalmongers. Meanwhile efforts were made to bring Alexianus forward to public attention, giving him prominent parts to play on ceremonial occasions. Well coached by his mother and grandmother, he acquitted himself in a manner that disguised his extreme youth. At last Maesa went to the Emperor with the proposal that he should adopt his cousin and give him the title of Caesar, Emperor designate. To sweeten the advice, she pointed out that Alexianus could take some of the cares of State off his shoulders and leave him more time to devote to the service of his god. This appealed to him. The calls of politics were a tiresome burden distracting him from his plans for the exaltation of Elagabal.

He performed the ceremony of adoption without demur in the presence of the senate. Although the proceedings were in accordance with ancient custom, there had never been an occasion before on which the leading players were both so young, a reigning Emperor of seventeen and an Emperor designate of twelve. The circumstances tickled the Emperor's sense of humour. He was in the best of spirits and invited the senators to congratulate him on fathering so well-grown a son. Afterwards he pleased his grandmother by changing the name of Alexianus to Alexander. It was a modification of the name common in the family, there were examples of both Alexianus and Alexander among his ancestors; but the change had peculiar value now in associating the boy with Alexander the Great, the hero worshipped by Caracalla. The allusion was the more timely because of a mysterious apparition reported on the lower Danube. A leader who claimed to be the famous Alexander reincarnate travelled with a band of revellers dressed as Bacchanals through Thrace, where they were entertained at public expense and no one, not even the governor of the province, dared to oppose them. They reached Byzantium and crossed the Bosporus by ship to Chalcedon. There, after performing sacred rites including the burial of a wooden horse, the leader vanished.

The story reveals the nostalgic force exercised in the East by the myth of Alexander enriched with accretions from an older age of heroic legend. This was the sentiment still powerful in men's minds that Caracalla wooed, and his father before him, when they paid so much attention to the cult. The twelve-year-old Alexander could make profitable use of support from the charismatic hero.

At first all went smoothly. The Emperor was fond of his cousin, finding him a biddable companion, and Maesa encouraged them to spend much of their time together. It created a good impression in Rome to see them on friendly terms. The friendship, however, had results less worthy of approval. Alexander consorted not only with his cousin but also with his cousin's friends, whose influence both Maesa and Mamaea deplored. When they complained the Emperor retorted that as adoptive father he had a duty to educate his son in the ways of the world. The world that he meant was that of his private circle, whose standards of speech and manners were notoriously permissive. Grave senators invited to dine at his table returned horrified by the impropriety of the opinions expressed and the subjects discussed. The effect on the pliable Alexander soon became apparent.

Maesa acted with resolution. Declaring that Alexander was neglecting his studies, she took him off to live in a separate wing of the palace with tutors to keep an eye on him, men chosen from the best teachers available. The most eminent of them, in whom she put greatest confidence, was the jurist Ulpian, pupil of her sister's friend and her own, the famous Papinian. Under his supervision Alexander was carefully protected. The brief exposure to his cousin's influence left no lasting impression. He was soon echoing his mother's and grandmother's opinions when they denounced the evils of the court. The studious life suited his natural bent, and he made rapid progress in every subject except Latin. Brought up to speak Greek, he never as long as he lived spoke Latin with fluency, and in spite of his love of reading he got no pleasure from Latin literature.

The Emperor bitterly resented his cousin's removal. He was well aware that the studies were an excuse to keep the boy out of his way, to prevent him from corrupting his morals, and he suspected that everything possible would be done to foster prejudice against him in the boy's mind. As he brooded over his wrongs, his former affection for his cousin yielded to hostility. It occurred to him that the purpose of the adoption was not to relieve but to replace him, and that he was the victim of a cunning intrigue devised by his grandmother. His only ally in the family on whom he could rely was his mother. She listened with unfailing sympathy to his complaints and shared his fears. Neither he nor she, however, had the skill needed to win public opinion and powerful interests to their side, whether by bribery or coercion. They were both too impulsive and indiscreet, helpless against Maesa and Mamaea.

Although Sohaemias, like her mother, bore the title of Augusta, she was unable to enter the senate to plead in person. That was a privilege enjoyed by Maesa alone, an unprecedented tribute to the strength of her personality. The best that the Emperor could do to give Sohaemias prestige was to establish for her benefit a women's senate, over which she presided on the Quirinal hill. The procedure was strictly modelled on that of the superior establishment; but the debates covered nothing more weighty than etiquette and sartorial fashion. There were arguments over the correct dress to be worn at an official sacrifice in the temple of Jupiter, and the very different style appropriate to the Hilaria, the orgiastic climax of the rites of the Phrygian Attis; over the order of precedence when the wife of the minister in charge of the corn supply at Rome met the wife of a former governor of Dacia or Britain; over the rank which entitled a woman to a carriage drawn by mules, and beneath which she must content herself with oxen. These were questions on which Sohaemias could express an informed opinion, and whose discussion amused her; but they had no bearing on the danger threatening her son, the political forces hostile to his authority.

Meanwhile Maesa was busily at work to turn public opinion against him and focus it on Alexander. Fearing to wait any longer, he went in person to the senate to demand that the title of Caesar given to Alexander should be withdrawn and the adoption annulled. The senate listened in grim silence. Not a voice was raised to propose the necessary resolution. If he had been sure of the loyalty of the Praetorians, he could have enforced his will, bullying the senators into submission; but he knew that intrigue was as active in the barracks as the senate-house, nourished by copious draughts of money from the treasury, over which his grandmother held control. Abandoning his purpose, he returned abashed to the palace. He consoled himself for the rebuff by dismissing Alexander's tutors, sending Ulpian into exile. When he heard that even Comazon was of Maesa's party, he deprived him of his post of Prefect of the City, breaking almost his last remaining link with the early days of hope and promise at Emesa.

None the less the victory was Maesa's. She might regret the loss of Ulpian, but he was not irreplaceable. There were other tutors whom she could engage for Alexander. The principal effect of the incident was to leave the Emperor discredited. The senate's refusal to accede to his demand put him to public shame, and she could persist with confidence in her plans to exalt Alexander to the purple. The title of Caesar which he retained gave him already a measure of authority.

As the rift in the family widened, and hope of reconciliation receded, the Emperor's feeling for his cousin turned to burning hatred. Convinced that his own life was in danger while the other lived, he bribed and cajoled some of the attendants in Alexander's part of the palace either to poison Alexander's food or kill him in his bath, whichever was most convenient. Meanwhile, without a word to anyone, even his mother, he set off alone for the Gardens of Ancient Hope, his suburban pleasure-ground, to await the course of events. It was a favourite haunt of his, so that the visit provoked little comment. All assumed that he had a homosexual assignation there.

On arrival he sent orders to the Praetorian barracks to deface all statues of Alexander and remove his name from inscriptions or at least obliterate it with mud. He was counting on the hope that Alexander already was dead, and that when the news reached the Praetorians they would understand how powerful he was and make haste to obey him. His plans, however, went awry both in the palace and at the barracks. The corrupt attendants failed to elude Maesa's vigilance, and the attempt to kill Alexander was thwarted. Meanwhile the Praetorians rejected the Emperor's orders with indignation. Guessing what was afoot, some of them rushed to the palace to protect Alexander, others to the Gardens of Ancient Hope to confront the Emperor in person.

They found him driving a chariot and team of horses round the raceground. He was eagerly awaiting news of his cousin's death, and at first when he saw the soldiers approaching he thought that they came to tell him that his orders had been carried out. Their drawn swords and threatening voices undeceived him as they approached. It was clear that his plans had miscarried. Urging the horses to a gallop, he fled to the temple, the scene of the sacred marriage between Elagabal and Astarte, where he drew up, leapt out and ran into the building to a little room which he used as a bedchamber. A curtain hung behind the door, and he crouched beneath it.

The soldiers came racing after him, and the few attendants on duty in the temple were unable to stop them. An angry crowd burst into the room, found him at once in his too obvious hiding-place and dragged him out. They would have killed him on the spot if the Praetorian Prefect, Antiochianus, had not intervened, reproving them sternly and reminding them of their oath of allegiance. Even so, they were unwilling to be pacified, and the Prefect's own life might have been forfeited if a messenger had not arrived from the detachment sent to the palace, who announced that Alexander was alive and well and that he was on his way with his mother and grandmother under secure escort to the barracks to be out of danger.

At this point the Emperor recovered his boldness of spirit. Cowardice was not among his faults. He declared with dignity that he was ready to accompany the soldiers to the barracks to meet his grandmother, cousin and aunt and listen to their complaints. The soldiers agreed to the proposal and led him off, treating him less as their Emperor than their prisoner. As the barracks lay outside the city the way was through open country, and they saw a woman running ahead of them on the path. They caught her up and found to their surprise that it was his mother Sohaemias. Left behind when the others departed, she had set off on foot in defiance of habit and decorum to follow them to the barracks, too frantic with anxiety for her son to wait for a litter to be prepared. She was overjoyed to meet him still alive and attached herself to the party, determined to fight for him to the death. As things turned out, her role on this occasion was no more than that of a helpless spectator.

At the barracks Antiochianus restored discipline. Instead of clamouring for the Emperor's life the soldiers demanded satisfaction of their grievances, especially the dismissal of his cronies whom they hated. Maesa took charge of the negotiations, less concerned to punish the attempt on Alexander's life than to avoid any encouragement of a mutinous spirit in the troops, any upheaval dangerous to the dynasty. She believed that it was to the interest of the State to put her younger grandson in the elder's place; but there was no need for the latter to come to harm. It was enough to strip him of political power and leave him, as he himself seemed to prefer, to occupy an honourable sinecure, reigning in the temple of Elagabal as Imperial hierophant.

For the present, however, she sought a more limited aim, to remove the venal and incompetent ministers responsible for his misrule and replace them with men of her choosing, who would do her bidding. She told him that if he agreed to this the soldiers would be appeased, and he could resume his reign. He protested and tried to bargain with her, offering to give up some of his favourites if others were spared. The most cherished of these was Hierocles, in origin a Carian slave, who had attracted him first by prowess on the racecourse, then by reciprocity of sexual tastes, so that he was accustomed to call him his 'husband'. He begged with tears to be allowed to retain him, if no one else, declaring that he would rather die than be deprived of his services; but when she pointed to the grim faces of the soldiers around them, whose expression warned him what to expect, he decided that life without a husband was preferable to deposition and death. He returned to the palace to reign under the supervision of his grandmother's friends. They were more capable than his old associates, but less congenial.

His discomfort was aggravated by the persistence used to bring Alexander into prominence. A result was that the cousins, adoptive father and son, were constantly obliged to appear in each other's company on official occasions, in spite of the strained relations created between them by the knowledge that the one had tried to murder the other. An embarrassing ordeal lay before them both when they were named together as consuls for the year beinning on 1 January 222. A senator who congratulated the Emperor on sharing the consulate with his son received the curt reply: 'Next year I hope I'll be luckier and have a real son to share it with.'

If he meant that Aquilia was pregnant, no record survives of her giving birth.

When the day came for the inauguratory ceremony he showed his ill-humour by refusing to accompany Alexander to the senate-house to attend it, and it was not till his mother, remembering with alarm the recent scene in the barracks, spent the morning pleading with him that he relented, put on the prescribed uniform of bordered toga, a garment that he detested, and presented himself late in the afternoon before the waiting dignitaries. For a time he was on his best behaviour to make amends for the discourtesy. He escorted his grandmother in person to a seat of honour. Then, as if the effort had been too much for him, his mood changed, his petulance returned, and he left abruptly without joining his fellow-consul in procession to the temple of Jupiter to take the appropriate oaths. The urban praetor had to act as his proxy, as was the custom in an emergency when the consuls were detained by urgent cares of state. There was no emergency on the present occasion, as everyone knew, to account for his absence.

The gesture of self-assertion seemed to restore his confidence. Having shown his contempt for the senate, he decided to press his advantage and achieve total victory over his enemies. Without consulting his new ministers he issued a decree ordering the senate into long recess, during which the members were forbidden under threat of heavy punishment to stay in Rome. A lively picture is offered by an eyewitness of the resulting scramble. Those without the means to own a carriage searched in haste for an animal to ride. There was a rush to hire or borrow any available horse or mule. Many fled carried ignominiously on the backs of porters. Among those unable to find a conveyance was a certain Sabinus, a senator of consular rank, a friend of Ulpian. The Emperor saw him standing at the gate of his house and called to a centurion who walked with drawn sword at his side, *Caede belle*, 'Give him a good slash'. The centurion, who was rather deaf, thought that he said, *Aede pelle*, 'Drive him out of the house'. He chased Sabinus along the street and into the next, then sheathed his sword and left him unscathed. Sabinus, elderly and portly, suffered nothing worse than unaccustomed exertion, a stitch in his side and loss of breath. The Emperor's anger turned to mirth.

The success of the measures taken against the senate encouraged the Emperor to renew his attempt to oust his cousin from power. He contrived things so that he appeared alone at ceremonies which the two of them would normally have attended together, and when anyone commented on Alexander's absence he replied that the boy was ill, hinting that the illness was likely to be fatal. His subtlety overreached itself, and the effect was not what he intended. A rumour spread through the Praetorian barracks that Alexander was being poisoned. The indignation provoked among the soldiers was such that they went on strike, refusing to serve the Emperor as bodyguard unless he produced Alexander alive and well and brought him to the altar of Mars in the barracks, where they all could see him. The choice of Mars, the Roman war-god, to preside over the event added to the provocation. He stood for everything least compatible with the Syrian Elagabal.

In spite of his experiences on the earlier occasion in the barracks, the Emperor boldly complied with the invitation to meet the men face to face. He put his trust in the sanctity of his office and his personal charm to impress them. The Imperial litter, a magnificent equipage inlaid with gold, was prepared, and he sat in it with Alexander at his side. He refused to be accompanied by his grandmother, unwilling to depend again on her mediation; but he yielded to his mother's insistence when she implored him to let her follow. This time Sohaemias travelled in state, in her own litter emblazoned with her title of Augusta.

As the procession approached the barracks and passed in through the gate the soldiers cheered with enthusiasm, but their cheers were all for Alexander. They peered into the litter to make sure that he was there, called his name and saluted him with good wishes for his health. There was no salute for the Emperor, they paid no attention to him at all. Nevertheless he carried on with the ceremony, and the cousins stood together in seeming concord at the altar of Mars to perform the appropriate rites of sacrifice.

The party spent the night at the barracks, while the Emperor brooded over the affront, pondering what to do to restore his authority. It seemed that his best hope lay in boldness, that if he took the offensive the example would win to his cause many who favoured him in their hearts but shrank from declaring themselves. In the morning therefore he ordered the Prefect Antiochianus, who had shown loyalty on the previous occasion, to arrest the most vociferous of those guilty of demonstrating against him and let it be known that they were to be punished, the rest spared. In spite of the prevailing disorder Antiochianus contrived to do as he was told. He chose the most incorrigible troublemakers and shut them up.

Instead of intimidating the soldiers and recalling them to discipline, the action exasperated their resentment and provoked them to mutiny. The victims chosen to be scapegoats were popular. When their friends heard that they had been seized and fettered, there was a rush to set them free. The uproar grew and spread, till the whole fortress was infected with riot. The few men who remained loyal were outnumbered and hemmed in, and most of them, including Antiochianus himself, were killed.

Sohaemias refused to leave her son in spite of the danger. She took advantage of the confusion to draw him away into a corner where there was an empty crate. It was of the sort used to hold military stores, long pikes and similar weapons. When he crept inside there was room for him to lie in it. She replaced the cover and told her bearers to carry the load out through the gate and declare, if anyone asked them, that it contained supplies for troops in another camp.

They were not allowed to proceed far. Their burden attracted curiosity, and their explanation commanded no belief. A crowd collected, suspecting that treasure was being smuggled out, a huge sum of money ready to be plundered. Eager hands wrested the crate from the bearers; hammers and crowbars smashed it open and revealed the Emperor huddled inside.

His mother, watching appalled, ran to him and clung to him tightly, bending over him to shield his body with her own. The soldiers stabbed both to death, stripped them naked and dragged them through the streets of Rome with jeers of derision. Sohaemias was left at last sprawled on a patch of waste ground, but her son's body was thrown into a sewer flowing down to the Tiber. So ended the reign of Heliogabalus. He died on 13 March 222, shortly before his eighteenth birthday.

A massacre followed of his friends, especially those associated with his pleasures, on whom the same refinement of cruelty was practised as in English history on King Edward II, a burlesque of the act of sodomy performed with a spear. The 'best people' in Rome were jubilant over their bugbear's downfall, and leaders of literary fashion earned laurels, titillating their patrons with scabrous anecdotes about him. Among the most zealous was Aelian, the 'honey-tongued' sophist who charmed Julia Domna's learned circle in the old days with stories of strange beasts. He prided himself now on the tirade that he composed to denounce her great-nephew, whom he nicknamed 'Gynnis', the She-man. Philostratus, to whom he recited it, told him: 'I'd have enjoyed the wit more if you'd published it while he was alive.'

10

The Prudent Princess

Maesa, prevented by her grandson from accompanying him to the barracks, was not present when he and his mother were murdered. Although her own efforts to tamper with the loyalty of the Praetorians were largely to blame, she was taken by surprise and appalled by the violence of the mutiny, which threatened the dynasty with disaster. The purpose of her schemes was to transfer Imperial power to Alexander, in whose name she herself would bear rule, while her elder grandson retired harmless and unharmed into an honourable sinecure of purely sacerdotal dignity. The latter's violent death was an unforeseen development, provoking dangers more formidable than any that preceded it. Even his misrule and his impossible friends were preferable to chaos.

For the moment habits of allegiance checked further excesses. The soldiers acclaimed Alexander as Emperor and escorted him back in triumph to the palace; but the extent of Maesa's alarm is revealed by her haste to present him to the senate, to have his title confirmed before the mutineers could substitute a candidate of their own, better qualified than a boy of thirteen to wear the purple. She even persuaded the senate to confer, in addition to formal recognition, a number of honorific titles borne by earlier Emperors which were not usually assumed till a later stage in the reign. To seal the continuity of the dynasty Alexander appended to his name the honoured cognomen of Severus. No one could fail to remark a connexion between Septimius Severus and Alexander Severus, even if the latter was only great-nephew to the former's wife.

The senate acceded readily to her will, as relieved to be rid of Heliogabalus as earlier of Caracalla. Like Macrinus, she earned favour by contrast with what went before. She was careful to encourage support by promising to treat the senatorial order with respect and make amends for the insolence that it suffered in the previous reign. To prove that she meant what she said, she appointed a council of sixteen senators to advise the Emperor on every aspect of policy. The impression was fostered that the creation of this body restored to the senate something of its old position under the Republic, or at least the share of power that it enjoyed when the Empire was founded; but in fact the new council had no executive authority, and the Emperor was free to accept or reject its advice as he chose. If respect was paid to its opinions, and they carried weight during the reign, the reason lay in the willingness to listen shown by Maesa herself, and later by Alexander when he was old enough to rule.

The members of the council were in any case friends of the Imperial house with a long record of loyalty behind them. Maesa chose for promotion and surrounded herself with men on whom she had relied in the old days at Emesa, or who had braved unpopularity in the senate to serve her sister in the reign of Caracalla. Comazon, commander of the army that defeated Macrinus at Antioch, was restored to his post of Prefect of the City. The chief of her confidants, however, was Ulpian, whom she recalled from exile not to resume his care of Alexander's education but to help her to administer the Empire. He was appointed Praetorian Prefect, a lawyer following the precedent set by Papinian, and to increase his authority she promoted him to consular rank, for which no one holding his office had hitherto been eligible. She put him on a level where he could deal with senators on equal terms.

He for his part supported with legal acumen her role, distasteful to Roman tradition, of female regent. Although her sister's example helped to reconcile prejudice, it was not a true equivalent. Caracalla delegated part of the work of government to his mother, whose decisions were taken subject to his will. Maesa, acting on behalf of a child, exercised supreme power. To validate her authority Ulpian added to the maxim that the Emperor is above the law the rider that, although the Augusta is not above the law, she can acquire from the Emperor the same privileges that he possesses himself. The boy Alexander, he argued, conferred these on his grandmother. Inscriptions surviving from the period show the care taken to accustom the Roman world to the idea. Alexander's lineage is traced in the maternal line, 'son of Julia Mamaea, grandson of Julia Maesa'.

The manners of the court were reformed. Neither Maesa nor Mamaea approved of the standards that prevailed in the previous reign. Guests henceforward could attend official banquets without fear of suddenly deflated cushions, a lodging shared with a bear or other tricks of Imperial puckishness. No team of pretty girls, naked and callipygous, obeyed the crack of the charioteer's whip, competing on the racecourse. Religion too resumed a soberer aspect. The black stone representing Elagabal was sent back to Emesa, and the temples built in his honour were re-dedicated to gods of the Roman pantheon, that on the Capitoline hill to Jupiter the Avenger. Grave citizens expressed relief, but the common people of Rome regretted the change. They missed Heliogabalus and his comic turns.

Maesa lived for only three years after Alexander's accession. She died in her middle fifties just when her ambition was achieved. Although she lacked her sister's beauty and charm and never shone as the presiding genius of poets and philosophers, she was her equal in strength of will and talent for statecraft. She saved the dynasty from disaster after the murder of Caracalla and was the architect of its restoration to power. It was her misfortune that, when the task was accomplished, a freakish grandson thwarted her efforts to make it bear fruit, and that when his death left the way open at last for a more amenable successor she herself survived so short a time to enjoy the opportunity.

Her daughter Mamaea, left alone to carry on the matriarchy, inherited much of her administrative ability. The Empire throve during the next ten years, while her son was nominally, she herself actually, in control of affairs. She lacked, however, her mother's formidable presence and was less capable of controlling the turbulence of the Praetorian Guard. The affection professed by the soldiers for Alexander and their concern to protect him lost force now that his cousin was dead and he himself their master, and the flow of bribes dried up, no longer needed to outbid the rival party in the family. The new Prefect, Ulpian, made himself unpopular by the severity of the measures that he imposed to maintain discipline, anxious to show that a lawyer could be as firm as a soldier. He followed the example set by Papinian, but unlike Papinian he had no Septimius behind him to reinforce his efforts.

Resentment mounted in the barracks, and an incident small in its beginnings brought matters to a head. A party of soldiers became involved in a drunken brawl with the citizens in a humble quarter of the city, and the quarrel grew into a battle as more and more of the local youths ran to join in on one side, and soldiers to help their comrades on the other. The Praetorians were disliked in Rome for their insolent manners, and it was a source of friction too that, since the reforms introduced by Septimius, they were recruited from distant provinces alien in customs and speech. The fighting lasted for three days with heavy casualties, till the soldiers getting the worst of it set fire in retaliation to the houses, and the inhabitants made peace for fear that the whole street would be burnt down.

On the first night of the tumult Ulpian came in person to try to stop it; but he had too few men with him to impress the rioters, and in the darkness and confusion he was cut off from his party and fled unattended through the streets with a mob of Praetorians on his heels. He ran to the palace and took refuge in the room where Mamaea was sitting with her son, the Emperor. Undeterred, the Praetorians still pursued, overpowered the servants on duty and burst in after him into the Imperial presence. Mamaea and Alexander protested in vain. He was killed on the spot under their eyes.

Ulpian was dead, but the Emperor and his mother were left unharmed. The soldiers had sufficient respect not to offer them violence and withdrew from the palace content with their night's work. The chief blame for the incident was traced to a freedman called Epagathus, who bore Ulpian a grudge and offered a reward for his murder. This Epagathus was a wealthy tycoon who owed his fortune to contempt for political scruples under successive régimes. Having enjoyed the favour of Caracalla, he changed sides on Caracalla's death and took service with Macrinus, who put such trust in his professions of loyalty that he charged him with the mission to escort his son safely into Parthia. Intercepted on a bridge over the Euphrates, Epagathus made a bargain with his captors to surrender the boy to be put to death in return for a pardon for himself. Thereafter he prospered again, acquiring such influence among vested interests of commerce and finance in Rome that in spite of his responsibility for Ulpian's murder Mamaea feared to order his arrest. Her vengeance was delayed, but his guilt not forgotten. She offered him the lucrative post of governor of Egypt, which he accepted with joy. As soon as he landed in Egypt he was hurried aboard a ship sailing to Crete where, out of sight of his cronies in Rome, the executioner awaited him.

Intermittent trouble with the Praetorian Guard continued during the reign, but never on a scale seriously to threaten the stability of the government. When Dio, having governed Pannonia with a severity that earned him a bad reputation among the soldiers, was appointed consul with Alexander for the year 229, he was warned by Alexander that the Praetorians were in a dangerous mood, fearing the same treatment to themselves, and it would be better for him not to venture into

Rome but to perform his consular duties from a safe distance at Rhegium on the toe of Italy. Dio boasts that, in spite of this, he visited Rome to meet the Emperor, and the soldiers saw him and did him no harm. He was careful, however, not to tempt fortune too long. The visit lasted only for a day or two. A convenient attack of gout gave him the excuse to cut it short.

Alexander was too mild and amiable to assert himself effectively. His dependence on his mother, persisting even when he grew to manhood, sprang from a congenital weakness of character, on which his upbringing and the habit that it fostered left an indelible impression. He had his cousin's example to warn him of the evil consequences of wilfulness, but he scarcely needed the admonition to persuade him to submit to guidance. Obedience came naturally to him, and there were few occasions when he and his mother failed to think alike.

When he was of an age to marry she chose the bride, Barbia Orbiana, a girl of impeccably aristocratic family. He was well satisfied with the choice, and the young couple lived happily together, till trouble arose between the girl and her mother-in-law. Mamaea became jealous when Orbiana received the title of Augusta, made equal in rank to herself. Alarm was added to jealousy when Alexander went on to confer the title of Caesar on Orbiana's father. In the circumstances, as with Gannys in the previous reign, it was never likely to be more than honorific, as the reigning Emperor was so much younger than his father-in-law designated to succeed him. Nevertheless Mamaea feared that her son paid too much attention to the interests of his wife's family, and that a rival power was growing that threatened her own. She knew Alexander too well to put confidence in his resistance.

The rift widened between her and her daughter-in-law, and Alexander's efforts to mediate had no success. At last after an especially bitter dispute ending im mutual recrimination Mamaea drove Orbiana out of the palace, and the girl fled in tears to her father, who, furious at the treatment that she suffered, set off for the Praetorian barracks, the unfailing resort of the disaffected. He insisted that he had no quarrel with the Emperor, to whom he was grateful for the honour shown him, but he called on the soldiers to support him against the Emperor's mother and avenge the insult put on the Emperor's wife. He hoped that by drawing the distinction he would avoid the guilt of sedition, but Alexander disappointed him. Compelled to choose between his mother and his wife, he yielded to the habit of filial obedience, and his appearance in person at the barracks at the head of loyal forces turned the scale. The waverers returned to their allegiance and the revolt fizzled out. Orbiana and her father were both arrested. The former was banished to Africa with her marriage dissolved, the latter put to death.

Alexander never married again. The picture that emerges of him from contemporary accounts is of a shy young man of quiet tastes, who shrank from responsibility and was glad to let his mother bear it in his place. If he had a fault in her eyes it arose from the informality of his manners, for which she reproved him in vain, as did his wife too while their short marriage lasted. He liked to meet his friends on familiar terms, visiting them and encouraging them to visit him without invitation. On all occasions his bearing was unpretentious; he hated to be addressed as *Domine*, 'Lord', and wished to be called simply by name as Alexander. Like Septimius, he presided with reluctance over a formal banquet, preferring to dine with a single congenial companion or by himself with a book beside him, usually Greek as he read Latin with difficulty. He was fond of music, had a good singing voice and could play with skill on various instruments, but he indulged the taste strictly in private to an audience of his household alone, for fear that the censorious might complain of conduct unbecoming in an Emperor. Another source of pleasure was his aviary, in which he kept pea-fowl, pheasants, partridges, ducks and doves. With a frugality inherited from his mother he covered the cost of upkeep by the sale of eggs and young birds for the table.

His mother was indeed notorious for the care that she took to save and accumulate money, earning thereby a reputation for parsimony and avarice. This trait in her character provoked one of the few disputes recorded between her and him. He protested with indignation when she used her powers to bar an inheritance and confiscate the property. Not enough is known of the circumstances to explain her motive with any certainty. The succession of political changes in recent years left many men of ambition discontented and unsettled, ready for subversive action to repair their fortunes, and the danger was aggravated when troublemakers could appeal to ancient prejudice against a government controlled by a woman, and a Syrian at that. Glad as she no doubt was to fill the treasury, there can have been wisdom too in Mamaea's confiscations, concern to nip treason in the bud by depriving it of funds. It does not convict her of injustice that the victims carried their woes to the soft-hearted Emperor to trade on his sympathy.

Her care for finance had useful results. She was vigilant in restraining corruption and peculation, and some at least of the saving effected in the cost of government was passed on to the governed in reduction of taxation. A well-filled treasury was able also to support schemes which encouraged the production of food by small farmers, rather than from estates cultivated by slaves on behalf of absentee owners. The purchase of land was aided by loans of public money granted at a moderate rate of interest, or in suitable circumstances even interest-free, whose repayment could be deferred till the farm was working at a profit (Pertinax, thirty years earlier, had a similar scheme in mind). At the same time a strict control was exercised on prices to forestall the fluctuations of the market. During a shortage of beef and pork an Imperial decree forbade the slaughter of cows and calves, sows and sucking pigs. The butcher had to be content with steers and hogs, while the farmer built up his livestock and restored the supply of meat.

Another field in which the government intervened to ease the burden of expense was that of public administration. Hitherto it had been obligatory for a magistrate assuming office to celebrate his inauguration with performances of gladiators and similar shows in the amphitheatre at an oppressive cost to himself. Under the new enactment the crowd still had their entertainment, but the bill was paid by the State. To save hardship to an officer appointed to a post in the provinces where a costly establishment was necessary, an old custom was revived, obsolete since the days of the Republic: the State provided a large part of the equipment, including servants, horses and mules, official robes, silverware, with the addition, if the officer was a bachelor, of a suitable concubine. Anyone earning approval in office was allowed to retain the outfit as a perquisite at the end of his term; but those guilty of extortion and embezzlement had to return everything in quadruplicate. If this included the concubine, the government ran the risk of accumulating an embarrassing surplus of second-hand girls.

Alexander's reign came to be regarded by later generations as a watershed, beyond which the time of troubles began, a succession of ephemeral Emperors and barbarian inroads. A golden glow bathed it in retrospect, so that its blemishes were forgotten. Nevertheless the impression left on popular memory was not wholly false. If the Praetorian Guard at times was unruly, and there were riots in the streets of Rome, the government was strong enough none the less to restore order, and except during the last years of the reign the frontiers of the Empire remained unbroken, the Roman world was at peace. The reforms introduced to conciliate the senate, such as the appointment of an advisory council, made little difference in fact to the balance of power, and the Emperor's will was still supreme; but they encouraged respect for traditional dignity and promoted harmony in the State. Mamaea could boast with justice that Rome wore a face never more Roman than under a Syrian dynasty.

Like her aunt, she combined political ability with a fervent interest in religion. It had nothing in common with her nephew's obsession with the cult of Elagabal, the tribal god of Emesa. Her purpose was closer to Julia's, to study the tenets of every religion, choose the best from each and compound them into an acceptable body of belief, in which all men could find comfort and a measure of truth. If she differed from her aunt, it was in the greater sympathy that she extended to the ideas of the Jews and Christians. In the shrine kept in the palace for private worship there were images not only of the deified Emperors but also of Abraham and Christ, as well as pagan heroes and teachers like Alexander the Great, Orpheus and Apollonius. A plan was even considered to build, with the Emperor's blessing, a temple to Christ in Rome, but it aroused too much opposition and had to be abandoned. Senators remembered too clearly the licence encouraged at the dedication of the temple to Elagabal, and the part that they themselves were compelled to play in the rites. They were determined not to risk a repetition, whether in honour of Christ or any other Eastern god.

Christianity at this time enjoyed a respite from persecution. There had been none of any extent since the reign of Marcus Aurelius. The spasmodic outbreaks under Commodus and Septimius Severus were confined to particular districts and depended on the attitude of the local authority. They ceased altogether when the Syrian Princesses controlled affairs. The Christian community had peace from external enemies, but its condition was far from peaceful within. A fierce struggle was raging between two factions in the Church at Rome, one of them with a Greek, the other with a Latin background. The latter was the larger, and its leader, Callistus, held the title of Bishop of Rome. His claim was contested by the leader of the opposition party, Hippolytus, who set himself up as Antipope.

The professed ground of dispute between them lay in doctrine defining the nature of Christ. Callistus, who insisted on the indivisibility of the Godhead, was accused by Hippolytus of the heresy that God the Father hung on the Cross. He retorted that the heretic was Hippolytus, who, by distinguishing the Divine nature of the Son from that of the Father, betrayed himself as a 'ditheist', a believer in two gods. The doctrinal subtlety was embittered by personal jealousy. Hippolytus denounced Callistus as an unscrupulous thruster usurping a title that should have been his own. The Christians were no longer a brotherhood of unworldly devotees relying on the spirit alone for cohesion. As the movement grew it attracted converts active in many branches of secular life, and to organize relations between them and with the world in which they lived office-holders were needed, a graded hierarchy. The topmost grade became an envied distinction, and frustrated ambition provoked strife.

The story of Callistus illustrates the conditions prevailing in the Church at this date. He was a slave employed in Rome by a certain Carpophorus, a freedman of Marcus Aurelius, to take charge of a banker's stall at the Public Fishpool, the financial quarter of the city. His master was a Christian like himself. Whether from incompetence or dishonesty the business was unsuccessful, and depositors losing their money complained of him to Carpophorus, who demanded to see his accounts. Callistus, unable or unwilling to produce them, fled to Ostia and boarded a ship that was taking on cargo, about to put to sea; but while the ship still lay at anchor in mid-harbour he saw Carpophorus approaching, ferried towards them in a boat. The ferryman was rowing slowly, and Callistus had time if he wished to hide; but he knew that the ship would be searched, and he himself found. In despair he jumped into the water, ready to drown as he could not swim. The sailors jumped in after him and pulled him out against his will.

They held him fast till the arrival of his master, who took him back to Rome and set him to work in the bakery grinding corn at the treadmill, a job that was not only physically exhausting but also much beneath the dignity of a cashier employed at a banking stall. After some time his friends in the local congregation went to plead on his behalf with Carpophorus, whom they reproached for behaving so harshly to a fellow-Christian. Carpophorus replied that he was less concerned about the loss of his own money than moved by the tears of the depositors, widows and other needy persons, whose trust Callistus had abused. Then the friends told him that Callistus had money of his own put away somewhere, and that if he were released from the mill he would be able to collect it to meet his liabilities. Carpophorus agreed to allow him time off for this purpose.

Callistus had invested his private hoard in a loan to a Jew, to whom he hurried to reclaim it; but it was the Sabbath, and the Jew was absent from home at the synagogue. Too agitated to wait for a more suitable occasion, Callistus followed him there, entered the room where the Jews were assembled at prayer and called to his debtor that he wished to speak to him on an urgent matter. The Jews, resenting the interruption and recognizing him as a Christian, supposed that he came deliberately to insult their religion. They set on him and beat him, then dragged him off to the City Prefect, complaining that this was a Christian who stirred up factious strife in the synagogue to disturb the peace to which they were entitled by Roman law.

When Carpophorus heard of the arrest, he feared that he would lose ownership of Callistus, because a slave convicted of a criminal offence was forfeited to the State. He made haste to the court, where he denied that Callistus was a Christian and identified him as his fugitive slave against whom he had a claim for missing money. The second part of the statement was true, but the first part a lie intended to refute the charge that Callistus acted from motives of sectarian malice. The Prefect, more convinced by the evidence of the Jews than by the pleas of Carpophorus, found Callistus guilty of riotous behaviour and sentenced him to be transported to the silver-mines in Sardinia. These workings in the south-west of the island near the modern town of Iglesias were notorious for the unhealthiness of the climate and the severity of the conditions to which the labour force, mainly consisting of convicts, was condemned. The galleries were narrow and ill-ventilated, liable to frequent flooding, and lit only by the glimmer of a lighted wick in a saucer of oil set in niches at distant intervals. For living quarters the men had a cave in which to eat and sleep. They spent months on end underground without a glimpse of daylight, and with little chance of escape as the only egress from the mine was by a ladder up a vertical shaft, with soldiers on guard at the top.

Callistus was still there when Marcia, the mistress of the Emperor Commodus, exerted herself, as has been related in an earlier chapter, to obtain relief for persecuted Christians. She persuaded the Emperor to pardon those condemned to the Sardinian mines, and the Bishop of Rome gave her a list of their names, which her foster-father, a Christian himself, carried with him to Sardinia, so that all named in it might be released. Callistus, however, was omitted from the list, because of the unfavourable report given of his character by Carpophorus. When he heard that the others were allowed to go free, but that he himself must stay in subterranean torment, he was in such despair that Marcia's foster-father, a merciful man, agreed on his own responsibility to add him to the party. In this way he returned to Rome, and as Marcia still enjoyed the Emperor's favour the irregularity was overlooked.

His return caused surprise and displeasure to many in the Christian community, especially Carpophorus. As his status was that of a convict pardoned by the Emperor, he could no longer be claimed as a slave and was free to do what he wished. To allay strife, the Bishop suggested that he should move to Antium some fifty miles to the south on the coast, and the community paid him an allowance to live there. It is evident that in spite of his misadventures he enjoyed sympathy and support from a large body, probably the majority, of the Church in Rome, those who were more concerned with the needs of daily life in a pagan world than with austere standards of doctrinaire purity. He was the leader of this party of compromise, and when the Bishop died he won the confidence of his successor, who consulted him over the management of the clergy and finally invited him back to Rome to take charge of the cemetery on the AppianWay which still bears his name. When the next vacancy occurred, Callistus himself was chosen to be Bishop of Rome, and his enemies protested in vain.

This was the man who presided over the Christians at the beginning of Alexander's reign. If the foregoing account of his life draws an unflattering portrait, much of the reason lies in the fact that the source is a work written by his enemy Hippolytus, leader of the opposing party in the Church. The account reveals even clearer animosity when it goes on to attack Callistus for his conduct in episcopal office, for enticing converts to his party with promises of indulgence to sin and re-admitting sinners whom Hippolytus had expelled from the congregation. Other charges are that he permitted second and even third marriages to the clergy (it was a tenet of strict Christians that the nuptial bond was not severed by death), and condoned the behaviour of an unattached woman if she sought a temporary union with a slave, which she could dissolve at will. In defence of his easygoing standards Callistus is said to have quoted the example of Noah's Ark, which contained specimens of unclean as well as clean beasts. The controversy is evidence of the stresses that arose in the Church as it tried to adapt itself to pagan society. Nevertheless, it seems that the worst offence committed by Callistus in the eyes of Hippolytus, far outweighing his shortcomings in discipline and in doctrine, was his occupation of the see of Rome. Hippolytus could not forgive him for leading the larger party and claiming the title with better right than his own.

Callistus died, killed in a riot, within a year or so of Alexander's accession; but Hippolytus, with claims still unrecognized, carried on the feud with his successors, and the jealousy persisted till the end of Mamaea's life. The event that at last brought reconciliation was the persecution following the fall of the dynasty, when the Christians, regarded as its friends, were singled out for vengeance. Both Hippolytus and his rival were arrested, and making common cause in common misfortune they put their quarrel aside. They were sent to the mines in Sardinia, where, older and weaker than Callistus at the time of his own ordeal, they succumbed to the hardships and died.

More than a century later the old enemies, Callistus and Hippolytus, Pope and Antipope, ascended to glory on equal terms. Both were recognized as saints and martyrs, and both are commemorated in the calendar of the Church, Callistus on 14 October, Hippolytus on 13 August.

The Christians were peculiarly liable to internal discord because their organization was comparatively new and the order of precedence less established by tradition than in most of the pagan priesthoods. To a student of their ideas like Mamaea a dispute over the tenure of an office could have little importance; but the doctrinal battle into which the rivals plunged to support their respective claims provoked a question of inescapable difficulty. Christianity insisted on the authority of revelation over reason. When pagan inquirers trained in Greek philosophy wished to argue the merits of the case, they received an answer in the words already quoted from Tertullian: 'We have no need to ask questions, having the Gospel.' The foundation of this certitude was shaken if Christians themselves could not agree what the Gospel taught.

Tertullian died early in Alexander's reign. Before his death he himself was accused of unorthodoxy by the majority of the Church because of his adherence to the sect known as Montanists. The issue, however, was more practical than speculative. The Montanists deplored any concession to the demands of the pagan world. They looked back with nostalgia to the days when Christians were a little group hidden in the multitude of mankind, like the leaven in the parable, setting an example of piety and virtue. Inflexible in obedience to the rules of their faith, they courted persecution and welcomed it as the means to a crown of martyrdom. This attitude brought them into conflict with mundane fellow-Christians, who wanted to live in peace with secular authority, and as the rift grew wider the Montanists hardened into a sect of zealots convinced of their exclusive claim to sanctity and so ascetic in their principles that unmarried girls were forbidden to show their faces unveiled.

Something of their influence can be traced in the violence with which Hippolytus attacks Callistus for his tolerance of human frailty; but the principal ground on which the two chose to denounce each other was that of opinions derived from interpretation of the doctrine of the Trinity. This was a question destined in years to come to split Christendom into warring factions, when Arius on the one side and

Athanasius on the other led their forces into battle over an iota—the letter '*i*' which alone distinguishes the Greek words *homoousios* and *homoiousios*, 'of the same nature' and 'of like nature', relating the second to the first person of the Trinity. At present, however, while the controversy provided fodder for clerics in dispute, it had little meaning for ordinary Christians, who were more concerned to practise their religion without offence to their pagan neighbours than to worry over theological subtleties. For Mamaea it had less importance still. Not being a Christian, she had no need to believe in the Christian Trinity at all.

Issues of wider appeal were raised by the Gnostic movement, whose doctrines had been active in the Church since the beginning of the preceding century and still commanded a large body of support in spite of efforts to condemn them as heresy. They had the attraction for Mamaea that, unlike orthodox Christianity, they borrowed ideas from the pagan religions of the East, also from the later schools of Greek philosophy. The problem that occupied the Gnostics was that of the origin of evil. They were not content with the crude dualism of God and Satan inherited from Jewish tradition. Like Plato, they identified perfection with spirit, imperfection with matter, and they asked how the perfect ever came to admit the imperfect, the spiritual the material.

Valentinus, the greatest of them, offers an answer in the form of a myth. The plenitude of the Godhead existed self-sufficient, till Wisdom, one of the Divine attributes, craved for love and descended into Chaos, the gulf of non-being, to find it. In consequence she was transformed into Achamoth, a fallen spirit, who conceived from the consummation of her love and gave birth to a son, the Creator of the material world. The fall of Achamoth and her redemption and restoration to the God-head are events belonging to eternity; but the redemption of the material world, for whose creation she was responsible, took place in the field of time through the intervention of Jesus Christ. This myth differs from the orthodox story of the fallen angels in the motive that it attributes. Satan yields to ambition, Achamoth to love. The revolt arises within the Divine nature itself from the need of the One to seek satisfaction in the Many. The purpose is explained in the words of Valentinus, that 'love is not love unless there is something to be loved'.

Valentinus died in the middle of the second century, and although the movement that he inspired still flourished in the early part of the next his ideas suffered distortion and accretion, imperfectly understood by many who called themselves his followers. The behaviour of the less enlightened brought Gnostic teaching into disrepute. Professing contempt for the carnal, the fruit of the fall, they alternated between a

G

rigid asceticism and the antinomian view that, as the flesh lacked reality, its indulgence could incur no blame. In addition, the air of superiority with which they set themselves apart from the common run of mankind gave offence to the main body of Christians and did more even than their doctrines to persuade the Church to condemn them as heretics. Nevertheless the Gnostic myth held seeds whose growth had a healthy influence on Christian thought. The redemption of Achamoth was not a restitution of things as they were before. Her fall brought the material world into being and revealed the Divine purpose more fully, to reconcile creation with the spirit of God.

An intelligent pagan like Mamaea studying Christianity could find more with which to sympathize in Gnostic heresy than in teaching bounded by a literal interpretation of the Scriptures, especially when these included the Old as well as the New Testament. Jehovah to her was a Baal similar in rank and function to her own Elagabal at Emesa. Even if Jewish tradition could make a contribution of value to truth, its local god had no right on grounds either of reason or moral excellence to claim superiority over others. Christian apologists themselves were often hard put to it to reconcile the message of Christ with Jewish national ambition. They could not afford, however, to cut themselves adrift and depend for evidence on the Gospels and Epistles alone. A background of venerable antiquity was indispensable to establish the credentials of a religion and win converts. Jehovah with all his faults helped to disguise the novelty of the movement founded in Galilee.

The most famous of the Christian teachers alive at the time, Origen, had a way of his own to get over the difficulty. When a passage from the Old Testament, or the New either, seemed to conflict with the doctrine that he taught, he explained that the words of the inspired book were allegorical, and that when the true purpose hidden beneath the literal meaning was uncovered conflict was eliminated. The method had the advantage that it retained the sanctity of ancient tradition without the embarrassment of obsolete ideas incompatible with morality or rational belief. Allegorical interpretation was in accord with accepted principles of contemporary thought. Many philosophers applied it to Homer to give authority to their views, as did Plutarch rather earlier to the Egyptian myth of Isis and Osiris. Origen, whose life and writings bear witness to the integrity of his character, could use it in good faith to promote a reconciliation of philosophy and Christian revelation. Later ages rejected a method that imposed a meaning on the Bible instead of accepting what was offered, and it smacks perhaps a little of Humpty Dumpty: 'When I use a word, it means just what I choose it to mean.' Nevertheless, if Origen had prevailed, mankind could have been spared much suffering inspired by fidelity to the letter of Holy Writ. Texts would have afforded less support to armed bigotry and sanctimonious acquisitiveness.

He was born at Alexandria in the reign of Commodus in 185. His parents were probably pagan at the time, as they gave him a name derived from Egyptian mythology, Origen meaning 'born of Horus'; but they were converted soon afterwards to Christianity, and he was educated at the famous school of Christian teaching which flourished at Alexandria under Clement, the eminent Father of the Church. Before he was twenty his father lost his life in a persecution when a Prefect unfriendly to the Christians held office in Egypt; but a rich woman in the congregation took a fancy to the orphaned boy, and with her help he was able to continue his education. Nevertheless he was so impoverished that he had to earn a livelihood copying manuscripts, and he sold all the books that he possessed on literature and philosophy, preserving only those that dealt with Christian doctrine. He parted with the books the more willingly because of an emotional crisis through which he was passing. Inspired by his father's martyrdom, he craved with ardour to become a martyr himself, rejected pagan learning with abhorrence and adopted a relentlessly ascetic way of life. In an access of frenzy against the temptations of the flesh he castrated himself.

It was an act for which later he suffered bitter remorse, condemning it as interference with God's will, depriving him of understanding of humanity. It brought its own punishment also in the obstacle that it created to his career. Tradition opposed the ordination of a eunuch as priest. When he outgrew the prejudices of adolescence, and became the leader of the movement to accommodate Christian revelation to Greek philosophy, his enemies were glad to have this lever to obstruct his promotion.

At first, however, he was regarded with benevolence by the dignitaries of the Church. From pupil he rose to be a teacher at the school and was able to earn an adequate income. His range of knowledge and gift for imparting it made so favourable an impression on the Bishop of Alexandria, Demetrius, that when Clement resigned Origen was put in charge of the school in his place. He held the post for twenty-eight years from 203 to 231, during which he attained such fame that pagans as well as Christians were attracted to his lectures. Hitherto Christianity had been despised in intellectual circles as a barbarous superstition, an offshoot of Jewry. Origen exalted its status, arguing with the philosophers on their own ground, offering his doctrine as a rival to theirs worthy to be judged by the same standards.

His work at the school kept him in residence at Alexandria except for a short period in 216 when he fled from Caracalla's massacre and its aftermath and travelled in Palestine. There is a record too of a visit that he paid in the course of these years to Rome, when he attended a sermon preached by the schismatic Bishop Hippolytus. Mamaea was on friendly terms with Hippolytus, whom she encouraged to write a treatise on the Resurrection; but she missed the chance to talk to Origen, a man better qualified to explain the tenets of Christianity in language that she could understand. He came and went without attracting attention, and thereafter he was busy in Egypt and she in Rome. Although she heard much of his growing reputation she was unable to meet him, till in 231 when she was at Antioch for the Persian war—of which more will be said in the next chapter—she took advantage of her proximity to summon him to visit her and sent a guard of honour of Praetorians to escort him.

He was no longer living at Alexandria but at Caesarea on the coast of Palestine in ecclesiastical disgrace. Ever since his flight at the time of the massacre there had been friction in his relations with Demetrius, his Bishop, who blamed him on his return to Alexandria for the fact that, while he was abroad, he, a layman, preached sermons in church. The Bishops of Jerusalem and Caesarea, less rigid in their views, had been willing to overlook a breach of the rule that reserved to priests the right to speak in church; but Demetrius would allow no such concession, least of all to Origen, whom he himself refused to ordain. He justified his intransigence on the ground not only of the mutilation inflicted on himself by Origen in his youth but also of the heterodoxy of his teaching, both in its method and its content. To pore over niceties of doctrine and elucidate them in voluminous tomes set an example, the Bishop declared, more fit for a pagan philosopher than a simple follower of Christ. The commentary on the Gospel of Saint John, on which Origen was engaged, was already into its fifth volume, having covered so far only ten verses of the first chapter.

Demetrius had a more serious complaint, however, which he did not put into words. He was jealous of Origen, whose reputation far surpassed his own. As time went by, the controversy became more and more embittered. The greater the respect that Origen enjoyed in the world, the more stubbornly Demetrius denied him ordination, till at last Origen took the matter into his own hands, went to Palestine and got a friendly Bishop there to ordain him. Demetrius was enraged, and when Origen returned he was summoned before a diocesan synod which deprived him of his post at the school and banished him from Alexandria. As the sentence hinted at threats of violence if he did not obey, he withdrew from the country, and a further synod convened in his absence proceeded to annul the orders conferred on him. Although the greater part of the Church accepted the decision of the Eygptian synod, the Bishops in Palestine, Phoenicia, Arabia and Greece stood firm on his side, and he settled at Caesarea to continue his teaching. The school that he founded there surpassed in renown that at Alexandria.

Mamaea, uncommitted to Christian belief, had no interest in the internal disputes of the Church, whether it was a question of Origen's ordination to the priesthood or of the conflicting claims of Callistus and Hippolytus to the title of Bishop of Rome. She invited Origen to meet her because he was the most eminent spokesman of Christianity alive at the time, and the likeliest to be in sympathy with her open-minded quest for truth. He himself, discussing those who ascribe divinity to the sun and moon and whole order of heaven, as did the lore inherited by the priests of Elagabal, declares that, although they err, their error is of a better sort than that of worshippers of gods made by hand. He is not among the Christians who opposed themselves utterly to the ideas and values of pagan society. He regarded these as a stage in the process whose culmination was the coming of Christ. His Christianity was no ruthless innovator sweeping everything away to make room for its own building. Its function was rather to complete the buildings already standing, to remove their blemishes and illuminate them with glory.

He sought an answer to the question; why does the world exist? Accepting from Plato the division of things into spirit and matter, and from the later Platonists the multiplicity of steps by which the former descends into the latter, he differed from pagan philosophy in insisting that men have freedom of will to climb back up again, and that God himself came into the world to teach them how to do so. In the Incarnation he sees the intervention of the Divine teacher or, in another figure of speech, of the good physician. The Cross bears no meaning of barter, it denotes only the pain that the effort cost. The pain will and must bear fruit, God's patience is never exhausted. If he cannot win a human soul in this life, he defers its cure to the next. Origen believed in an innumerable succession of worlds, in the pre-existence and re-incarnation of the soul. The Divine teacher has no need to hurry. He has infinite time for the accomplishment of his loving purpose.

There is present here, as in the Gnostic myth of the fall of Achamoth, the implication that good comes of evil, that the soul climbing back up the steps enters a state better than that from which it fell. In later ages the Church condemned this idea as heresy. It was incompatible with the doctrine which, borrowed from the ancient religion of Persia, had become an essential article of Christian faith, that of war between God and the Devil. In any case, if all souls are destined to be saved, where are the enemies for the Church militant to fight? What becomes of hell without prisoners to torment? Questions of this sort were already being asked in Origen's lifetime, especially in the synod which expelled him from the school at Alexandria. He was accused of teaching that even the Devil will find salvation at last. He denied the heresy, but admitted that he might have said something like it in the heat of argument. It was not in his eyes a matter of importance. The Devil was less real for him than the image of the good physician at work among his patients, of whom some are still bedridden, others already convalescent.

All that is recorded of his meeting with Mamaea at Antioch is that they had a long conversation, in which he said what he could to show her 'the glory of the Lord and the value of the Divine teaching'. Then he returned with the same guard of honour to escort him to Caesarea to resume his work in the school. So bald a report does scant justice to an event without parallel in the history of the pagan Roman Empire, an official invitation to a Christian leader to confer with the Emperor's mother, who held more effective authority than the Emperor himself. Origen's teaching offered much that was likely to appeal to her. Crude symbols played no part in her religion. The black stone was sent back to Emesa as soon as her nephew was dead, and her son, ashamed of the associations, took it as an affront to be described as 'Syrian high priest'. Her interest lay in ideas, and like her aunt she was ready to listen, no matter where they came from. While the Christians, however, with whom Julia Domna came in contact repelled her by opposing faith to reason, Origen was able to link revelation to philosophy and fit it into the familiar background of ancient culture. Texts were no longer a stumbling-block, when allegory was at hand to explain them away.

A hundred years later the Emperor Constantine was converted to Christianity, which soon became the official religion of the Roman Empire. The Church triumphed, but it was not a victory in which Origen would have felt at home. Constantine needed a spiritual ally to support his new model of Empire arising from the ruins of the old after half a century of chaos, a Church militant organized for the conflict between God and the Devil, Truth and Error, in which the interests of the former were at one with those of the State. The purpose called for strict discipline, a hierarchy of absolute authority, a code of sacrosanct doctrine. The Prince of Peace of the Gospels recruited soldiers for a holy war, and the Church earned its reward, temporal power, wealth and dignity. History records the price paid from one end of the world to the other by victims of religious intolerance and strife.

Would Christianity have adhered closer to the spirit of Christ if Mamaea and Origen had been given the time to collaborate, and the new religion had attained recognition while the tolerant atmosphere survived of the Age of the Antonines? The condition of the times was favourable. Men were satisfied no longer with the impersonal formality of official cults. They sought a god able to comfort and inspire them. The Syrian and Egyptian mysteries and similar forms of worship attracted devotees because they gave purpose to human life. In his detailed account of the ideas prevalent at the time, *La Religion à Rome sous les Sevères*, the French scholar, Jean Réville, observes: Human nature, which has religious as much as intellectual and aesthetic needs, takes revenge sooner or later for a religious famine imposed on it and turns with the hunger of the starving to beliefs and rites able to afford satisfaction.'

The world had to wait too long for the satisfaction that Christianity afforded. In the interval the message lost much of its sweetness. Four years after the meeting at Antioch Mamaea was dead. It was left to Constantine to set the seal of Imperial approval on the Church and dictate its marching orders.

11

Doom of a Dynasty

During the reign of Heliogabalus and for the first ten years of Alexander's there was peace on the Parthian frontier. Artabanus and Vologaeses had urgent problems at home to distract them, not only those arising from fraternal strife but also from the insurrection gathering power among their Persian subjects. The leader of the insurgents bore a name honoured in Persian history, Ardashir rendered into Greek as Artaxerxes. Appealing to national and religious sentiment, he attracted a growing body of support in the province on the eastern coast of the Persian Gulf, the heartland of the old Persian Empire destroyed by Alexander the Great. The quarrel between the Parthian brothers contributed to his success. Defeating each in turn, he proclaimed himself Great King of Persia intent on resuming the ancestral rights and powers lost more than five hundred years earlier on the death of Darius, last of the Royal line, and on strict observance of the national religion founded by the prophet Zoroaster, which had suffered neglect from the apathy of the Parthian overlord. The dynasty that he founded became known as the Sassanids, derived from his forebear's name, Sassan.

Some years were needed to translate his claim into fact. Even when Artabanus and Vologaeses themselves were dead, the sons of the former kept up resistance in Armenia and the eastern provinces beyond the Caspian, and it was not till 230 that the last flicker of Parthian defiance was extinguished and Artaxerxes free to turn his attention to the West. The ancient Empire of Darius had extended as far as the Aegean coast of Asia Minor. Many conquerors had occupied this territory in the course of the intervening half-millennium, the last of whom were the Romans. Artaxerxes, demanding restitution of his patrimony, led his army across the Tigris into the Roman province of Mesopotamia.

The Romans were taken by surprise. The frontier had been quiet so long that no plans were ready to repel aggression. Dio asserts that discipline was lax, and he contrasts his own stern measures to keep the soldiers in order when he was in command on the Danube with the ease and licence that prevailed in the army here in the East. It is possible that self-esteem tempted him to exaggerate. There is evidence of a mutiny occurring at Edessa, in which the legionary commander was killed; but the men concerned were transferred to another frontier, where they served without further complaint. Local incidents of the sort were not uncommon in a Roman army without active engagements to sustain morale.

Whatever the reason, the Persians succeeded in piercing the Roman defence. Alexander was appalled when news of the invasion reached him at Rome. He was a man of peace, comfort-loving and studious, for whom war held no attraction. His mother shared his feelings, and an envoy was sent to Artaxerxes to remind him of the formidable power of the Roman Empire and of the many victories won by Roman armies over the Parthians, and to offer terms to persuade him to withdraw. He refused, however, to be deterred or conciliated. He was not a Parthian but a Persian, and his success in subjugating Parthia to Persia, reversing an order that had lasted for centuries, elated him and inspired his ambition with fanatical zeal. He saw himself as the champion appointed by Ormuzd, supreme power of Good in the Persian religion, to avenge ancient wrong and scatter the forces of Ahriman, the power of Evil, represented by the Romans. With a sense of mission encouraged by abundance of plunder, he overran the country between the Tigris and Euphrates and threatened the neighbouring province of Syria.

Regretfully but resolutely, Alexander prepared for war. Levies were raised from Italy and the provinces to bring the legions up to strength, and when a sufficient force was mobilized he went in person to review the men on parade on open ground outside the Praetorian barracks. The contemporary historian puts a speech into his mouth which, in accordance with the custom of ancient writers in history, is almost certainly fictitious; but it has phrases that ring true of his attitude to the war. He tells the soldiers how uncongenial the occasion is for him, and how much rather he would address them in the tone to which years of peace have accustomed him. Nevertheless, he adds, 'men of courage and sense must pray for the best but put up with what comes'. War is hateful, but there are circumstances in which it becomes a necessary task. He reminds them that he did his best to avoid conflict, sending an envoy to dissuade Artaxerxes, who has added to the crime of killing his own overlord, the Parthian Artabanus, that of unprovoked aggression on Roman territory. The barbarian treated his appeal with scorn and deserves to be punished. The Roman army, having a just cause, can fight with the confidence inspired by an easy conscience.

They are words directed less to inflame martial ardour in his hearers than to resolve his own doubts as he braced himself for efforts repugnant to his nature; but having made his decision he acted on good advice with vigour and firmness. An able and distinguished officer was appointed governor of the threatened province of Syria, and a naval command set up to crush the pirates who, counting on Roman weakness, troubled communications at sea and endangered the transport of men and supplies. In spite of his lack of military experience Alexander followed the example set by Emperors in the past, accompanying the army when it left Rome for the seat of war. Crowds lined the road to watch him depart. His gentle manners endeared him to the people, and he had reigned long enough for habit to regard him as a fixed institution. Many wept as he rode away from them, and he himself looking back at the city wept too, wondering if he would ever see it again. His mother carried in a litter at his side preserved her dignity. She disliked war as much as he did, but she was determined to go with him and see it through to the end.

The Emperor and his army travelled round the head of the Adriatic, then across the Balkan peninsula to Thrace and the Bosporus and down through Asia Minor to Antioch, arriving in the late summer of 231. This was to be their headquarters while final arrangements were made for the campaign, and Mamaea was kept busy during her stay there. Even if details of strategy were left to the military experts, there were urgent questions of policy that demanded her attention, arising not only from the Persian war but also from the wider interests of the Empire. It is an indication of the importance of religion in her scale of values that she found time nevertheless for the interview with Origen described in the previous chapter. She sought refuge from cares of state and the distasteful prospect of war in contemplation of the eternal verities.

Even now, with preparations complete for military action, Alexander made a final attempt to negotiate peace, hoping that Artaxerxes would be in a more amenable frame of mind when he heard of the approach of the Roman Emperor with a huge army, an Emperor who bore the name of Alexander, fatal in the past to the Persian Great King. He sent envoys to propose an alliance between Rome and Persia.

They returned with the message that a Persian embassy would follow, bringing the answer; but there was nothing conciliatory in the appearance of the representatives of Artaxerxes, who came to Antioch four hundred strong, all of enormous height, splendidly dressed and mounted, armed with bows. They announced that there could be no peace till Rome restored to the Great King the satrapies of the Persian Empire, including Syria and the Asian coast of the Aegean, stolen from his ancestor Darius. The arrogance of a claim raked up from the distant past and the evident intention of the Persian giants to impress and intimidate gave offence in the Roman camp and provoked violence against the ambassadors, till Alexander intervened, sparing their lives to respect diplomatic immunity, while he vindicated Roman dignity by stripping them of their finery and sending them to villages in Phrygia to work on the land.

The army set forth on the campaign without further delay. The plan was to deliver a three-pronged attack on the enemy. The first column would advance in a northerly direction through the mountains of Armenia, where a few supporters of the Parthian cause—allies against the Persians—still held out. The second would aim southwards to the Euphrates, then travel down the river in boats to its confluence with the Tigris. The third and largest, led by the Emperor himself, would follow the direct route which lay between them, striking across the desert to Hatra, the town that successfully resisted Septimius in his own war against Parthia, and which now stood fast for the Romans against the Persians. The effect intended was to divide and confuse the Persian defence, till the three columns meeting and joining forces advanced together into the Persian heartland to inflict crushing defeat.

All went according to plan at first. The northern force made steady progress through the mountains in spite of the rough going, which was less disadvantage to them marching on foot than it was to the Persian cavalry sent to oppose them, but unable to charge effectively among the crags and ravines. The Persians suffered further setback when news came of a second invasion, a Roman army sailing down the river and already approaching the sea. Artaxerxes, whose home province lay vulnerable to an attack from the coast, recalled a large part of his forces to meet the new danger, leaving only a weak defence in the north. The Romans watching the retreat assumed that both the other columns had reached their destination and were keeping the enemy fully occupied. They relaxed their vigilance and descended plundering at their ease into the valley of the Tigris.

Their confidence was premature. The third and largest column, which should have filled the gap in the middle, was missing, and Artaxerxes, finding only a small force threatening him in the south, drove it off without difficulty, then led his army back quickly to deal with the northern invaders. Incautious and secure, intent on plunder, they were caught unaware and surrounded. The Persians outnumbered them, showered them with arrows from all sides and pressed them inwards into a tight mass, where they crouched beneath a wall of shields, packed too closely together to use their weapons and offering a helpless target to arrows that pierced the interstices of the screen. In this desperate plight the spirit of the Roman soldiers was broken, and they put up little resistance when the Persians charged in on them, thrusting the shields aside and killing the men underneath. Heaps of corpses mounted, and only a remnant of the army escaped to take refuge in the cheerless wilderness of the mountains. It was the worst disaster suffered by Roman arms for centuries.

Blame for the event fell on Alexander. He was in command of the column which upset the plan of operations by failure to arrive at the rendezvous. His route was the shortest of the three, and it was free from obstacles of the sort that retarded the northern column in the mountains. A large part of the journey, however, lay across desert, where, as other Roman armies had learnt to their cost, the men were tormented not only by heat and thirst but also by diseases endemic to the climate. Many succumbed to an epidemic of dysentery, and as supplies ran short their suffering was aggravated by an inadequate and unsuitable diet. Relief, rest and refreshment could be expected at Hatra; but the town was still a long way off, and the pace of the sick army cruelly slow.

Alexander himself was among the victims of the disease, carried groaning in a litter. These were conditions to which he was wholly unaccustomed. He enjoyed the comforts and amenities of life and had never before been without them. Weakened in body and dejected in spirit, he was incapable of sustaining the effort to overcome his hatred of war. He longed for the campaign to be over, and his mother, watchful at his side, less heeding her own discomfort than prompted by anxiety on his behalf, played her part in sapping his fortitude. She told him that it was not the duty of an Emperor but of the soldiers who served him to endure an ordeal like this.

He accepted her argument the more readily because it was what he wanted to believe; but he was ashamed to turn back and leave the soldiers to go on without him. She suggested the solution to the difficulty, that he should order the whole force to retreat as it was in no fit state to fight an enemy. When the decision was announced the soldiers at first were jubilant, thankful to be spared further hardship; but on the march back, as their health improved in easier country, their conscience reproached them for leaving their comrades in the lurch and they sneered at the Emperor's faint-heartedness to cover their own. The feeling against him was reinforced when they reached Antioch by news of the disaster suffered by the northern column on the Tigris. Survivors of the battle straggling back across the mountains into Syria described the confusion and slaughter, the ignominious end of the expedition. They were outspoken in condemning the main body led by Alexander, whose absence left them an easy prey to the Persians.

A generous distribution of largess did much, however, to repair his credit, and the outlook improved when it was reported that Artaxerxes, instead of following up his victory, was disbanding his army. The Persian, like his Parthian predecessors, relied on vassals to support him with their retainers when he went to war. The horde that obeyed his summons could not be kept indefinitely under arms, as the men were needed to till the land and care for the livestock. On the other hand, once disbanded, it was not easy to mobilize again, so cumbrous was the procedure, so inconvenient the disturbance of productive work. Alexander could assume with reason from the information brought him that for the present the Persians had no aggressive plans.

The refreshing climate of Antioch, wholesome food and civilized pleasure soon restored him to health, and as his spirits revived he was able to persuade himself that the purpose of the campaign had in fact been achieved. The loss of a battle, no matter how regrettable the circumstances, could be forgotten. The Persians had retired to their own country, and the frontier was quiet. It is clear that they were impressed by the size of the forces mustered in reply to their challenge, and they knew that the Roman Empire had the power to send other expeditions more formidable than the last to enforce its will. Artaxerxes was not yet so secure in his newly-won position at home that he could count on repeating his success. Years passed, more than Alexander was destined to see, before Persia renewed its claim to the lost realms of Darius.

Alexander returned to Rome in the summer of 233, greeted by the people with joy as exuberant as the sorrow shown at his departure. Among those who cheered loudest were the wives of the soldiers whom he led back from the desert. He increased his popularity by lavish distribution of largess, games in the amphitheatre and performance of mimes and similar pastimes on the stage. His mother, whose thrift was unused to such expenditure, was appeased by the foundation of a youth organization bearing her name, *Mamaeani* and *Mamaeanae*, Mamaea boys and Mamaea girls. The climax of the festival was a triumphal procession to the temple of Jupiter on the Capitoline hill to celebrate the victorious conclusion of the Persian war. Hating formality, he insisted in defiance of tradition on walking on foot, while his chariot, drawn by four elephants, symbols of conquered Persia, followed behind him. Enthusiastic crowds raised him to their shoulders, crying: 'Rome and the commonwealth are safe, while Alexander lives.'

In their eyes he represented peace and stability, but soldiers who remembered him in the Mesopotamian desert joined with less conviction in the chorus.

Fresh trouble arose before the year was over. The governors of the provinces of Noricum and Rhaetia between the upper Danube and upper Rhine sent urgent appeal for help to repel an invasion of German tribesmen. This was the region that had suffered depredation in Caracalla's reign; but by the victories that he won over the invaders, the personal impression that he made and the measures that he took to strengthen the defences he succeeded in restoring order, and the settlement that he effected had lasted for years undisturbed. The blame for the danger now threatening it lay in part with the Persian war. The garrisons on the Rhine were stripped to muster an army of the size needed in the East, and the tribesmen took advantage of their weakness to burst through. It is clear, however, that there were other reasons as well to provoke the sudden outbreak of restlessness on the frontier. These were no mere sporadic raids inspired by lust for plunder. The attacks which the Roman defences tried with scanty success to repel were on the scale rather of an invasion, a movement of population. Events taking place at the time in the unexplored hinterland of Central Europe are unrecorded, and it is not known what pressure from beyond drove the Germans on the Rhine, hitherto content for the most part with their own homes, to covet territory in the Roman provinces. It was an impulse, however, destined to continue with gathering momentum along the whole frontier of the Rhine and the Danube for the rest of the century. Recurring in later centuries, it was the principal cause of the fall of the Western Roman Empire.

Alexander, thankful to be back in civilization after the uncongenial experience of war in the East, was most unwilling to depart for another term of military service; but the danger threatened the frontier at the most sensitive point, where it lay within shortest distance of Italy, and there were still people alive old enough to remember the alarming occasion in the reign of Marcus Aurelius when a similar incursion penetrated before it was checked to the shore of the Adriatic. Another reason urging Alexander to intervene was the impatience that his hesitation provoked among the legions recently withdrawn from the Rhine to fight against the Persians. In accordance with the policy encouraged by Septimius the soldiers had intermarried with the native population on the German frontier, and most of them left wives and children settled there, whose fate aroused their anxiety. They asked indignantly why they were detained in the East when the war was over, and demanded to be led back home to protect their families and property.

Alexander dared not refuse. Recalling his army from Syria except for a few essential garrisons, he left Rome as soon as the fighting season opened in 234 and set off for the new scene of hostilities. His mother accompanied him, indefatigable in sharing his hardships. In spite of his distaste for the duty he acted with energy and decision, travelling at great speed to the Rhine, which he reached at Moguntiacum, the present-day Mainz. To cross the river, he had a bridge built of boats lashed together and covered with planks, and his army, both men and supplies, passed over to the other bank to carry the war into hostile territory. The German tribesmen, hitherto the raiders, found themselves raided in their turn, and their dismay was increased by the unfamiliar weapons used to attack them. The Roman army included contingents recruited in the East, many Parthians who preferred the service of Rome to that of Artaxerxes. These men were skilled archers, able to pick off with their arrows the bare heads and tall figures of the Germans from a great distance. There were javelin-throwers too from Africa whose accuracy of aim achieved a similar effect at long range. The Germans, accustomed to fight at close quarters and charging in massed formation, offered an easy target to the missiles.

Intimidated by the success of the Roman offensive, they sent envoys to treat for peace, and Alexander met them in an accommodating spirit. It was in his nature to prefer negotiation to war, and in present circumstances his military advisers agreed with him, anxious to patch up peace here so that they could transfer forces to other parts of the frontier, especially the upper Danube, affected by the prevailing unrest. His mother too was in favour of a conciliatory policy, hoping that it would put an end to the war and enable them both to return to more congenial work at home. At his meeting with the German envoys he offered a large sum of money as the price of their good behaviour, and they accepted his terms. The procedure was no different from Caracalla's in similar circumstances. It was the habit of Rome to maintain peace by a judicious combination of force and gold.

Nevertheless, when the terms became known, there was indignation in the army, especially among men who regarded this country as their home and were glad of the opportunity that brought them back to their wives and children. They feared that, as soon as quiet was restored, they would be sent again to the East. Grievance arose too from the contrast between the lavish bribe conceded to the tribesmen and recent economies enforced in military pay to cover the cost of bringing the legions up to strength for the Persian war, and of making good the losses suffered during it. The soldiers neither knew nor cared how much the treasury and taxpayers could afford. When bonus and other privileges were reduced, they laid the blame on Mamaea's avarice, and they jeered at the Emperor for his dependence on her. Caracalla too was accustomed to leave financial administration to his mother; but no one suggested of the 'Ausonian Beast', as they did of the amiable Alexander, that he was tied to his mother's apron-strings.

Among those who condemned the negotiated peace most strongly was an officer called Maximinus, a giant of a man, conspicuous not only in stature but also in the size and piercing glare of his eyes. Beginning life as a shepherd-boy in a semi-barbarous district of Thrace, he joined at an early age a troop of auxiliary horsemen in the Roman army, where in spite of his lack of education his talent and fire earned him rapid promotion. Transferred to legionary service, he rose from the ranks to hold the office of military tribune and later to command a legion. During the Persian war he was in Mesopotamia with the duty of co-ordinating the movements of all the legions in the province. His rapid rise to distinction inflamed his ambition, and when his son came of age for marriage he tried to obtain him the Emperor's sister, Theoclia, as his bride. Even the open-minded Alexander was taken aback, and in a letter informing his mother of the proposal he expresses doubt whether the Thracian's son, however handsome and seemingly well educated, would make a congenial husband for Theoclia, a girl of intellectual tastes. Mamaea had no doubt at all. She married her daughter off at once to a more eligible suitor of senatorial rank. Maximinus neither forgot nor forgave the affront.

In the army on the Rhine he held the office of *praefectus tironibus*, charged with mustering and training the fresh intake of forces needed for the campaign. The post not only carried responsibility: it afforded him opportunity also, of which he took advantage, to gain an influence over the recruits in his care. He dazzled them with feats of strength and inspired them by his example, sharing and taking the lead himself in the tasks that he set them. They learnt to regard him with adoring devotion, expecially those of them, a large proportion, who came from provinces on the lower Danube related in speech and customs to his own birthplace. As they contrasted his herculean figure with that of the sedentary and studious Alexander, it seemed to them that he was far the better fitted of the two to wear the Imperial purple. They expressed the opinion freely in the canteens where they mixed with other branches of the army, pouring facetious scorn on the part played by Mamaea in the Imperial council. Their conversation was infectious, loosening discontented tongues. Men from other units joined in, some to complain of the Emperor's weakness in negotiating with the Germans, others to scoff at his faint-heartedness in the Mesopotamian desert. Maximinus did nothing to stop the talk.

The recruits were encamped at a distance of several miles down the river from Moguntiacum, while the Emperor's headquarters lay on the outskirts of the town. The treasonable speeches and mounting disaffection escaped notice, and the plot grew in secret till a day came when the recruits assembled on parade were joined by a great number of other soldiers in full armour. As Maximinus arrived to take command, several stepped forward to meet and salute him, and one of them threw a purple cloak over his shoulders. At the same time the parade-ground rang with concerted applause, and all present shouted in unison, acclaiming him Emperor.

He made as if to resist and pull the cloak off again; but in spite of his known strength the soldiers were able to restrain him without difficulty, and with a few perfunctory exclamations of surprise and dismay he submitted to their will. Towering above them, magnificent in Imperial purple, he declared that Alexander was deposed and he himself the rightful successor.

Prompt action was needed to make the *coup d'état* an accomplished fact. Those who took part in it were only a small fraction of the army assembled on the Rhine, among which much loyalty to Alexander still prevailed. The insurgents were anxious to take him by surprise and dispose of him before sufficient forces had time to gather for his defence. They set off at once with their new Emperor to march to Moguntiacum. Nevertheless, in spite of their efforts, the news preceded them. A man faithful to Alexander slipped away to the lines where the horses were picketed, mounted the fastest and galloped to Moguntiacum to warn him.

On arrival he rode straight to the Emperor's tent, speaking to no one on the way, so that nothing was known of his message till Alexander himself came running out, calling to all indiscriminately in his agitation, raging against Maximinus and blaming him especially for his treachery in seducing the loyalty of the recruits and taking advantage of their youth and inexperience. His mother hearing the outcry hurried from her own tent to join him, and as she calmed him down and his voice recovered coherence he revealed what the messenger had told him. By now a large crowd of his retinue stood watching and listening with curiosity. He addressed a passionate appeal to them, imploring them to protect him and promising that, if they had any grievance against him, he would put it right. Most of them had been a long time in his service, attending on him personally during a reign that extended already to thirteen years. He was well liked for the considerate way in which he treated them, and they assured him of their support.

The spring evening was verging towards dusk. As much as possible was done in spite of the lateness of the hour to strengthen the defence of the Imperial headquarters with forces summoned from elsewhere to reinforce the guard. Night fell without sign of Maximinus. The defenders, standing idle hour after hour on watch, whiled away the time in conversation, in which those added as reinforcements, strangers without personal attachment to Alexander, betrayed doubtful interest in their task. They repeated phrases picked up in the canteens to which recruits resorted. Old complaints against Alexander were rehashed, and many paid tribute to the soldierly qualities of Maximinus. Even if the loyalists remained unconvinced their zeal was discouraged, and the emotion aroused by Alexander's appeal began to wane.

Meanwhile Maximinus, fearing to attack in darkness on unfamiliar ground, had halted his men a short way off and was waiting for daylight. At the first glimpse of dawn he advanced, and the watchers on the rampart protecting the Imperial headquarters reported a cloud of dust on the skyline. Soon a clamour was heard of men cheering, growing louder as it approached. Few defenders, however, took up arms to make ready for battle. A deputation went to Alexander's tent to inform him that the soldiers refused to fight for him unless he granted their demands in full. On the previous evening, speaking to his trusted retainers, he had promised to rectify any wrong of which they complained; but strange faces accosted him now, men unknown to him, and the ultimatum that they presented covered matters of discipline and policy far beyond anything that he was able to concede. They brought a list of officers whom they blamed for unpopular decisions, and they insisted that all those named on it should be put to death. It included his closest friends and confidants.

Frantic with dismay, he pushed past the deputation and climbed up himself on to the rampart to plead with the garrison; but already the followers of Maximinus were swarming beneath over the field. As he stood there, they caught sight of him and pointed, yelling derisive insults, inviting the soldiers beside him to throw him down, to choose a real man as Emperor—raising their arms in salute to Maximinus, a purple-cloaked giant—instead of a 'money-grubbing milksop, Mother's puling puppet'. Alexander tried to speak, but his voice was lost in the din. Beneath him, rank behind rank, jeering faces stared up at him, and the expression was reflected in the eyes of those at his side. Contempt and hatred rang in his ears from attackers and defenders alike. 'Money-grubbing milksop,' they taunted, then in a roar of full-throated exultation,

'Hail, Maximinus Emperor!'

Alexander turned quickly, climbed back down to the ground and fled into his tent.

His mother waited there, listening to the noise outside and trembling for the outcome. As he entered she clasped him to her breast, and he clung to her, weeping. His nerve failed him, only self-pity remained. He reproached her with tears for leading him to his doom.

They still clung together, he bemoaning his fate, she vainly trying to soothe him, when a military tribune with several centurions burst into the tent, sent by Maximinus as executioners. Alexander shrank from them with a scream, but they seized and stabbed him to death. Mamaea stood impassive, till they turned from her son's dead body and killed her too.

The date was 10 March 235. Alexander died at the age of twenty-six, having reigned thirteen years. Mamaea was in her early forties. She was the last of the Syrian Princesses who ruled in fact, but not in name, over the Roman Empire.

12

Epilogue

Maximinus lasted as Emperor for three troubled years. Murdered in a military insurrection, he suffered the fate that he himself inflicted on Alexander. The story was repeated again and again through the years that followed. Emperor followed Emperor in rapid succession, most of them imposed and, when the time came, murdered by the soldiers. Few reigns attained as much as five years, many were limited to a few months. On occasions there was more than one Emperor at the same time, while rival claimants fought each other for the purple. The anarchy from which Septimius Severus saved Rome was triumphant. The safety of the Empire depended on the army guarding the frontiers, as he understood in his dying advice to his sons; but when there was no longer an Emperor capable of controlling the soldiers, or a binding spell like that of the dynasty that he founded, the watchdogs turned into a pack of ravening wolves.

Internal strife was not the only torment in this time of troubles: the barbarian menace that summoned Alexander and Mamaea to Mainz grew after their death, till not only the fringe but even the heart of the Empire suffered invasion. Goths from beyond the Danube overran Thrace and pressed on to the Aegean to plunder the rich provinces of Asia Minor. The Germans, not content with raids on the western bank of the Rhine, penetrated through the Brenner pass into Italy. In the East the Persian Kings, successors of Artaxerxes, renewed claims which the distracted Roman Empire no longer had power to resist. Roman prestige sank to its lowest ebb when the Emperor Valerian, entrapped by a Persian army, was led away captive to Persia and put to work as a slave, and on his death his skin stuffed with straw hung adorning a Persian temple.

The time of troubles lasted for fifty years. In 284 Diocletian became Emperor, and having the means and the ability to maintain himself in power he set about rebuilding the Roman Empire. His work, carried on and completed by Constantine the Great, was destined to endure for another two centuries in the West, and another twelve in the East. The new Empire, however, was very different from the old, from whose ruins it rose. The State founded by Augustus, and surviving till the death of Alexander Severus, inherited the traditions of Republican Rome. Despite the steady encroachment of Imperial power the structure of a self-governing society remained, in which everyone except for the slave (but even he was beginning to acquire rights towards the end) enjoyed freedom within the limits of his rank and income to live as he chose. In the new Empire this freedom ceased to exist. The Emperor no longer even pretended to be a magistrate responsible to the people. He was an autocrat in command of a totalitarian government, under whom everyone's livelihood and career were subject to official direction. Constantine's Rome had much in common with the dictatorship exercised by the State in the Soviet Union today.

The year 235, when the last of the Syrian Princesses was murdered, has its place among the decisive dates of history. It was the end of the old Roman Empire, of a political achievement that gave peace, order and as much freedom as the human condition can reasonably expect to the majority of the population of a territory whose bounds were those of the civilized world. In an earlier century the Latin poet Juvenal, protesting at the influx of Eastern races and customs, used a phrase that was often quoted, *In Tiberim defluxit Orontes*; 'The Orontes has flowed into the Tiber.' On the upper waters of the river Orontes stood the city of Emesa with its temple of Elagabal. Rome had reason to mourn when the flow was cut off.

Bibliographical Appendix

Most of the record of this period of Roman history is derived from two Greek writers, contemporaries of the events. The first is Cassius Dio Cocceianus (to whom I have referred throughout as Dio), a well-to-do citizen of Nicaea in Asia Minor, who was born about 150 and died shortly before 235 after a distinguished career in public service. He wrote a history of Rome in eighty books from the mythical days of Aeneas to the reign of Alexander Severus, of which only those survive intact which cover the end of the Republic and the reigns of the first three Emperors. Fortunately, before the later books were lost, a Byzantine monk in the eleventh century called Xiphilinus made an epitome of them, rather in the manner of the *Reader's Digest*, and his work is still available. He cuts ruthlessly, but the material that he retains is left in Dio's own words, and it is evidence of first-hand authority as Dio was present himself on many of the occasions described. The Greek text with English translation by Earnest Cary is published in the Loeb Classical Library under the title *Dio's Roman History*, of which volume 9 contains the years relevant here.

Less is known about the other contemporary historian, Herodian, not even his full name. His history covers the years from the death of Marcus Aurelius to the accession of Gordian III in 238, all of which fell within his own lifetime. He was of provincial birth, probably from the East, and of lower rank in society than Dio. His narrative lacks Dio's immediacy. It is that of a student of events observed from a distance; but they are the events nonetheless of his own times, and as his work survives in full it is a valuable supplement to the too fragmentary epitome of Dio. He is published in the Loeb Classical Library with an English translation by C. R. Whittaker, who adds informative footnotes discussing the text in the light of parallel passages from Dio and of the epigraphical evidence. I owe a great debt to Mr Whittaker's footnotes for help to piece together Dio and Herodian into a coherent story.

There is a third source available to students of the period, the Augustan History, a collection of Latin biographies of the Roman Emperors beginning with Hadrian and ending with the accession of Diocletian. Its date and authorship have been much disputed. Although it claims to be a compilation of the work of several authors, and the various lives are divided between them, some attributed to one, others to another, the generally accepted opinion today is that their names are fictitious, appended for the sake of verisimilitude, and that the whole work is in fact from a single hand, a literary *tour de force* written in the last years of the fourth century. Very little reliance can be placed on its authority, except for a short passage in the *Life of Heliogabalus*, chapters 13 to 15, relating the events of the last year of this Emperor's reign, where the pace and coherence of the narrative, contrasting with the pedestrian style that prevails elsewhere, suggest that the account is a transcript from the lost work of an earlier historian founded on accurate information. The question is examined by Sir Ronald Syme in a recent book, *Ammianus and the Historia Augusta* (Oxford, 1968).

Among secondary authorities the most famous is Gibbon's *Decline and Fall of the Roman Empire*, but the period relevant here is so small a portion of the immense range covered by his work that inevitably it receives from him only cursory treatment. A recent biography of Septimius Severus is *Septimius Severus, the African Emperor* by Anthony Birley (Eyre and Spottiswoode, 1971), from which I have derived much help, especially with regard to the campaign in Britain. An earlier work, *The Life and Reign of the Emperor Septimius Severus* by Maurice Platnauer (Oxford, 1918) is also of interest. I know of no biography of the Emperor Caracalla, but the events leading up to the massacre at Alexandria in his reign are discussed in an article by P. Benoît and J. Schwarz in *Etudes de Papyrologie* 1948. The next Emperor is portrayed in *The Amazing Emperor Heliogabalus* by J. Stuart Hay (Macmillan, 1911). My account of the death of Gannys in that reign is founded on Captain Hay's reconstruction of an otherwise unintelligible passage in Dio. The reign of Alexander Severus is described in *Etudes critiques sur la vie et le règne de Sevère Alexandre* by Auguste Jardé (Paris, 1925).

The works of Julia Domna's friend, Flavius Philostratus, both his *Life of Apollonius* and *Lives of the Sophists*, are published in the Loeb Classical Library, as are also those of two other members of her circle, Aelian and Oppian. The ideas of Philostratus are discussed in *Philostrate et son école* by Edouard Bertrand (Paris, 1886). Galen's medical and philosophical works are published in the Greek original with Latin translation in the series *Scriptores Medici Graeci* edited by Karl Kuehn

(Leipzig, 1821). There is an English translation of his treatise *On the passions and errors of the soul* by Paul W. Harkins published by Ohio State University, and light is thrown on his philosophical ideas in *Galen on Jews and Christians* by R. Walzer (Oxford, 1949).

The account given of events in the Christian Church in Rome is founded on the evidence of the contemporary Bishop Hippolytus, *Philosophumena* book 9 section 12, of which the Greek text is available edited by Emmanuel Miller (Oxford, 1851), and an English translation by F. Legge (SPCK, 1921). The works of Origen, those still available in the Greek original and those that survive only in Latin translation, are edited in 25 volumes by Karl Vincent Delarue (Berlin, 1831–48). Information about his life and ideas is to be found in *La jeunesse d'Origène* by René Cadiou (Paris, 1935) and *Origen and his work* by Eugène de Faye, translated by Fred Rothwell (Allen and Unwin, 1926). Two books on the religion of the period from which I have derived much help are *La religion à Rome sous les Sevères* by Jean Réville (Paris, 1886) and *Personal Religion among the Greeks* by André-Jean Festugière (University of California, 1954).

Index